STRATEGIC STALEMATE: NUCLEAR WEAPONS AND ARMS CONTROL IN AMERICAN POLITICS

Council On Foreign Relations Books

The Council on Foreign Relations, Inc., is a nonprofit and nonpartisan organization devoted to promoting improved understanding of international affairs through the free exchange of ideas. The Council does not take any position on questions of foreign policy and has no affiliation with, and receives no funding from, the United States government.

From time to time, books and monographs written by members of the Council's research staff or visiting fellows, or commissioned by the Council, or written by an independent author with a critical review contributed by a Council study or working group are published with the designation "Council on Foreign Relations Book." Any book or monograph bearing that designation is, in the judgement of the Committee on Studies of the Council's board of directors, a responsible treatment of a significant international topic worthy of presentation to the public. All statements of fact and expressions of opinion contained in Council books are, however, the sole responsibility of the author.

STRATEGIC STALEMATE: NUCLEAR WEAPONS AND ARMS CONTROL IN AMERICAN POLITICS

Michael Krepon

St. Martin's Press   New York
A Council on Foreign Relations book

ISBN 0-312-76434-0

Library of Congress Cataloging in Publication Data
Krepon, Michael, 1946–
    Strategic stalemate.

    "A Council on Foreign Relations book."
    Includes index.
    1. United States—Military policy.   2. Atomic
weapons.   3. Strategic Arms Limitation Talks.
4. United States—Politics and government—
1981–   .   5. World politics—1975–1985.   I. Title.
UA23.K777   1984   355'.0335'73   84–13323
ISBN 0-312-76434-0

IN MEMORY OF MY PARENTS
HARRY AND OLLA KREPON

Honesty may not always be the best policy, pragmatically speaking, but it is usually commendable. Let me therefore state at the outset that this book—though I hope it is respectably analytical and even objective—presents an argument. I have tried to be fair to opposing arguments, but I have been conscious of taking part in what may loosely be described as a debate. . . .

—Bernard Brodie, introduction to
Escalation and the Nuclear Option

Contents

Forewords

Brent Scowcroft

To a great many concerned citizens, nuclear weapons and arms control matters are too important to be left in the hands of the "experts." To many experts, these issues are far too complex and serious to be left to the variable winds of public opinion. For some who advocate arms control, the most serious problem facing the planet is the bomb. For others, the most serious problem we face is the Soviet Union. As Michael Krepon points out in *Strategic Stalemate,* these countervailing forces have made it exceedingly difficult for any administration to carry out a long-term strategy that has both popular support and broad-gauged leadership.

Most Americans and their elected officials reject either/or characterizations of current problems and solutions. Yet increasingly, political choices and public debates are being framed in black and white terms — terms fit only for caricatures. One is either for a nuclear weapons freeze or for nuclear weapon modernization programs across the board. The treaty barring effective anti-ballistic missile defenses must either be immutable or abandoned in favor of space-based defenses against nuclear attacks. We must either achieve deep reductions in Soviet nuclear forces of concern, or we must significantly increase the size and capabilities of our stockpile.

The American public deserves more than this menu of stark

choices, but the political dynamics of nuclear weapons and arms control debates continue to serve them up. Long experience over several administrations — including most recently in President Reagan's Commission on Strategic Forces — persuades me that attempts to forge alliances between opposing camps on these issues are extraordinarily difficult enterprises.

The difficulty lies not in partisan friction, for Democrats and Republicans are found in both camps and in varied positions along the entire spectrum Mr. Krepon describes. Nor is the problem primarily one of institutional division between Congress and White House or Pentagon and State Department. Different individuals in each of those institutions have adopted each of the policy stances depicted by the author. Yet the challenge of framing a durable national security policy involves all of those divisions — legislative-bureaucratic, Republican-Democrat, ins and outs — and more. To meet it demands of all participants not only clear thought but open minds. Each of us can hold to his convictions but each must recognize that we can best serve the nation's security only by reconciling or accommodating the differing convictions of responsible people.

Rather than amplifying the disputes over strategic policy which separate Americans from Americans, we must seek to work out some means to build coalitions on future nuclear weapons and arms control choices. Otherwise this nation will become less secure as time passes. Security can come only if we as a nation are able to make intelligent choices that incorporate arms control with prudent measures to maintain our military strength.

That sense of policy balance and of political accommodation is the hallmark of Mr. Krepon's study. Participants in the longrunning debate in the United States may quibble over details in the work but they will find that the author has tried conscientiously to present their views fairly and to frame the real issues intelligently. Only through such a process of honest inquiry and search for effective policies accommodating a reasonable range of divergent strategic beliefs and preferences can America devise a steadfast and steady course on these fractious questions.

I do not subscribe to every prescription Michael Krepon offers in this perceptive book, but I heartily subscribe to his analysis of the current dilemma of strategic stalemate and to the penalties of our failure to move away from either/or debates over nuclear weapons and arms control. We need to think long and hard over the criteria for national security policies that can promote sustained public support, while guiding us through contentious political debates. This book offers a roadmap of how to get from here to there.

Paul C. Warnke

In his perceptive study of the nuclear arms control debate, Michael Krepon tells a sad story — not quite, or at least not yet, a tragedy. Despite increasing acceptance of the fact that nuclear war between the United States and the Soviet Union would mean their mutual destruction, efforts to achieve negotiated limits on the weapons and the threat they pose have achieved remarkably little.

Mr. Krepon's analysis shows why this is so. While the Soviet Union has not been an easy negotiating partner, the reason for recent failures to achieve significant arms control is not simply Soviet intransigence. The major concessions leading to both the SALT I agreements and the unratified SALT II Treaty were made by the Soviet leaders, notably by General Secretary Brezhnev when he met with President Ford at Vladivostok in November of 1974. Nor are these failures the result of legitimate concerns about the ability of the U.S. to monitor Soviet compliance. Sophisticated monitoring capabilities as well as ingenious negotiating provisions — such as counting rules for multiple independently targetable re-entry vehicles (MIRVs) — can provide sufficient confidence for verification of most kinds of agreements.

The major problem barring significant progress to date in arms control has been the deep difference of opinion between those who oppose any agreement that would seriously limit new U.S. nuclear weapons systems and those who feel that a virtually unrestricted competition between the two nuclear superpowers can only mean less stability and a greater risk of nuclear war. This debate has raged in Democratic as well as Republican administrations.

The political roadblocks associated with these domestic debates were, it should be noted, helped along by Soviet international misbehavior. Advocates of the military utility of nuclear weapons prevented President John F. Kennedy from going beyond the atmospheric test ban to a comprehensive ban on the testing of nuclear weapons. But it was the movement of Soviet troops and tanks into Czechoslovakia, on the very day in August of 1968 when Moscow and Washington were to announce the initiation of strategic arms limitation talks, that delayed the SALT negotiations for a year. And during that year the first U.S. missiles with MIRVs were deployed, to be matched a few years later by Soviet MIRVed missiles. In a sorry replay, it was the Soviet invasion of Afghanistan in late 1979 that dealt the final blow to hopes for ratification of the SALT II Treaty.

But the SALT negotiations had for many years been beset by political attacks from within the United States. It is, I think, instructive to note that the only strategic arms agreements approved by the U.S. Congress have been the Limited Test Ban Treaty, ratified after President Kennedy faced down the Kremlin during the harrowing Cuban missile crisis, and the ABM Treaty and Interim Agreement on control of offensive arms — SALT I — overwhelmingly approved in 1972 when Richard Nixon was at the height of his political powers. Buoyed by the break-through to China, and not yet burdened by the break-in at the Watergate, President Nixon lost only a handful of votes for the SALT I accords in the Congress.

Presidents Gerald Ford and Jimmy Carter never found themselves in a position of comparable political strength. After the Vladivostok meeting, where Secretary General Brezhnev accepted the principle of equal ceilings on U.S. and Soviet strategic forces and the exclusion of American forward based nuclear systems in Europe, a SALT II Treaty should easily have been completed within the next two years.

But President Ford heard thunder on the right, in the challenge of Governor Ronald Reagan for the Republican nomination. President Carter's concern about appearing weak in the face of Soviet and Cuban involvement in Africa and elsewhere delayed the completion of the SALT II Treaty and stalled other arms control negotiations, most importantly those on a comprehensive ban on the testing of nuclear explosive devices. By the time that the SALT II Treaty was completed, President Carter's political fortunes were on the decline. Even before the dispatch of Soviet troops into Afghanistan, the ratification process had been slowed to a crawl by the political posturing about a Soviet brigade that had been in Cuba for many years.

The unsatisfactory record of negotiations on controlling strategic nuclear arms is not, as I see it, the result of some flaw in the process. New negotiating strategies are not the key to improving the prospects for success in the future. What is needed is a national decision to start pulling together to make this nation and the world a safer place. This cannot be done by relying solely on nuclear weapon modernization programs. Progress in arms control is also needed, and progress will come only with the recognition that neither the United States nor the Soviet Union is going to give up something for nothing.

In this carefully reasoned book, Michael Krepon offers guidelines to narrow the differences of opinion that have divided us and prevented forward progress in this field. Even one who does not find them as persuasive as I do should appreciate the cogency of his analysis and the utility of his approach.

Acknowledgments

This book could not have been written without the benevolent support of two institutions and many kind individuals. I am grateful to the Council on Foreign Relations for offering me a year-long fellowship to do research and write, and to the Center of International Studies at Princeton University for providing me a congenial and stimulating working environment.

These institutions have much to offer the occasional interloper because of the people in charge. Winston Lord at the Council makes it clear by example that young professionals in the International Affairs Fellowship program have the full run of the house. Alton Frye and Kempton Dunn, who administer the fellowship program, manage to service a broad range of needs in addition to their numerous other responsibilities. Paul Kreisberg, the Director of Studies, was instrumental in helping me revise the manuscript, while David Kellogg and Grace Darling helped shepherd the finished product to market. Andrew Pierre offered sound advice at numerous stages in the creation of this book. Janis Kreslins and other members of the library staff helped me sift through the Council's treasure trove of obscure documents and press clippings from early arms control and nuclear weapon debates.

Cyril Black at the Center of International Studies allows Visiting Fellows free rein to experience the richness of academic life at Princeton. Because of the many courtesies he extended, my year on campus was especially rewarding.

If this book has value, it is based on the contributions of many readers who pointed out the need for revisions in earlier drafts. I am especially indebted to the Council on Foreign Relations for assembling a group of articulate and thoughtful reviewers: Richard Betts, Barry Blechman, Anthony Cordesman, Robert Einhorn, Stephen Flanagan, Robert Gallucci, Michael Mandelbaum, Frederic Morris, Barry Posen, Strobe Talbott, and Samuel Wells. I would also like to thank Len Ackland, Harold Brown, Richard Falk, Robert Gilpin, Robert Osgood, Richard Ullman, Paul Warnke, and Jasper Welch for their helpful suggestions which improved earlier drafts. The assistance of Gladys Starkey, Kathrin Black, and Sara Goodgame is also gratefully acknowledged.

I am especially indebted to Alton Frye for the multiple roles he played as editor, adviser and practitioner of the art of the possible. Without his gentle wisdom, the realization of this book would not have been possible.

Authors usually close their acknowledgments with a public note of gratitude to their spouses. Now I know why. During the extended gestation of this book, my wife and best friend, Sandra Savine, waited patiently amidst the subdivisions and soybean farms of central New Jersey for my distractions to pass. Other writers should be so lucky.

1 Two Camps

The catechism repeated dutifully in official speeches is that defense programs and arms control must work together to advance the nation's security. The reality is far different: our attempts to integrate the two have consistently failed, a conclusion on which advocates of new nuclear weapon programs as well as passionate supporters of arms control can readily agree.

The reasons for failure cannot simply be explained by obstreperous Soviet behavior or by administrative incompetence within the executive branch. As difficult as the Kremlin is to deal with on nuclear weapons and arms control, its actions have not been so excessive in one sphere and so recalcitrant in the other to explain how badly disjointed U.S. policies have become. The problem goes far deeper, to contrary impulses within the body politic and deep divisions among those who express our hopes and fears on the nuclear issue. We want arms control, but we don't trust the Russians. We feel that current stockpiles are high enough, but we don't wish to fall behind in the arms race. We hope for progress, but we are skeptical of the process by which we can achieve it.

These conflicting impulses are reflected by a continuum of views in domestic debates over nuclear weapon programs and arms control agreements. At one extreme are those who wish to place heavy reliance on military forces, including nuclear weapons, to secure U.S. interests when it is necessary to do so. At the other are those who wish to stop and then to liquidate the nuclear arms competition. Most of the public and their elected officials have usually fallen well within the two ends of the political spectrum; but over the last decade their ranks have been depleted and their choices as well as the terms of debate have been dictated with greater frequency by those with more extreme views.

Increasingly, debates over nuclear weapons and arms control have little room for those who argue for a prudent mid-course combining arms control with new nuclear weapon programs. The two domestic camps — one advocating increased reliance on weaponry, the other on negotiations to serve U.S. interests — have substantially lost their overlapping center. Most of the operationally-minded strategists who once comfortably drifted back and forth between the camps have now been labeled as partisans. The political center has lost considerable ground to the politics of exclusion.

Neither camp sees its preferences as standing alone, but each is increasingly skeptical about the initiatives favored by the other. The arms control community rejects the assumption that nuclear weapons can provide military advantage, and questions their political utility as well. Members of this camp are predisposed toward controls and reductions in nuclear forces. Nuclear weapon strategists are, in turn, deeply skeptical that arms control agreements can alter fundamentally hostile Soviet political or military objectives. They prefer to see the United States protect its interests by military forces that are best left unconstrained.

The familiar pattern of these domestic contests allows for an intellectual taxonomy of the debaters, although one that admittedly works better in the abstract than in specific cases. The framework chosen here divides the participants into camps of arms control and nuclear weapon strategists. Each camp is subdivided into two wings of operationally- and ideologically-minded activists. Within the arms control and disarmament community, there is a natural division between those who accept the existence of significant constraints to unbounded progress (operationalists) and those who do not (ideologues). In similar fashion, the community of nuclear weapon strategists can be split between those who are prepared to work out limited rules of the nuclear arms competition with the Soviet Union, and those who are not. Operationally-minded nuclear weapon strategists are prepared to accept some arms control arrangements as a management tool in the geopolitical struggle; ideologues view the entire contest in zero-sum terms — one side wins only at the expense of the other. (See the chart on pp. 14–15.)

Arguments over nuclear weapons and arms control began to surface within the scientific community during the last stages of the Manhattan Project. At the outset of this enormous undertaking, there was little debate about the need to build nuclear weapons. A war was going on, and it didn't take too much imagination to consider the implications of an atomic bomb in German hands. Many individuals were instrumental in responding to this challenge; the public eye has focused mostly on two men, and an odder couple could not have been imagined. One was making his mark in the prosaic activities of the Army Corps of Engineers when he was entrusted with the job of carrying out a sprawling and ambitious program to build the bomb. The other, a man of great intellect, no administrative experience to speak of, and leftist views, was tapped to lead the final design and engineering effort.

These two men, General Leslie Richard Groves and J. Robert Oppenheimer, worked well together as a team. The work they shepherded to a successful conclusion has forever altered traditional equations of national power and security. Their contrasting political orientations and sensibilities demonstrated how such differences were submerged in a simpler time, when questions of political ends and military means were somewhat easier to calculate. The means chosen to end World War II forever clouded the picture, sparking a debate which continues to this day.

Then, the question for some scientists was whether or not a demonstration shot of the A-bomb would suffice in convincing the Japanese to surrender. A small group of scientists at the University of Chicago, led by James Franck, Eugene Rabinowitch, and Leo Szilard, argued that it would be morally reprehensible to use the weapon they helped develop against the Japanese people. In their deliberations over the social and political implications of the new weapon, they wondered how the United States could lead an effort to ban the bomb after using it first as an instrument of war.

This was a minority view, both within the scientific community and the upper echelons of the War Department. The majority view was that a demonstration shot might not be carried out effectively, and even so, might lose its desired shock effect. With Germany defeated and Japan's capitulation sure to follow, the objective in 1945 was to hasten the war's end in the Pacific and save lives that would be lost in an invasion of the home islands. The bomb could accomplish these objectives, and most of those deeply engaged in its development assumed in 1945 that it would be used to break the back of the Japanese war effort.

This decision rested first on the shoulders of Henry L. Stimson, a man of judicious temperament and high ideals. Stimson was also the personification of public service, having entered the Army as a Major during World War I at the age of forty-nine, serving earlier in the more elevated capacity as Secretary of War. In his second stint as head of the War Department, it was Stimson's burden to recommend the use of A-bombs against Japan as the "least abhorrent choice"[1] available to President Harry S. Truman.

The scientific community was more seriously divided in deliberations four years later to undertake a crash program on the hydrogen bomb. The H-bomb would provide a quantum leap in destructive power over the A-bomb, just as the A-bomb overshadowed the destructive power of conventional weapons. Again, the debate took place in private, among those appointed to the highest positions in government and their advisers. This time, to many scientists now privy to the debate, another crash effort was something to be resisted strenuously.

Their leader, by virtue of his position as Chairman of the Atomic Energy Commission's group of scientific advisers, as well as by his powers of intellect and suasion, was J. Robert Oppenheimer. A number of the atomic scientists took to citing passages from Scriptures after the cumulative shock waves of Hiroshima and Nagasaki. In the glare of Alamogordo, New Mexico, where the first atomic test took place, Oppenheimer's mind flashed instead to a passage from the Bhagavad-Gita: "I am become Death, the shatterer of worlds." Oppenheimer was blessed with the genius to help unlock the power of the atom and cursed with the sensitivity to rue that which he helped discover.

On the first anniversary of the atomic age, Oppenheimer was called the sorcerer's apprentice by a Dutch newspaper,[2] and the young head of the Los Alamos team that designed the bomb could not entirely dismiss the notion. Oppenheimer himself later confided that "in some sort of crude sense which no vulgarity, no humor, no overstatement can quite extinguish, the physicists have known sin; and this is a knowledge which they cannot lose."[3] A good number of Oppenheimer's colleagues shared this sense of unease, which was periodically expressed along with affirmations of the potential benefits of atomic power.

In the private debate over the development of the H-bomb, Oppenheimer and his like-minded colleagues were in a unique position to make their concerns known through the Atomic Energy

Commission's General Advisory Committee, or GAC. Many government agencies have such committees which can be used for a variety of purposes. The Atomic Energy Commission's GAC was used as a sounding board for decisions that could benefit from extremely scarce and valuable scientific advice. Oppenheimer and his colleagues on the GAC were essentially unanimous in the judgment that a crash effort to build the H-bomb was inadvisable. Again, opposition was couched strongly in ethical terms. The scientific advisers "hoped" that development of the hydrogen bomb could be avoided, and were "reluctant" for the United States to pursue the opposite course. The majority pushed for an unqualified commitment not to develop the H-bomb; others wished that U.S. restraints be made conditional on a positive response from the Soviet Union to our efforts to renounce the new weapon. If the Soviets did not show similar restraint and eventually developed and used H-bombs, the United States could respond with its large stockpile of A-bombs. As further insurance and as an alternative to a crash H-bomb effort, the GAC endorsed proposals to expand production facilities for the materials needed to make atomic weapons. Oppenheimer and his colleagues further endorsed intensified development efforts on tactical nuclear weapons and a program to provide a bigger bang for A-bombs. These efforts, they argued, would be more cost-effective and more likely to provide early returns than a crash effort to produce the "super."[4]

The GAC's arguments sat well with the Chairman of the Atomic Energy Commission, David Lilienthal, but not with President Harry S. Truman or his other key Cabinet advisers. Secretary of State Dean Acheson couldn't see how delaying our research would have a similar effect on the Russian research program, nor how the American public would tolerate unilateral restraint when U.S. and Soviet interests appeared so diverse and when a successful policy of accommodation appeared so remote. Secretary of Defense Louis Johnson agreed on both counts. His staff supplied further arguments for a crash program: it would be "intolerable" for the Soviets to have the H-bomb first, and it was folly to argue the ethical consequences of relying on one type of nuclear weapon as opposed to another. Moreover, there were potential military benefits to be gained from a stockpile of H-bombs, allowing substitution for a larger number of A-bombs, the more efficient use of scarce resources, and added "flexibility" to U.S. planning and operations.[5]

Here then, nearly four decades ago, were the core arguments

elaborated by arms control and nuclear weapon strategists in the long procession of debates that have followed since. With the H-bomb's public unveiling, the debate emerged very much in the open, with themes so constant over time that any recapitulation of them risks tiresome repetition.

Nuclear weapon strategists have wished to challenge the expansion of Soviet power on broad fronts from positions of military strength. In this view, the Soviets appear to place credence in the power of nuclear weapons to accomplish their objectives, preferably as instruments of coercion but, if need be, as military means to accomplish political ends. Thus, the United States must, at an absolute minimum, have nuclear weapon capabilities second to none in order to block the Soviets from achieving their goals. Mere parity in nuclear weaponry poses risks because of Soviet advantages in non-nuclear forces. Given this view of Soviet objectives, it follows that negotiations are not the most appropriate way to defend Western interests. Our good intentions and our readiness to negotiate place us at a real disadvantage before cynical Soviet negotiators whose primary objective is to secure advantage.

The arms control community has reached opposing conclusions to each of these central questions in the strategic debate. For this camp, the close of World War II ushered in a threat larger than that posed by the Soviet Union—the threat of nuclear weapons. The specter of the mushroom cloud in turn led to the primacy of arms control and disarmament as U.S. policy objectives, imperatives that continued to grow with the sophistication and size of nuclear weapon inventories. Otherwise, an unregulated competition would at the very least magnify tensions between the superpowers and raise the alarming prospect that nuclear weapons would again be used.

To those in the arms control camp, the goal of regulating the arms race repeatedly was at odds with the objective of securing positions of strength. For some, a policy of "no first use" of nuclear weapons was indispensable; virtually all rejected the premise that weapons of mass destruction could be controlled on the battlefield to secure political and military objectives against a similarly armed (and presumably resolute) adversary. The only solution to the arms race, then, lay in cooperative agreements. Nuclear arms control negotiations could succeed for the basic reason that it was also in the Soviet interest to make them succeed.

When representatives of the two camps argue over the nuclear question, they have their own internalized set of assumptions that makes for a coherent world view. Whatever results from new weap-

ons programs or arms control negotiations can readily be assimilated
into these views. Assumptions clash with each other in ways that
allow both sides to claim self-fulfilling prophecies in a self-perpetu-
ating debate.

Nuclear weapon strategists believe they are right because the
Soviet build-up has dwarfed the restraints imposed by arms control, requiring responses in kind. Arms controllers believe they are
right because the accelerated arms race is a testament to the in-
sufficiency of partial measures. For "hawks," if increased defense
spending does not bring about added security, the proper remedy
is still higher defense spending. For "doves," if arms control measures do not provide for increased stability, the proper remedy is
more comprehensive arms control.

Debates between the two camps have therefore become highly
ritualized. At every treaty debate, opponents caution that the agreement in question would pose greater risks than benefits, harm alliance relations, and lull the public into a false sense of security. At
every weapon decision, opponents argue that arms races, not arms
control, pose the greater risks. One camp thinks that negotiations
will bear fruit only if the United States rejects attempts to gain advantage. The other thinks that negotiations will succeed only if the
United States bargains from a position of strength. Underlying these
differences is the notion of arms controllers that the Soviet Union
won't accept an inferior position. For many of their opponents, the
Soviets won't accept arms control agreements unless they have
managed to secure superiority or unless they are threatened with
inferiority.

Both sides long ago developed a filtering process to support their
judgments. Some filtering mechanism is necessary, if only because
it is so difficult to decipher what the Soviets really mean through
the layers of ideology, history, and military culture that go with their
pronouncements in this field. The Kremlin, after all, has long been
a proponent of both disarmament and dominance over the West.
These mixed messages do not confuse partisans in both camps: each
side in the strategic debate tends to take literally those Soviet pronouncements that support its assumptions, while interpreting loosely
those that do not. Each weighs military capabilities against Soviet
intentions in very different ways. For one camp, intentions can be
inferred from the Kremlin's growing military inventories. For the
other, a more relaxed view of the Kremlin's intentions takes much
of the menace out of the Soviet military build-up.

Neither camp presents a united front at all times; each has its own internal divisions. Both have what may be described as operationally- and ideologically-inclined wings. The arms control and disarmament community naturally divides between those who are content in managing the arms race and those who wish to liquidate the competition in its entirety. Arms controllers are very much operationally-minded. They accept as a given the presence of nuclear weapons in modern-day arsenals. Their operational goal is "strategic stability"—a situation where neither superpower feels its security threatened because of rough nuclear balances and the ability to create "no win" situations even in the event of a surprise attack, whether conventional or nuclear. Threatening political gestures or weapon developments are to be avoided to foster a condition of strategic stability and to serve as a basis for arms reductions; new weapon systems that provide for stability and balance are acceptable.

The disarmament wing of the arms control community questions the very concept of deterrence based on the threat of mass destruction. From this perspective, operational concerns are subordinate to the primary objective of getting rid of nuclear weapons. In turn, political disputes would become easier to resolve because the disarmament process would remove an important source of tension in superpower relations. Because they are heavily weighed down by operational concerns, arms controllers are quite sensitive to the limitations of their craft. For partisans of disarmament, these preoccupations themselves become constricting. In this view, far more can be accomplished if we remove our self-imposed bonds.

Each wing has been pre-eminent at different times. At the outset of the strategic debate, "arms control" wasn't a part of the popular lexicon. After V-J Day, the issue for concerned citizens was abolishing U.S. stockpiles and preventing other nations from following in our footsteps.

A complicating factor in disarmament discussions was the appearance of the H-bomb, a progeny that could easily be 1,000 times more powerful than its parent. Subsequent disarmament initiatives continued to be cast in sweeping terms, and desultory negotiations over general and complete disarmament continued for almost two decades, despite the increasing implausibility of this goal. The first of several editions of Grenville Clark's and Louis Sohn's work, *World Peace Through World Law* appeared in 1958, arguing for wholesale disarmament; the last official U.S. proposal for a "Treaty on General and Complete Disarmament in a Peaceful World" was tabled before the U.N.-sponsored Eighteen Nation Disarmament Committee in April 1962.

Starting in the mid-1950s, the focus of public and scientific concerns began to shift from grand disarmament schemes to more limited approaches. President Dwight David Eisenhower appointed a Cabinet-level adviser, Harold Stassen, to head up these efforts. Stassen's views generated considerable opposition within the executive branch; his constituency came from an aroused public, which focused on the need to stop atmospheric tests of nuclear weapons. The ensuing public health debate was encouraged by the creation of national organizations promoting arms control, like the National Committee for a Sane Nuclear Policy (SANE). Popular pressure on behalf of arms control found a legislative channel when Senator Hubert Humphrey convinced his colleagues to form a Special Subcommittee on Disarmament. In hearings held in 1956–58, Humphrey's Subcommittee advocated graduated measures to relieve tensions and reduce the threat of nuclear war.

While Eisenhower showed some receptivity to partial measures of arms control, the initial operational success of this strategy as well as the intellectual basis for it are associated with the Kennedy Administration. The first tangible result of this approach was the Limited Test Ban Treaty, ratified in 1963. By rejecting a comprehensive treaty banning all nuclear tests and avoiding the political and technical problems associated with such a treaty, President Kennedy accepted a limited solution to one part of the overall problem. But he was also breaking a good deal of new ground.

A rich literature appeared during the early 1960s explaining the principles and possibilities of arms control. The most important was probably *Strategy and Arms Control*, written by two Harvard University professors, Thomas C. Schelling and Morton Halperin. Arms control, the authors felt, was a "promising," but "dimly perceived" tool. It could work, even in the adversarial superpower relationship, because both the U.S. and the U.S.S.R. had a "mutual interest in the avoidance of a war that neither side wants, in minimizing the costs and risks of the arms competition and in curtailing the scope of violence of war in the event it occurs."[6]

Subsequent contests over anti-ballistic missiles (ABMs) and multiple independently targetable re-entry vehicles (MIRVs) were debates over arms control, not disarmament. The language of President Jimmy Carter's inaugural address, calling for the elimination of nuclear weapons from the face of the earth, sounded strange after ro many years of official disuse. The staffing plans of the new president were also unusual: the designees for Secretary of State and Director of ACDA were both deeply committed arms controllers, as were many of their key lieutenants.

When the Reagan Administration generated another wave of public involvement in national security issues, arms controllers were in a weak position to take blocking action. Their management practices and formulas yielded meager returns when given the chance. Working at the margins of the arms race no longer seemed an appropriate strategy to many new foot soldiers in the debate. For them, the practices of the arms control community appeared more exclusionary than effective; what was needed was not a theology of arms control, but a stop to the arms race.

The Reagan Administration's initiatives therefore generated a different mix of the opposition, one more reminiscent of earlier debates over nuclear weapons than the classic confrontations over ABMs and MIRVs. Once more, the debate shifted from relative to absolute terms. In lieu of calls for immediate disarmament, the popular cry was for a freeze in the testing, production and deployment of nuclear weapons.

Again, books appeared in print warning, as Linus Pauling had done during the test ban debate, of the human consequences of nuclear warfare. The most celebrated among them, *The Fate of the Earth*, was sold to the public at reduced cost, as was the case with an earlier manifesto, *One World or None*, which appeared after the close of World War II. The author, Jonathan Schell, stressed the theme that the concept of deterrence by nuclear weapons was a hoax and a failure, "because at the crucial moment it requires nations to sacrifice mankind for their own interests — an absurdity as well as a crime beyond reckoning."[7] Schell's prescription was complete nuclear disarmament; "abolition" again became a rallying cry.

Joining the nuclear freeze movement was George F. Kennan. During the heyday of the Humphrey Subcommittee on Disarmament, Kennan warned that political settlements were a precondition to disarmament; in 1958, he stated his preparedness to "concede that the atomic deterrent has its value as a stabilizing factor until we can evolve some better means of protection."[8] Kennan always drew narrow bounds for the utility of nuclear weapons; when the roles which others ascribed to these weapons continued to grow and when political solutions appeared increasingly remote, his prescription for relief became increasingly bold. In 1981, Kennan called for an immediate 50 percent reduction in nuclear arsenals, leading eventually to complete nuclear disarmament:

> I see the danger not in the number or quality of the weapons or in the intentions of those who hold them but in the very existence of weapons of this nature, regardless of whose hands they are in. I believe that until we consent to recognize that the nuclear weapons we hold in our own hands are as much a danger to us as those that repose in the hands of our supposed adversaries there will be no escape from the confusions and dilemmas to which such weapons have now brought us, and must bring us increasingly as time goes on. For this reason, I see no solution to the problem other than the complete elimination of these and all other weapons of mass destruction from national arsenals; and the sooner we move toward that solution, and the greater courage we show in doing so, the safer we will be.[9]

Despite differences of view and varying positions of political strength, advocates of disarmament and practitioners of arms control have at critical moments joined together in common cause against many programs favored by nuclear weapon strategists. Policy disputes between the two wings within the arms control community usually can be narrowed to matters of timing and degree, particularly when juxtaposed against the policy preferences of those of the hawkish persuasion. Both wings within the arms control camp are concerned about strategic balances, broadly speaking, although they readily differ in the amount of weight that should be attached to "perceptions" of military balances. Often, each wing directed its attention to different audiences: arms controllers tried to work with policy-makers directly, while advocates of disarmament were more inclined to affect policy via the grass roots. Arms controllers often framed their proposals with "credibility" (such as what constituted a credible deterrent) very much in mind. Advocates of disarmament generally believed concerns over credibility to be more of a hindrance than a help in achieving positive results.

These were important distinctions, but not of a kind to bar a collaborative relationship. Most of the time, the two wings have held overlapping positions. Arms controllers are committed to dismantling nuclear weapons, just as those committed to disarmament have respect for the management tools of their operationally-minded colleagues. Working together, both wings within the arms control community could point to limited successes—improved communication channels with the Soviet Union, some curtailed nuclear weapon programs, and an occasional symbolic gesture—taken together, welcome change from years of empty rhetoric and fruitless negotiations. The lack of greater success was not linked to failures of collaboration, but to long spells of public indifference to the nuclear peril.

Within the opposing camp of nuclear weapon strategists, there have also been two wings: those who accepted limited arms control agreements as management tools in the strategic competition, and those who opposed almost any agreement on its face. Nuclear weapon strategists also differed over the role that ideology played in Soviet behavior. One wing placed heavy emphasis on ideology in explaining Soviet actions and the futility of arms control. For them, dealing with a sworn adversary was essentially a zero-sum game in every respect.

Ideologically-inclined nuclear weapon strategists could trace their roots back to NSC-68, the interagency study prompted by the discovery, in 1949, that the Soviet Union had in all probability joined the nuclear club. The themes expressed in NSC-68 were repeated in conferences and publications linked to academic centers founded in the 1950s and early 1960s, like the Foreign Policy Research Institute of the University of Pennsylvania and the Georgetown Center for Strategic Studies. These institutions moved over time to the mainstream. The pronouncements of nongovernmental organizations like the American Security Council and the Heritage Foundation retained a harder edge. The rhetoric of those most inclined to view the contest in systemic terms has often found its way into official pronouncements, but control over decisions governing nuclear weapons and arms control has usually rested in the hands of operationally-minded strategists. The role of their ideologically-inclined colleagues was usually relegated to braking or prodding initiatives within the executive branch. It was not until the Reagan Administration that ideologues came in from the cold, obtaining multiple and critical positions in the White House and Pentagon.

Operationally-inclined strategists have not denied an ideological element in shaping Soviet activities, but they generally placed this within the context of the more traditional impulses and objectives of a great power. Operationalists could also trace their roots to NSC-68, but they tended to avoid organizations formed by their more ideologically-inclined brethren to influence the course of U.S.

national security policy. When they did join such organizations, such as the Committee on the Present Danger during the Carter Administration, it was out of a sense of extraordinary circumstance, not natural habit. For the most part, operationalists affected policy not through pressure groups, but from positions of influence held in either the executive or legislative branches of government. Their campaigns to affect American public opinion usually resulted in changing their unaccustomed status from outsiders back to practitioners. Such men did not see themselves as rigid anti-communists; they believed they were highly sensitive to operational concerns.

As is the case with the arms control community, distinctions between ideologically- and operationally-inclined nuclear weapon strategists are far from neat. Differences have become widely blurred on a number of issues, views have changed over time, and the context of each debate has been important in determining the positioning of some key participants. It is not too difficult to find public statements of prominent figures which confer upon them the title of rigid ideologue or flexible practitioner of the art of *Realpolitik*.

Distinctions within the camp of nuclear weapon strategists—like those within the arms control community—have periodically had political import, but not of a lasting kind. When nuclear weapon strategists hold the reins of power, their intramural differences can be quite sharp and politically divisive. The disagreements can usually be traced back to varying degrees of emphasis placed on ideology as a guide to Soviet behavior. However, when opposing the policies of an arms control-oriented administration, the two wings usually have little difficulty closing ranks: the distinctions they draw between themselves are far less significant than their quarrels with the domestic opposition. There is every reason for hawks of all persuasions to unite because they tend to view the contest in universal terms. Despite the differing emphases they may place on motivations for Soviet behavior or on the possibilities of blending diplomacy with military preparedness, all agree that the United States is faced with a global challenge for the largest conceivable stakes.

Divisions between and within the two camps can be summarized as in the accompanying chart. Without question, the two camp/two wing classification scheme oversimplifies the spectrum of views present at arms control and nuclear weapon debates. Most of the debaters hold textured views on these complex issues. A few individuals, like Harold Brown, could be classified as hybrids of the two camps. Some important public figures have changed camps

POSITIONS TAKEN IN DEBATES OVER ARMS CONTROL AND NUCLEAR WEAPONS

ISSUES	NUCLEAR WEAPON STRATEGISTS		ARMS CONTROL AND DISARMAMENT STRATEGISTS	
	IDEOLOGUES	OPERATIONALISTS	OPERATIONALISTS	IDEOLOGUES
DEFINITION OF THE PROBLEM	The Russians	Managing geopolitical competition	Managing the arms race	The bomb
DEFINITION OF THE SOLUTION	Superiority	Strategic advantage	Strategic arms control	Disarmament
POLITICAL UTILITY OF NUCLEAR WEAPONS	Significant	Likely, with disparities in nuclear capabilities	Possible, with significant disparities in nuclear capabilities, otherwise as a deterrent	Counterproductive
MILITARY UTILITY OF NUCLEAR WEAPONS	Significant	Possible, with significant disparities in nuclear capabilities	Unlikely, except to aid conflict termination	Counterproductive

WILLINGNESS TO TAKE RISKS FOR NEW NUCLEAR CAPABILITIES	Major	Measured	Minimal	Counterproductive
UTILITY OF ARMS CONTROL NEGOTIATIONS	Counterproductive	Measured	Major	Measured but can be counterproductive
DESIRED OUTCOME OF NEGOTIATIONS	Superiority	Stability and parity in key indices	Stability and reductions in armament and cost	Major reductions in armament and cost
WILLINGNESS TO TAKE RISKS FOR NEW ARMS CONTROL AGREEMENTS	Counterproductive	Minimal	Measured	Major
UTILITY OF UNILATERAL INITIATIVES	Counterproductive	Minimal	Measured	Major
NUCLEAR WAR-FIGHTING OBJECTIVES	War-winning	Gain most advantageous position	Avoid disadvantageous position	Counterproductive

in the course of the extended debate. Stuart Symington switched camps during his years of public service, moving from friend to foe of the Pentagon's strategic weapon programs. Donald Brennan reversed his support for arms control after the SALT I accords were signed. Others, like George Kennan, moved from one wing to another within their camps. The public postures on arms control of some individuals, like Paul Nitze, suggest a correlation between positions held in or out of government. Some key figures in the debate defy classification. Others have assumed widely varying positions over the extended course of debate. For example, Henry Kissinger has made important contributions to arms control, but his positions on specific issues have hardly been a model of consistency over time.

Despite these shifts, paradigms like the one delineated here can provide insight into the political dynamics of debate. With all the necessary caveats, there remain established themes for each contest, articulated by individuals who have become familiar champions of them. Current nuclear weapon and arms control debates can be gauged by following the previous positions of influential senators, scientific luminaries or distinguished public servants. When key individuals break with their pasts, we take note, for they signal important changes in the domestic political climate and provide clues to the outcome of debate. To simplify the process of recognition, some analytical framework is needed. The one offered here, it is hoped, gains more by providing clarity than it loses in accuracy. This framework succeeds if it illuminates the political dynamics of current debates and provides clues on how to alter their outcomes. It fails if it serves merely to pigeonhole the views of various participants. Most of the individuals who are quoted in the following pages hold views that are too complex to fit neatly into analytical cubbyholes. Only the "true believers" in both camps have continued to hold rigid positions on the issues, regardless of changed political circumstance.

What follows is not a history of strategic arms control or nuclear weapon developments, but an analysis of political debates over the nuclear question. To illuminate each camp's basic premises and the political dynamics that result, themes are stressed, not chronology. Wherever possible, key participants speak for themselves. Not all of the prominent spokespersons in prior debates are represented here. Some figures may appear too prominent; others not prominent enough. Quotations are chosen to illustrate themes, not to reflect the relative weight of their authors' arguments.

2 The Soviet Threat

The Hawkish Persuasion

Stationary threats do not lay claim to the emotions or arrest the attention for very long. What makes the Soviet threat so compelling to nuclear weapon strategists is its expansionary character. Even those strategists who acknowledge the attenuation of Soviet ideological fervor and its limited export market have not contended that this in any way diminishes the dangers facing the West. On the contrary, in its weakened condition (or in reaction to the weakened condition of the West) the Soviets can be expected to continue their implacable hostility and opportunistic expansionism.

In one debate after the next, nuclear weapon strategists have stood together in their prescriptions for dealing with this problem. All have emphasized the critical role of military power generally and nuclear weapons specifically in foiling Soviet designs, and all have expressed skepticism over the utility of arms control agreements in dampening the Kremlin's appetite for military hardware and unwarranted political access.

For those who stressed the theme of ideological confrontation, the entire postwar period of decision over nuclear weapons and arms control could be viewed as a constant ideological struggle. NSC-68, the source document for post-Korean War policy toward the Kremlin, framed the contest in just these terms, noting that "the Soviet Union, unlike previous aspirants to hegemony, is animated by a

17

new fanatic faith, antithetical to our own, and seeks to impose its absolute authority over the rest of the world."[1]

In the ideological struggle against communism, relativism tended to give way to absolutism. Admiral Arleigh Burke voiced these themes when he became the first Director of Georgetown University's Center for Strategic Studies. Writing at the time of the Partial Nuclear Test Ban Treaty debate, Burke warned, "Between the free West and the Communist movement, there can be no reconciliation, no real coexistence. The confrontation is absolute. For the two centers of power hold fundamentally different views of the process whereby order is established and preserved."[2]

To ideologues, the Partial Test Ban Treaty meant that an American President had joined a political compact with a sworn adversary, the "Red Russians." The symbolism behind even so limited a first step was rather profound: The United States was denying itself the unilateralism it had previously insisted upon for its nuclear weapons programs. This warning has been echoed at every key decision point for nuclear weapons and arms control ever since. By the time the two superpowers began the process of Strategic Arms Limitation Talks (SALT), the ideological tenor of the competition had faded for most, but not for the right wing. At the outset of the SALT negotiations, the American Security Council took it upon itself to remind the American public of what it saw as a fundamental truth: "In both word and deed, the Soviets have shown that they regard the world struggle as a fight to the finish between two diametrically opposed social systems. Moreover, it is a fight the Soviets intend to win."[3]

This message was broadcast from several academic centers, but most vigorously at the University of Pennsylvania's Foreign Policy Research Institute during the first two decades of its existence. Established in 1955, the Institute was very much an extension of its first Director, Robert Strausz-Hupé. Born in Vienna, Strausz-Hupé received his doctorate from the University of Pennsylvania at the age of forty-one, while World War II was drawing to a close. The Foreign Policy Research Institute remained his base of operations when he was not holding ambassadorial posts abroad.

Strausz-Hupé gathered around him a number of like-minded souls in Philadelphia, and together they published numerous manuscripts. The two books that probably had the most impact bracketed the transition between the Eisenhower and Kennedy Administrations. Appearing at a time of domestic turmoil over Sputnik and the general state of the strategic balance, these two books, *The Protracted Conflict* and *A Forward Strategy for America*, could hardly be ignored. The first diagnosed the problem: The U.S. and the U.S.S.R. were engaged in a protracted conflict on all fronts and for the largest conceivable stakes — "domination of the earth . . . outer space and over the future of human society."[4] The second book offered prescriptions — a total effort, seizing every initiative to transform communist societies, short of military liberation. "We cannot tell whether, in the future, the communists will see the wisdom of prudent retreat," cautioned the collective authorship, who closed by asking their readers to "cultivate the dour virtues which alone sustain a people in mortal combat."[5] For members of the Foreign Policy Research Institute, hostile Soviet pronouncements had to be taken at face value. In 1963, Strausz-Hupé warned: "The West can make no graver error than to assume that Communist leaders speaking *ex cathedra* do not mean what they say, and, like Western leaders, are willing to accept a 'reasonable' compromise between idea and reality."[6]

This hard line necessarily changed during Khrushchev's pronouncements of "peaceful coexistence." Nuclear weapon strategists who viewed the struggle largely in ideological terms then began to suggest that Soviet pronouncements not be taken at face value; rather, they should be discounted, as feints in the continuing struggle between communism and the West. President Ronald Reagan's first National Security Adviser, Richard V. Allen, began his professional career around this time, interpreting Khrushchev's remarks for the Georgetown Center and for the American Bar Association's Standing Committee on Education Against Communism. Allen's message then was that peaceful coexistence was a ruse, "the strategy which will carry forth the Communist revolution to the final overthrow of the free world and the establishment of worldwide Communist rule."[7] Soviet pronouncements may change, but their expansionist goals remain constant. President Ronald Reagan was therefore working from a script at least as old as NSC-68 when he stated at his first press conference that he, too, accepted the Kremlin at its word, that its "goal must be the promotion of world revolution and a one-world Socialist or Communist state."

Interpretations of Soviet ideology profoundly bored operationally-minded strategists, but the accumulation of raw military power by the U.S.S.R. commanded their attention. Such capabilities could allow the Kremlin to advance its geopolitical objectives unless the West was properly prepared to counter them. This was, after all, what the policy of containment was all about.

The post-World War II intellectual roots of the containment policy can be traced to the dispatches of George Kennan — a man who parted company with nuclear weapon strategists as he saw how they were implementing his precepts. But immediately after the war, Kennan's policy prescriptions were quite different than they later became. "It is clear," he wrote anonymously in the famous "X" article in *Foreign Affairs*, "that the main element of any United States policy toward the Soviet Union must be that of a long-term, patient but firm and vigilant containment of Russian expansive tendencies."[8] This thought has sustained numerous offspring, much to the despair of its author. One direct descendant was the Committee on the Present Danger, which opened for business thirty years after the "X" article appeared with the declaration that "the principal threat to our nation, to world peace, and to the cause of human freedom is the Soviet drive for dominance based upon an unparalleled military buildup."[9]

Kennan's recommendation for dealing with "Soviet pressure against the free institutions of the Western world" was through "the adroit and vigilant application of counter-force at a series of constantly shifting geographical and political points."[10] For those entrusted with the operational responsibilities of containing Communism, counterforce meant, first and foremost, military preparedness. Without big sticks, the United States lacked the leverage to modify Soviet behavior. While Kennan increasingly pressed for nonmilitary approaches and limited objectives, the policy of containment proceeded largely on a military basis and on a global scale.

When NSC-68 was drafted, the concerns weighing most heavily on the minds of defense strategists were the status of Germany and China. These twin concerns faded as the Cold War progressed, and the cockpit of U.S.-Soviet rivalry turned to the Third World. Still, the theme of the Soviet drive for dominance remained constant. Thirty years after taking the lead in drafting NSC-68, Paul Nitze saw a difference in Soviet tactics, not grand strategy:

> For many years the focus of Soviet strategy has been on Western Europe. By achieving dominance over the Middle East, they aim to outflank Europe. They propose to outflank the Middle East by achieving controlling positions in Afghanistan, Iran, and Iraq

on one side, South and North Yemen, Eritrea, Ethiopia and Mozambique on the other, and by achieving the neutrality of Turkey on the north. Concurrently, they are attempting to encircle China by pressure on Pakistan and India, by alliance with Vietnam, and dominance over North Korea.[11]

It wasn't necessary for nuclear weapon strategists to share Nitze's particular scenario of the Soviet drive for dominance to join with him in instigating blocking action. Nor was it necessary to agree on Soviet motives in order to form a common front of operationally- and ideologically-inclined strategists. The goal that the Soviets were seeking made it somewhat beside the point to argue the question of motivation, especially when there was next to no disagreement over the consequences, nor the means to counter Soviet designs.

The Arms Control Perspective

For the arms control community, the problem posed by the Soviet state can be characterized more in terms of a challenge than as a threat. To be sure, one did not have to be a certified hawk to be concerned about the military power of the Kremlin and the steady output of Soviet military production. Where arms controllers usually drew the line with their adversaries in the domestic debate was over the end use of the Kremlin's abundant military hardware. Many took their cues from seasoned veterans of the U.S. diplomatic corps who viewed the accumulation of Soviet military power as defensive, more than offensive in nature. It was, said Charles Yost, a former U.S. Ambassador to the United Nations and champion of SALT II ratification, a reflection of, "on the one hand, a national psychosis and, on the other, real vulnerabilities."[12]

Men like Yost concluded long ago that there were other, more plausible explanations for the consistently high level of defense spending since the Khrushchev era. At or near the top of the list was the division of bureaucratic power and resulting budgetary trade-offs within the Kremlin. The Soviet military bureaucracy was strong and exceedingly well-fed, a status Brezhnev fostered and benefited from in return. It was also a condition unlikely to be changed in the near term by his successors. Another explanation offered was the habit (no less notorious in the Kremlin than in some circles in Washington) to build defenses based on bleak estimates of adversarial capabilities and intentions. Perhaps, too, the Soviet build-up was a conscious effort to stress the one output of the Soviet economic system from which a measure of political gain abroad could be derived, although this must be judged a subsidiary motivation. According to commentary in the West, at least, the size and equipment of Soviet military forces were the most salient features in the changing "correlation of forces," so central to Soviet ideology and political objectives.

For arms controllers, ample Russian military capabilities had to be judged within the context of Soviet political intentions. Those advocating a more relaxed view have sometimes been helped by official intelligence estimates, as was the case immediately after the first Soviet atomic bomb test. Then, the Central Intelligence Agency held,

> It has been asserted that only the existence of the U.S. atomic bomb prevented the USSR from carrying out an intention to continue its military advance to the Atlantic in 1945. There can be no doubt that the U.S. atomic bomb had a sobering and deterrent effect on the USSR. There is no reason to suppose, however, that the USSR had any such intention in 1945 or subsequently.[13]

While intelligence assessments are usually held privately, those of disillusioned former diplomatic and public officials have been meant for public consumption. At the height of the Cold War, George Kennan continued to stress the need to distinguish between what the Soviets "could conceivably do" and what "they actually do."[14] For Kennan, even then the Kremlin leaders were acting as sound-minded men, not as ideologues.

One reason why the arms control community held to this view lay in their assessment of the Kremlin leadership as a group of cautious pragmatists. When it came to the use of military force at their disposal, ideology took a back seat to more narrow calculations of self-interest. "The Soviet approach to these matters is characterized by a considerable degree of sobriety,"[15] wrote Marshall Shulman, a Kremlinologist who practiced his trade at Harvard, Tufts, and Columbia Universities in addition to serving as an adviser to Secretary of State Cyrus Vance. Shulman's assessment was offered shortly after the SALT I accords were signed.

SALT provided confirmation that the Soviet Union was not carrying ideological baggage into the negotiating sessions. The SALT negotiations were a model of businesslike exchanges, a world apart from the public posturing that accompanied U.N. negotiations on general and complete disarmament. For arms controllers, this negotiating process confirmed the premise that ideology mattered a good deal less to the Kremlin than the objectives of avoiding nuclear war and stabilizing the strategic competition. For both wings of the arms control and disarmament camp, ideology had become the rationale rather than the animating force behind Soviet actions. Communism as an ideology had lost its power; Soviet society was no longer viewed as a beacon for others except in the most deadened official pronouncements. Certainly, the Soviets were no longer a role model for their communist state neighbors both East and West. Instead, the power of the Soviet state was tied to an assortment of significant liabilities, and the writings of Marx and Engels didn't provide a clue to solving them.

When the Soviets consolidated their control over Eastern Europe, they placed themselves in the position of having much to lose, rather than gain, in a military offensive on the Continent. The arms control community had difficulty envisioning the Soviets using their massive conventional capabilities to overrun Europe, just as they could not foresee how any Kremlin leadership could give the orders to start a nuclear exchange. To be sure, the Third World presented wholesale opportunities for gaining advantage at the expense of the West. But there too, Soviet progress was uneven, and attempts to expand the Kremlin's reach have been characterized not so much by adventurism, as by cautious opportunism. Even the Soviet invasion of Afghanistan, a move that troubled many as establishing a dangerous new threshold for Soviet intervention if not a new drive to the Persian Gulf, could be interpreted as defensive maneuvering. In the view of men like George Kennan and Richard J. Barnet, the Soviets moved into Afghanistan to avoid losing a friendly government, or worse, to block the ascendancy of another hostile government on their periphery.[16]

Soviet weapon programs can likewise be explained by a deep sense of insecurity, or responses to specific technological and military challenges posed by the West. True, the Soviets had been the first to usher in some new phases of the strategic competition (such as flight testing of intercontinental ballistic missiles) and the first to resume dormant phases of the competition (such as antisatellite warfare). But these initiatives have been rare and have generated immediate, technologically advanced responses by the United States. More often, the Soviets have lagged behind the United States in reaching critical technological milestones. Most notably, the Soviets were clearly inferior in MIRV technology until the late 1970s. When the Kremlin deployed MIRVs in abundance on land-based missiles, this, too, could be explained in nonthreatening terms: the Soviets could hardly depend on their inferior forces of ballistic missile submarines and propeller-driven heavy bombers. Soviet bureaucratic interests and military culture all pointed to a top-heavy reliance on ICBMs.

For the arms control community, Soviet weapon programs did not reflect a grand design; they represented how deeply ingrained the strategic competition had become. Former Secretary of Defense Robert McNamara once referred to this phenomenon as "a kind of mad momentum intrinsic to the development of all new nuclear weaponry. If a weapon system works — and works well — there is a strong pressure from many directions to procure and deploy the weapon out of all proportion to the prudent level required."

McNamara unburdened himself of these thoughts in one of the oddest official addresses ever given by a Secretary of Defense — his announcement of the decision to deploy a "light" nationwide anti-ballistic missile system. The Secretary of Defense explained his decision in terms of a challenge far different from the Soviet threat: "We each have reacted to the other's build up with very conservative calculations . . . simply because both wanted to be able to cope with the worst plausible case." The build-up of strategic forces out of proportion to military needs evoked a matching build-up from the other side. "What is essential to understand here," said McNamara, "is that the Soviet Union and the United States mutually influence one another's strategic plans. Whatever be their intentions, whatever be our intentions, actions . . . necessarily trigger reactions on the other side. It is precisely this action-reaction phenomenon that fuels an arms race."[17]

Others used different phraseology to describe this causal chain: David Lilienthal thought the U.S. and U.S.S.R. were "caught in a seesaw." Paul Warnke likened the competition to two rivals on a treadmill.[18] All agreed that the United States bore a special burden by intensifying the arms race in attempting to maintain a qualitative edge. Whether for this reason or because we were more enlightened, the chain could not be broken without U.S. initiatives.

When asked about initiating accommodating measures toward the Kremlin, President Ronald Reagan replied, "It takes two to tango." Arms controllers were prepared to take the first steps. The importance of choosing the arms control option rather than its alternative was most succintly stated by General Maxwell D. Taylor in retirement: "any increase in any kind of strategic weapon stimulates the Soviets to emulation and fuels the arms race."[19] The U.S. and the U.S.S.R. were deeply engaged in the competition, but only the U.S. might muster the foresight and the political agility to lead both nations out of the arms race.

While their domestic opponents were pointing out numerous reasons why it was difficult or unwise to do business with the Soviets, the arms control community was focusing on the penalties of not reaching cooperative agreements. In this view, the bars to progress were more domestic than external, since there was a clear and common interest to make headway. If the United States could demonstrate the political will and cohesion to press forward, the Soviet Union would eventually be accommodating.

In the arms controllers' calculus of benefits and risks, there has been no need to change this assessment over time because Soviet national interests have remained, in the most fundamental sense, complementary to our own: we both needed to avoid a cataclysmic finale to the strategic arms competition. The very nature of this mutually threatening relationship—two scorpions in the bottle, to use Robert Oppenheimer's phrase—made arms control at the same time essential and possible. True, the Soviet state has been an opportunistic and difficult adversary, but it was an adversary that had as much at stake in defusing this deadly competition as the United States had. This was Kennan's assessment of the Soviet state under Stalin; it was Averell Harriman's conclusion during his negotiations with Khrushchev over a nuclear test ban, and it was Charles Yost's view of Brezhnev and his colleagues during the SALT decade:

There could be no shadow of a doubt in the mind of any Soviet leader that to initiate a general war—that is, almost certainly a nuclear exchange —would jeopardize the security of the Soviet Union in the highest degree, would lead to the destruction of most of the great industrial base they have built up over sixty years, and very likely to the overthrow of their own regime. It is almost impossible for any sober observer to imagine any Soviet leadership, particularly the present array of septuagenarians and sexagenarians, risking such hazards. Soviet doctrine requires them to nudge history along in their direction but not to give it so brutal a shove as to send it sprawling — very possibly with themselves underneath.[20]

The famous "X" article in *Foreign Affairs* by George Kennan offered to policy makers a management theory to deal with the Soviet challenge. The United States had to counter Soviet expansionism and clarify for the Kremlin leadership that there was no profit to be gained from flagrant misbehavior. The object of statecraft was thus "to force upon the Kremlin a far greater degree of moderation and circumspection than it has had to observe in recent years, and in this way to promote tendencies which must eventually find their outlet in either the break-up or the gradual mellowing of Soviet power."[21]

Kennan's "X" article became the leitmotiv for policy toward the Soviet Union. Much to the chagrin of the author, military considerations immediately and persistently dominated the policy of containment, while the United States "failed to take advantage of the opportunities for useful political discussion" that were opened up over time.[22]

Central to this point of view was the premise that the West could affect the way the Soviet leadership approached national security issues. "This problem of the possibility of a different and preferable Russia," Kennan wrote shortly after President Truman's decision to press ahead with the H-bomb, "is not really a question of war or peace. War in itself will not bring about such a Russia." A change in Soviet attitudes would not come from offensive military preparations, but from a combination of adroit political initiatives and a nonthreatening defense posture that secured vital Western interests against communist encroachment.

At this time, Kennan's policy objective wasn't arms control, per se, but a basis for some sort of political accord with the Soviet Union from which arms control would surely follow. In Kennan's view, the process of normalization would require far more of the Soviet Union than of the United States, and would largely be an internal affair. Nevertheless, the United States had a constructive and essential role to play in the evolution of Soviet attitudes and our possibilities for influencing the outcome were "significant."[23]

From the overriding objective of avoiding a war with the Soviet Union, the pursuit of arms control agreements with a committed

adversary naturally followed. For the entire arms control community, it did not particularly matter whether the Soviets shared our
world view or our military doctrine, although active and prolonged
debates continued on these topics. For the purpose of conducting
arms control business, it was sufficient that Soviet leaders simply
accepted the same basic premise that nuclear war must be avoided.
Because sane Soviet leaders would share a common calculus of relative loss and gain in the event of a nuclear war, the road to political accord seemed open, if U.S. leaders were willing to travel it.
The constant search for strategic advantage blocked this road, and
continually foreclosed progress in the political realm.

Throughout the four nuclear decades, the arms control community viewed the actions of nuclear weapon strategists as constituting
one foreclosure after the next to improved political relations — a continuing sequence of missed opportunities to shape Soviet attitudes.
James Franck and his colleagues who opposed the A-bomb's use
against Japan were less concerned with its shock effect against the
Japanese than with its shock effect on the Russians. For these men,
the benefit of a quick Japanese surrender had to be weighed against
the risk of stimulating a U.S.-Soviet atomic weapons competition
after V-J Day. The choices facing Truman, Stimson, and their advisers were certainly not this stark. It was unclear how long the
Japanese could hold out and how many U.S. casualties would result,
even with Russian entry into the Pacific campaign. Nor was it clear
at the time how much the Soviets actually knew about the Manhattan Project as a result of their espionage activities. But on the
basis of the information available to them, Franck and his colleagues
concluded that short-term military gains in dropping atomic bombs
would be outweighed by long-term losses. Few agreed with them.

For those who wished to stop the arms race, President Truman's
decision to develop hydrogen weapons was another example of the
wrong way to manage the Soviet challenge. Oppenheimer and a
majority of his colleagues advising the Atomic Energy Commission
gave an unqualified judgment to forego development of the super
bomb. The minority view was to make this decision conditional on
a similar renunciation by the Soviets. When Truman decided otherwise and made his decision public, he succeeded in defusing a potentially nasty and volatile domestic political debate. But he also
succeeded, in the view of Hans Bethe and others, in ensuring an
intensified competition with the Soviet Union. "It would be wrong
for us to believe," Bethe wrote, "as we often seem to, that their

successes are independent of our own. Our decision to make the H-bomb indicated that we consider this project feasible and may well have caused them to make the same decision."[24] Bethe, formerly head of the Theoretical Division at Los Alamos, agonized over what role he should play in developing the H-bomb, first refusing to participate, then spending some time on the bomb project to prove that it could not be accomplished. Still later, when it was clear that hydrogen bombs could be built, Bethe worked full-time to prevent the Soviets from building one first.

At the time the H-bomb decision was taken in 1950, it was by no means certain whether or how the United States and the Soviet Union could reach some accommodation over a weapon of such extraordinary destructive power. When a Soviet H-bomb test followed close on the heels of the first U.S. explosion, it became clear that, for all intents and purposes, the two nations had been proceeding concurrently with their programs. The arms control community responded in unison to the prospect of a thermonuclear arms race: regardless of the state of U.S.-Soviet relations, it was necessary to reach some form of political accommodation on disarmament.

The necessary actions weren't forthcoming. Further refinements in thermonuclear weapons and their means of delivery continued to be pursued and achieved; attempts at disarmament were merely pursued. For those on the losing side of the H-bomb debate, their failure was not so much due to the intractability of Soviet strategic objectives as to the defective nature of U.S. initiatives.

3 How Much Is Enough?

Strategic Advantage

At least until the late 1960s, the need for a dominant military posture over the Soviet Union was a self-evident proposition to nuclear weapon strategists of all persuasions. Soviet ideological or geopolitical objectives could not be countered *without* positions of military strength. In the shorthand of the strategic debate, the unadorned requirement was one of superiority. A dominant military posture was not simply the means needed to check Soviet expansionism; it was a source of suasion to encourage moderation and accommodation to Western interests broadly defined.

NSC-68 described the relationship between containment and superiority in this way: "It was and continues to be cardinal in this policy that we possess superior overall power in ourselves or in dependable combination with other like-minded nations . . . Without superior aggregate military strength, in being and readily mobilizable, a policy of containment — which is in effect a policy of calculated and gradual coercion — is no more than a policy of bluff."[1] President Harry S. Truman saw no choice but to brush aside the ethical reservations of some of his scientific advisers in deciding to go forward with the H-bomb. The question of establishing an arms control regime based on prohibiting tests of H-bombs wasn't a live option before the President.[2] The technical obstacles and opportunity costs involved in a crash effort to produce the "super" paled before the dangers of trying to deal with an autocratic ruler named Stalin who, with all his divisions, could also be in sole possession of the new weapon. In this view, there was no way to maintain a superior military position except by having the H-bomb first, and then to build on that lead.

Whatever the military dominance and means of suasion available to the Eisenhower Administration, they rested heavily — and incorrectly in the view of a great many strategists — on nuclear weapons. Eisenhower and Secretary of State John Foster Dulles waged the Cold War on pronouncements of massive retaliation and explicit threats of nuclear weapons use, while the Secretary of Defense and the Chairman of the Joint Chiefs made public statements that smaller-yield nuclear weapons might just as well be considered conventional weapons. A good many strategists flayed the doctrine of massive retaliation as a caricature of the policy of bluff that NSC-68 said should be avoided. But in reality, Eisenhower and Dulles waged the Cold War with only eleven fully equipped Army divisions and a tight lid on defense spending. How else were they to project a dominant strategic posture?

The requirement of strategic superiority carried over to the Kennedy Administration, as well. It was clear that Khrushchev wasn't Stalin, but it was not at all clear what to make of Stalin's unpredictable successor. After years of constrained defense budgets, JFK lifted the lid on military spending. Secretary of Defense Robert S. McNamara vetoed some strategic weapon programs, but authorized considerable increases in U.S. nuclear capabilities.

For all the controversy he engendered at the Pentagon, McNamara was not vulnerable on the issue of relinquishing strategic superiority. On the contrary, McNamara emphasized, whenever asked, that despite his doubts about the political and military utility of nuclear superiority, he had no intention of testing his theories by allowing U.S. superiority to lapse.

The issue for nuclear weapon strategists during these years was not whether, but how much superiority would be adequate. Prescriptions varied, depending on assumptions of the military and political benefits of nuclear weapons and on the fragility of the current balance. For those who viewed the contest more in ideological terms, such as Stefan Possony, massive superiority was the answer. In 1949, Possony wrote a brief for strategic air power in the atomic age, dedicated to those "who fight with the conviction that on the greater glory of the United States rests the sole hope for the future of Western civilization."[3] His thesis then, shared fervently by the newly created U.S. Air Force, was that air superiority was essential both to avoid and to win an atomic war. Later, Possony's focus turned to technology, but his prescription was the same: "due to the unpredictability of technological change, a 'balance' based upon moderate superiority might be easily upset, hence, the hazards of such a strategy are very high."[4]

During this period, arms control agreements were not considered a bar to the maintenance of strategic superiority. On the contrary, the Partial Nuclear Test Ban Treaty was presented to the Senate in 1963 on the grounds that it would help preserve superiority: by forcing Soviet tests underground, it would take the Kremlin longer to catch up to the U.S. level of technological superiority. In hearings on the treaty, Senator Henry Jackson asked every key Administration witness virtually the same question: "Can the United States afford a position of parity or equality with the Soviet Union in nuclear weapons technology and systems?" The answers were uniformly in the negative. Air Force Chief of Staff Curtis LeMay's response was most succinct: "I would never be happy with a situation where we had parity with our enemies."[5]

A majority of the Senate Armed Services Preparedness Investigating Subcommittee rejected the Kennedy Administration's assertion that the Test Ban Treaty would preserve the then-current measure of superiority. With only one dissent (by Senator Leverett Saltonstall), the subcommittee stated that "only because we have maintained clear military superiority and the ability to inflict unacceptable damage upon him has the would-be aggressor been deterred. The basis of our deterrence is military superiority which, in turn, is based on our nuclear weapons programs and nuclear retaliatory forces." To Senators like Stennis, Thurmond, Jackson, Goldwater and Symington, it was difficult to see how U.S. superiority could be maintained by placing clamps on the nation's weapon programs. "At the very least," they argued, "it will prevent the United States from providing our military forces with the highest quality of weapons of which our science and technology is capable."[6] (Senators Jackson and Symington ultimately swallowed their reservations about the Partial Test Ban Treaty and voted for ratification, citing broader political and foreign policy reasons for doing so.)

Thus, in the first twenty-five years of U.S.-Soviet strategic competition, nuclear weapon strategists debated the degree of U.S. superiority needed in nuclear forces, not the requirement for it. In 1969, all of this changed. President Richard M. Nixon announced that hereafter, and despite campaign rhetoric to the contrary, the U.S. goal would be "sufficiency" in strategic forces. Others had foreshadowed this development, but Nixon give it the force of national policy. McNamara had taken the critical first steps by prefacing official policy on U.S. vulnerability in the atomic age — that there was no way to win a nuclear war "in the normal meaning of the word 'win.'"[7] It was left to a conservative Republican Administration to embrace the concept of parity. Secretary of Defense Melvin Laird proceeded to explain the criteria of "sufficiency" to Congress, and the preconditions for strategic arms limitation — acceptance of superpower vulnerability and parity — appeared to be in place. President Nixon and his National Security Adviser, Henry Kissinger, began planning for upcoming SALT negotiations.

The SALT process placed nuclear weapon strategists in somewhat of a dilemma. They had always felt that the best way to contain Soviet expansionism was from positions of strength. As Henry Jackson once said, "it isn't the balance of power that preserves the peace. We must have an imbalance of power in favor of ourselves in order to maintain it."[8] The SALT process was suspect on precisely these grounds.

Would SALT preclude the United States from adopting an optimal military posture? Could agreements based on the principle of rough parity negate a critical source of leverage on Soviet behavior? SALT would probably mean codifying the loss of U.S. strategic superiority without drawing down Soviet advantages in conventional forces. How then could SALT help check Soviet expansionism and adventurism?

Ideologically-inclined strategists rejected the notion offered by the Nixon White House that somehow a pattern of cooperative relations could secure from the Soviet Union what U.S. strategic superiority could not. "Détente" needed to be resisted as much as the premise of equality in strategic forces. Organizations such as the Coalition for Peace Through Strength, an arm of the American Security Council, stressed the need for superiority throughout the SALT negotiations. The Coalition stressed the goal of "overall military/technical superiority over the Soviet Union" in its public education campaign against SALT. Another of the Coalition's "basic principles" was that the United States "accept no arms control agreement which in any way jeopardizes the security of the United States or its allies, or which inhibits a superior defense."[9]

Most of the operationally-inclined strategists had difficulty asserting the need for superiority during the SALT negotiations. For one thing, many of these individuals were allied to or an integral part of the Nixon Administration which was touting sufficiency. There was also the recognition that superiority meant in the popular mind a turning away from the objective of strategic arms control and a clarion call for an all-out arms race. The debate was therefore cast by most opponents of SALT not in terms of regaining superiority, but of assuring parity. For men like Henry Jackson, this was more than just a debating tactic. In Jackson's view, the SALT I Interim Agreement limiting offensive weapon systems allowed the Soviet Union a greater number of strategic weapon launchers. This, combined with the much larger payload of Soviet missiles, would place the United States at a real disadvantage when the Soviets caught up with U.S. technology in MIRVing ballistic missiles.

While the SALT II agreement codified equal ceilings, it did not constrain other measurements of strategic power — such as the "throw-weight" that could be lifted by strategic missile, a decided advantage in the Kremlin's favor. At the SALT II hearings, Alexander Haig expressed the wistful notion that the United States could have retained strategic superiority by spending a few billion dollars more per annum on strategic forces.[10] By then, however, the ostensible concern for SALT skeptics was how to ensure parity, not how to regain superiority. In ratifying the first SALT agreement, the operative mechanism became the Jackson Amendment, calling for "levels of intercontinental strategic forces" in subsequent agreements that were not inferior to those allowed the Soviet Union. SALT II provided for equal levels in various categories of strategic forces, but was still found wanting according to supporters of the Jackson Amendment. Hawks of all persuasions agreed that parity could not be assured in the future unless many billions of dollars more were spent annually on strategic programs. At the very least, this was a precondition to ratification, one that the Carter Administration, like those before it, was willing to pay. But the hawkish community was now divided as to whether this was sufficient payment.

During the SALT II debate, those inclined to view the strategic competition in ideological terms continued to press for superiority, a goal that was clearly incompatible with the proposed treaty. Operationally-inclined critics of SALT explicitly rejected this goal, at least in the near term. For Paul Nitze, the object was simply not to concede strategic superiority to the Soviets.[11] Having "lost" superiority, many operationally-inclined hawks found themselves

wishing to lay the basis for a reinvigorated defense effort by wounding the treaty severely, but not by taking the onus for killing it. The
dilemma for these men was how to regain positions of strength without discarding negotiations altogether.

After all, negotiations for strategic arms limitation have become,
if in only the most narrow sense, a political prerequisite. As Henry
Kissinger said in his SALT II testimony, "No democratic leader
deserves the public trust if he fails to make a genuine effort to reduce the dangers of nuclear holocaust and to free national energies
for dealing with the many urgent problems of mankind."[12] Moreover, all our NATO allies were uncomfortable with a narrow, con-
frontationist posture toward the Soviet Union. A refusal to engage
the Soviets in arms control talks widened the distance in alliance
relations, weakened U.S. leverage for having others share in the
burdens of collective defense, and played into the hands of Soviet
propagandists.

How then could the United States secure adequate positions of
strength while working within a negotiating context that called for
equality? Before assuming positions in the Reagan Administration,
SALT critics proposed deferring negotiations or accepting only those
agreements that rectified the strategic balance. After all, the Pres-
ident-elect and his new advisers repeatedly claimed that the Soviet
Union had achieved a position of strategic superiority under SALT;
for equality to be reestablished, it followed that unequal strides by
the two sides had to be allowed. Before assuming his new responsibilities in the State Department, Richard Burt railed against the
"mad momentum" of arms control during the Carter Administration, while calling for a "nuclear battle management" posture to defend U.S. interests.[13] Before becoming START negotiator, Lt.
General Edward Rowny counseled that "we have put too much emphasis on the control of arms and too little on the provision of arms."
Rowny added, "arms control should be allowed to enter the process only when and where it does not interfere with the provision
of adequate defense for the United States."[14]

The Reagan Administration initially chose to defer negotiations
for as long as the traffic would bear. While the Comprehensive Test
Ban and anti-satellite negotiations remained suspended, Intermediate-range Nuclear Forces (INF) negotiations were resumed after
11 months; the Strategic Arms Reduction Talks (START) began
18 months after President Reagan assumed office. In contrast, President Kennedy resumed test ban negotiations after a three-month
review. At the outset of negotiations, the Reagan Administration's

position called for equality at much lower levels in those categories of forces where the Soviets held a decided advantage. If a negotiated settlement couldn't be reached on these terms, the onus could be placed on the Kremlin for failing to agree to meaningful arms reductions to equal levels.

As much as some members of the Reagan team wanted to redefine the balance of nuclear forces, they encountered predictable pressures that made it impossible to do so. Key members of the legislative branch naturally wondered whether the Reagan Administration's conception of equality would also permit negotiated agreements on terms both sides could find acceptable. These concerns were compounded by public and private statements by Administration officials inferring expansive strategic force requirements, capped by Secretary of Defense Weinberger's directive that American nuclear forces "must prevail and be able to force the Soviet Union to seek earliest termination of hostilities on terms favorable to the United States."[15]

In response, Congress again set conditions for the procurement of new nuclear weapons; unlike the early 1960s, legislative conditions were not so much predisposed for the maintenance of strategic superiority as for progress in arms control negotiations. Critics of the Reagan Administration's proposals noted that the Soviets had long been difficult to negotiate with, but this had not prevented earlier presidents from succeeding. Skeptics suggested that perhaps one reason for President Reagan's lack of success related to his negotiating positions that protected U.S. force advantages while mandating deep cuts in areas of Soviet advantage. Congressional moderates made some progress in altering the Administration's negotiating posture and prompting some internal considerations of trade-offs, but little headway was made before the Kremlin pulled out of INF and START in late fall 1983, after Pershing II and ground-launched cruise missile deployments began. With the Soviets absent at Geneva, it was difficult for congressional skeptics to apply leverage on the Reagan Administration, or to place the onus for failure on the President.

The Advantage of Parity

While nuclear weapon strategists calculated how many weapon systems to buy, the arms control community debated how few were needed. Opinions varied because views of the military risks facing the United States and the utility of military force differed considerably. One wing of the arms control community was reflected in the writings of Richard Barnet, a cofounder of the Institute for Policy Studies. In *Real Security,* Barnet wrote that the nation had entered an era of "unprecedented limitations on military power." Military power was far from useless, but much less useful than a stable international order that "cannot be imposed by any nation." It followed then, that "the most crucial elements of [national] power are a strong economy and strong spirit."[16] Harold Brown's actions as Secretary of Defense during this period characterized the other wing of the arms control community. To Brown, military forces were an integral part of the nation's real security. Military strength continued to have its many purposes in direct defense of U.S. national interests, negating Soviet political leverage, and enhancing the prospect for arms control agreements.

Traveling left along the political spectrum, the perceptual rationales for military forces were increasingly suspect. Within the disarmament wing, concerns over perceptions invariably led to open-ended military requirements, while reinforcing the interventionist tendencies of the domestic opposition. Moreover, large standing armies cost an extraordinary amount of money. It was infinitely better to rely on wise political leadership averse to interventionism and sensitive enough to events abroad to block opportunities for Soviet gains. The success of our efforts in checking Soviet expansionism, as George Kennan said time and again, had less to do with the U.S.-Soviet military balance than with our own domestic vitality and with the nature of our relations with the targets of Soviet opportunism.

The two wings of the arms control community also had different degrees of enthusiasm for redirecting defense spending to meet social needs. Operationally-minded strategists were often content to rechannel nuclear weapon spending to conventional forces. This was not the disarmament wing's idea of revising national priorities. These intramural differences periodically led to friction, since periods of tight defense spending in the past have also been those of the greatest reliance on nuclear weapons.

When Secretary of State John Foster Dulles unveiled the doctrine of massive retaliation, his speech was studded with no less than eleven references to the necessity for fiscal restraint and the burden of defense expenditures. The resulting force posture was most congenial to the budget priorities of many in the arms control community, but not to their goal of decreasing the likelihood of nuclear weapons' use. Even in times of less severe budget constraints, strategic modernization programs were to some extent funded at the expense of improvements in conventional forces: even though strategic forces consumed less than one-fifth of total defense expenditures, these programs usually have had the highest budget priority. They also consumed more than one-fourth of the Pentagon's research dollars. The situation is most acute in the Air Force, where two dollars are spent on research for strategic forces for every dollar spent on conventional forces.

Over the four nuclear decades, the arms control community continually stressed the theme that new nuclear weapon developments should not be pursued at the expense of alternative diplomatic approaches. This was at the heart of the General Advisory Committee's recommendation against a crash program to develop the H-bomb. As Oppenheimer wrote to James B. Conant, President of Harvard University and fellow member of the Committee, "What does worry me is that this thing appears to have caught the imagination both of the Congressional and of military people, as the answer to the problem posed by the Russian advance . . . that we become committed to it as the way to save the country and the peace appears to me full of dangers." Kennan made the same pitch within the State Department, arguing that "the removal of our dependence on the weapon will not alone alleviate this unhealthy preoccupation [of a defense based on nuclear weapons]; but it is a first step toward it."[17]

Oppenheimer wished to emphasize smaller-yield nuclear weapons as a substitute for hydrogen bombs. His former colleague at Los Alamos, Robert F. Bacher (the first scientist to become a Commissioner of the AEC), argued that developing antisubmarine warfare capabilities would be a far more useful expenditure of funds in the event the Soviets invaded Western Europe.[18] Much of the arms control literature subsequent to the H-bomb controversy opposed the developments proposed by Oppenheimer on the grounds that they, too, would lower the nuclear threshold and suggest dangerous military solutions to political problems. Bernard Feld, another veteran of the Manhattan Project who went on to become Editor-in-Chief of the *Bulletin of the Atomic Scientists,* warned in 1961 against an almost irresistible pressure to replace conventional forces by a tactical nuclear force. Thus, in the event of an armed conflict by the major powers over any one of many existing sore spots, the probability is alarmingly great that nuclear weapons will be employed at some point."[19]

Subsequent debates over fine-tuning nuclear weapons effects

("neutron bombs" being the most prominent example) evoked thi
theme most strongly. For arms controllers, the preoccupation o
weapon strategists with escalation control had long been mis
placed. A more useful preoccupation would be with political ini
tiatives to prevent the nuclear threshold from being crossed in th
first place.

Heavy reliance on nuclear weapons had another unfortunate re
sult: it helped convince the Soviets to adopt a similar strategy. The
arms control community has generally held that the power of the
U.S. example applied to doctrinal issues as well as to arms contro
initiatives. Having heard continuously from U.S. officials and nu
clear weapon strategists about the political benefits to be derivec
from a dominant posture in strategic weapons, how could the Soviet
not be affected to adopt a similar doctrine?

Both wings of the arms control community have long questionec
how a position of nuclear superiority would promote a stable anc
lasting peace. Instead, they stressed the benefits of rough parity
Advocates of disarmament called for phased and balanced reduc
tions to zero weaponry, accompanied by the build-up of some sor
of supranational authority to monitor compliance and maintain au
thority. Arms controllers agreed with advocates of disarmamen
about the goals of stability and nonthreatening force postures, bu
they were quite prepared to achieve them through the maintenanc
of military balances.

The notion of rough parity in nuclear weapons as a means tc
stabilize great power relations was expressed even before the Sovie
Union joined the atomic club. It first appeared in a book publishec
in 1946, *The Absolute Weapon*, in which, Arnold Wolfers, then at Yal
University, hypothesized the conditions of mutual deterrence
"Nothing could be less tempting to a government, provided it wer
in possession of its senses, than a war of mutual destruction end
ing in stalemate. It would not be surprising, therefore, if a high de
gree of Soviet-American 'equality in deterring power' would prov
the best guarantee of peace and tend more than anything else tc
approximate the views and interests of the two countries."[20] On
of Wolfers' colleagues, Bernard Brodie, provided the corollary: "su
periority in numbers of bombs does not endow its possessor witl
the kind of military security which formerly resulted from superi
ority in armies, navies, and air forces."[21] For arms controllers, th
two nations had rather simple and stark choices. They could eithe
manage their relations and their nuclear weapon programs in a wa

conducive to stability, or they could both suffer consequences without historical precedent.

It was not until the SALT I accords that the thinking of men like Brodie and Wolfers was reflected in numerically-based agreements that rejected the notion of strategic superiority. Marhshall Shulman articulated the working principle behind SALT shortly after the negotiations began: "The pursuit of superiority, in the belief that it offers putative political if not military advantages, is an anachronistic mode of thought which leads inescapably to a higher level of competition."[22] To Gerard Smith, former ACDA Director and chief SALT I negotiator, "The strategic competition was not unlike a game of tick tack toe. If one knows how to play it and makes no mistakes, one cannot lose. And if both sides know how to play it, and make no mistakes, neither can win."[23]

To proponents of arms control, failures to reach meaningful agreements were directly traced to decisions by political leaders to pursue strategic advantage rather than parity. Jerome Wiesner, President Kennedy's science adviser, lamented that for too long, the United States had "tried to have it both ways," in its attempt "to maintain a superior nuclear force and to get the Soviet Union to enter into an agreement which would preserve our superiority."[24] Wiesner's lament was expressed at a time when the U.S. was seeking to retain a technological edge over the Soviet Union by deploying MIRVs rather than attempting to limit them by agreement. But Wiesner's complaint was a timeless one. Statements by President Ronald Reagan about his Administration's intention to secure a "margin of safety" for the United States evoked the same twinges from the arms control community. Paul C. Warnke, President Jimmy Carter's Director of ADCA and chief SALT II negotiator, was thus speaking with thirty painful years of arms control history behind him when he told his Congressional antagonists, "I believe . . . that the Soviet Union is not going to be willing to sign an agreement that consigns them to inferiority . . . so from that standpoint, a situation of equivalence may be a precondition to an arms control agreement that is going to be durable."[25]

4 The Political Utility of Nuclear Forces

Political Clout

For those of the hawkish persuasion, a nuclear weapon is not the absolute weapon; it is an instrument of statecraft and, if need be, an extension of national will on the modern battlefield.

This view is the mirror image of that which nuclear weapon strategists ascribe to the Kremlin and Soviet miliary planners. At one level, a dominant strategic posture can serve as a "compellant," as suggested by Richard Pipes and others,[1] a critical factor in being able to resolve crises in a manner most congenial to national interests. As Raymond Aron once observed, crises have become the substitute for armed contests in the atomic age. The superpower that emerges triumphant from a crisis earns the spoils of allegiance and perceptual deference that traditionally have been reserved to the victor on the battlefield. The Soviet drive for strategic dominance could readily be understood by nuclear weapon strategists in this light. The Soviets were operating on the premise, according to Eugene V. Rostow, then Chairman of the Committee on the Present Danger, that "clear nuclear superiority is the ultimate weapon of coercive diplomacy."[2]

Men like Rostow and Pipes could draw on analyses by Thomas Schelling and others to back up their assertions about the political utility of nuclear weapons. But they were far more interested in the real world of power politics than in texts about game theory. For them, satisfactory resolution of the Cuban missile crisis and the Berlin crises offered proof of the compellant power of strategic advantage: the Soviets backed down in these crises because of clear-cut U.S. strategic dominance. For those who wish to argue the particulars about local conventional superiority in explaining the withdrawal of Soviet missiles from Cuba, nuclear weapon strategists rested their case on the subject of Berlin. Here, the Soviets enjoyed a dominant position on the ground, obvious geographical advantages, and in Edward Luttwak's phrase, "something close to 'parity' in the balance of declared interests."[3] Once again, U.S. strategic dominance was instrumental in achieving a Soviet retreat over Berlin in the Kennedy years. Both Pipes and Rostow joined the Reagan Administration to prevent a reverse Cuban missile crisis from occurring—Pipes as the resident Soviet expert on the National Security Council Staff, Rostow as Director of the Arms Control and Disarmament Agency.

For these men and others on the Reagan national security team, the compellant power of Soviet ICBMs was a pre-eminent concern. New Soviet land-based missiles carried an unequivocal message. Their combined yield, accuracy, and warhead numbers placed the entire inventory of American ICBMs at risk during the initial round of a nuclear war. U.S. bombers and submarines not in the air or at sea would also be lost. This would leave an American president in the intolerable situation of striking back indiscriminantly with his remaining forces (and receiving indiscriminant blows in return against his cities) or of capitulating after the first round of warfare. Alternatively, an American president would face the threat of escalation dominance: because of its superior numbers of quick-strike, accurate forces, the Kremlin would always be in the position either to dictate the peace or the extent of U.S. disadvantage in succeeding rounds of warfare.

These arguments may seem increasingly improbable with the passage of time, but they had considerable force before, during and immediately after the SALT II debate. Before they were dismissed by a blue ribbon presidential commission chaired by former National Security Adviser Brent Scowcroft in 1983, the themes of potential vulnerability and coercion were articulated by nuclear weapon strategists of all persuasions. An authoritative document like the Scowcroft Commission report, blessed by four former Secretaries of Defense, three former CIA Directors and two former Secretaries of State, was required to counter pessimistic notions of the strategic balance. While the Scowcroft Commission noted Soviet advantages in land-based missiles, it also confirmed U.S. advantages in sea-based forces and strategic bombers.

For hawks of all persuasions, the political dimension of nuclear weapons extended to the technological sphere, as well: the United States faced severe risks if we were not the first to exploit the rapidly evolving technology of nuclear warfare. Weapon strategists have long argued that nuclear weapon developments could have profound impacts on the balance of power and the outcome of conflict. The potential development of "clean" nuclear weapons has been an argument against signing a Comprehensive Test Ban in the 1970s and 1980s, just as it was an argument against the Partial Test Ban Treaty in 1963. Even those who discount the value of technical weapon refinements argue that the United States has no choice but to compensate for deficiencies in conventional forces with modern nuclear weapons.

One reason to push technology was that the strategic balance has always been defined by perceptions, as well as by forces in being. Therefore, the side that exploited military technology first gained advantage in the minds of men, a feat that could have far more practical effect than the actual use of weapons on the battlefield. In effect, strategic arms races as well as crises have become a functional equivalent of war. This was a point made by Henry Kissinger in his first book on the subject:

> nuclear technology makes it possible, for the first time in history, to shift the balance of power solely through the developments *within* the territory of another sovereign state. No conceivable acquisition of territory—not even the occupation of Western Europe—could have affected the strategic balance as profoundly as did the Soviet success in ending our atomic monopoly. Had a power in the past sought to achieve a comparable strategic transformation through territorial expansion, war would have been the inevitable consequence. But because the growth of nuclear technology took place within sovereign territory, it produced an armaments race as a substitute for war.[4]

One impetus behind every U.S. initiative in the strategic arms race has been the belief that the Soviets would not hesitate to exploit technological advances, if given the chance. Our adversary was different, but our impetus was the same during the Manhattan Project. Arthur Compton, a key scientific and administrative figure in the crash program to build the A-bomb, saw this effort as a "competition for survival." He undoubtedly reflected the thinking of most of his colleagues in science and government when he wrote "the choice before the American scientists was thus not whether the age of atomic energy should be ushered in. It was whether the possibilities of atomic energy would first be made known and available to the Allied nations . . . or whether we would wait for these possibilities to be developed elsewhere."[5]

Compton devoted his efforts after the war's end to controlling nuclear weapons. Others continued to press for political or military benefits from new technological developments and avoid the penalties of failing to do so. When President Truman was deciding whether to proceed with the H-bomb, he reportedly asked his key advisers, "Can the Russians do it?" They all nodded in the affirmative. General Omar Bradley, speaking for the Joint Chiefs, argued that "possession of a thermonuclear weapon by the U.S.S.R. without such possession by the United States would be intolerable," having a profoundly demoralizing effect upon the American people" and providing a "tremendous psychological boost" to the Soviets.[6] In effect, Truman's decision to build hydrogen weapons was a foregone conclusion.

Twenty years later, Secretary of Defense Melvin Laird was proceeding with the ABM and MIRV programs from this same calculus of benefits and risks. After warning publicly that not to press ahead with deployments of both would pose "intolerable risks," he sent a memorandum to his subordinates that "there must be no speculation which would indicate, or even imply, that a MIRV or ABM deployment moratorium is desirable."[7] (The Senate had earlier passed a resolution urging President Nixon to propose a mutual freeze on weapon developments to improve SALT prospects by a vote of 72 to 6.) Laird's warnings were repeated by Senator Henry Jackson during the decisive debates in 1974 and 1975 over improving missile accuracy to silo-busting dimensions: "In the absence of a foolproof agreement with the Russians . . . does it make any sense for us to deny our Government unilaterally the opportunity to improve our own ICBM systems, which are limited both in size and numbers, in comparison with those of the Soviets?"[8]

For ideologically- and operationally-inclined hawks, seeking new technological advances was also a necessary condition for successful arms control since the Soviets would sign agreements upon the realization that the United States would either beat them to deployments, or follow them with technologically more advanced systems. It followed, then, that the United States had two realistic options in nuclear arms competition: deploy new strategic weapons first, or deploy them second — and suffer the political, if not the military, consequences.

Whether the Soviet Union was motivated by ideology or by the more traditional impulses of a great power, strategic advantage could embolden the Kremlin leadership to take risks. This theme became more and more pronounced with the advent of shifting strategic balances in the 1970s. AdmiralThomas Moorer raised this warning flag during the SALT I debate in his capacity as Chairman of the Joint Chiefs of Staff: "The mere appearance of Soviet strategic superiority could have a debilitating effect on our foreign policy and our negotiating postures . . . even if that superiority would have no practical effect on the outcome of an all-out nuclear exchange."[9] By the late 1970s, nuclear weapon strategists of all persuasions widely feared that Moorer's warning had been confirmed by events. The Senate's most vocal critic of détente, Henry Jackson, intoned during the SALT II debate that, "The real dangers ahead, as I see it, are the Kremlin's political use of strategic superiority as an umbrella under which to pursue a series of probes aimed at expanding Soviet power and weakening the position of the United States."[10] Henry Kissinger yielded on this point, a nearly complete reversal for a chief architect of détente, who helped conceive SALT as the centerpiece for a "broadly based accommodation of interests with the U.S.S.R."[11] That was said prior to the Senate's review of SALT I; during the SALT II debate, Kissinger asserted that a willingness on the part of the Soviets to run greater risks in regional conflicts was "a minimum consequence of what is ahead."[12]

In order to block Soviet political gains resulting from their strategic build-up, nuclear weapon strategists pushed again for the adoption of greater flexibility and more options to employ nuclear weapons, if necessary. Herman Kahn had added the phrase "thinking about the unthinkable" to the popular lexicon in 1962, but the kind of nuclear war-fighting options he advocated were not new. In the late 1950s, many strategists offered a series of convincing arguments about the folly of a strategic and conventional force posture based on the doctrine of massive retaliation, and succeeded in reorienting national strategy toward graduated concepts of using military force.

Secretaries of Defense McNamara, Schlesinger, Brown, and Weinberger all moved in this direction. In order to counter presumed political, if not military, disadvantages stemming from new Soviet strategic programs, the United States needed more options and more flexibility to use nuclear weapons in defense of Western interests. Succeeding nuclear war plans became increasingly variegated in consequence. As often as not, increased flexibility in war plans did not bar political vulnerability: incoming administrations continued to be heralded into Washington amid rhetorical flourishes over the failures of their predecessors to provide adequately for the common defense.

Military Problems, Political Solutions

Moving to the right along the political spectrum, views concerning the political utility of nuclear weapons become increasingly affirmative; moving to the left within the arms control community, they become increasingly narrow. If conventional weapons were unsuitable instruments to combat ideas or for counterinsurgency operations, what possible role could nuclear weapons play in this realm, either in conditions of battle or in the preconditions leading toward it? And on a conventional battlefield, how could nuclear weapons be used to accomplish political objectives? Many arms controllers would grant the point that the numbers of tanks and aircraft accumulated by opposing sides mattered. After all, one assumption of conventional arms control negotiations is that gross imbalances can generate insecurity and be destabilizing, politically if not militarily.

A transference of this principle to nuclear weapons was rejected without qualification by the disarmament wing of the arms control community. For them, nuclear weapons were not convertible currency on the modern battlefield, because their use would destroy both societies. It followed that weapon inventories, whether in balance or not, did not assist one side to gain advantage or the other to forfeit it. Neither did it follow that an imbalance in nuclear force would consciously lead either side to take risks. It was one thing to take risks; quite another to take suicidal ones. Rational leaders took risks on the basis of calculations far-afield from computer simulations of nuclear exchanges. Since no rational leader could expect military gain arising from using nuclear weapons, what conceivable political leverage did these weapons provide? Operationally-minded strategists could sometimes support this thesis in the abstract. As Paul Warnke once said, "Where a numerical advantage in any part of the arms arsenal is without military meaning, it should have no real political potential."[13] In actual circumstances, however, most arms control strategists were inclined to hedge these assertions. There were no intramural differences, however, in rejecting the goal of superiority in an age of vulnerability.

In an earlier phase of the strategic competition, this premise generated a good deal of political heat. Alain Enthoven, then one of McNamara's top civilian officials, created a stir in the Senate Armed Services Committee when he volunteered, "It has never been possible to develop a clear concept for translating nuclear superiority into political power or international advantage, once the other side has an assured destruction capability against us."[14] Four years after Enthoven made these remarks in 1968, the ABM Treaty was ratified, which left both societies open to retaliation, and succeeding rounds of competition increased each side's retaliatory capabilities many fold. Still, the search for advantage continued. In a moment of exasperation, Henry Kissinger asked the memorable question, "What in the name of God is strategic superiority? What is the significance of it, politically, militarily, operationally at these levels of numbers? What do you do with it."[15] Kissinger later amended these remarks; others saw no need to.

Was there a single crisis when the outcome hinged on the strategic balance? Most of the veterans of the Cuban missile crisis have consistently asserted that the balance of nuclear weapons had little to do with Khrushchev's about-face.

McGeorge Bundy's thesis was that crises were resolved by questions of will and purpose, and not by inventories of strategic weapons.[16] (Bundy was the President's National Security Adviser during the Cuban missile crisis.) Kennedy's Secretary of Defense, Robert McNamara, came to the same conclusion, warning Congress after the crisis was over not to place too much stock in the favorable strategic balance then existing. As McNamara told the House Armed Services Committee,

It did not deter them from putting pressure on Berlin when we had a near nuclear monopoly in the early part of the decade of the 1950s. It did not deter the Communists from invading Korea. It did not deter them from building a wall in Berlin. It did not deter the Communist . . . attempt to subvert Southeast Asia . . . It did not deter their attempt to move offensive weapon systems into Cuba . . . I should go one step further, to say that . . . the strategic nuclear power which we are proposing, large as it is and superior as it is, is not a universal deterrent to all forms of Soviet political and military aggression.[17]

For nuclear weapon strategists, the Cuban missile crisis provided an airtight case to support the contention that the strategic balance mattered a great deal in resolving disputes short of war. Some arms control strategists saw an inverse correlation: Khrushchev, fearing the strategic balance that was then emerging, attempted to deploy intermediate-range missiles in Cuba as a "quick fix," one that, as Maxwell Taylor pointed out, "our strategic superiority did not deter him from initiating . . . in the first place."[18] Khrushchev's retreat, in the view of Taylor and others, came not as a result of U.S. strategic superiority, but because of the local preponderance of U.S. conventional forces. As six participants in the crisis concluded twenty years after the event, "The Cuban missile crisis illustrates not the significance, but the insignificance of nuclear superiority in the face of survivable thermonuclear retaliatory forces. It also shows the crucial role of rapidly available conventional strength."[19]

For operationally-minded arms controllers like Paul Warnke, the positive political utility of nuclear weapons was "very special," but extremely limited. "Essentially, they give the other side pause before launching any sort of attack on us or our allies, and also, and perhaps most important of all, they ensure that the other side won't dare use their nuclear weapons. They basically serve the purpose of neutralization."[20] The role of nuclear weapons is that of a deterrent, no more. They convey the not so subtle message that the costs of using nuclear weapons will far exceed whatever benefits might be contemplated by the user. Attempts to convey more discrete political messages via improvements in accuracy, escalation control, and finely tuned weapons effects invariably get garbled in transmission: when filtered by an adversary, they become war-fighting, not deterrent messages.

If nuclear weapons did not have positive political utility, they most certainly had negative political effect. For those most operationally-inclined, imbalances in force levels and characteristics could undermine negotiating objectives or support on the home front for agreements reached—even if the disparities had no military significance. Thus, for political rather than military reasons, gross imbalances had to be avoided. The disarmament wing rejected this premise and its results. For them, new weapon procurement for perceptual reasons might help in the domestic arena, but harm the prospects for future agreements while prompting counterdeployments on the other side.

Both wings of the arms control community also expressed differences of view on the question of whether armaments caused tensions or whether political tensions caused arms races. Each group agreed in principle to both propositions, but with distinctly different emphasis on cause and effect. The disarmament wing stressed the special role of nuclear weapons in generating tension in international politics; success in removing these weapons would help resolve political differences. The operational wing emphasized that tensions needed to be defused before significant progress in arms control could be realized.

Hans Morgenthau articulated the point early in the H-bomb controversy: "Disarmament is indeed an indispensable step toward pacificiation, but it cannot be the first step. It is the result of political settlement, never its precondition."[21] Senator Hubert Humphrey did not contest this point during the Eisenhower Administration in his path-breaking hearings within the Special Subcommittee on Disarmament. In the decade that followed, nuclear weapon arsenals became so bloated and menacing that operationally-minded strategists could argue that the relationship between cause and effect had been thoroughly blurred. The special characteristics of the weapons —their destructive power, long-term effects, and swift means of delivery—had not simply transformed the potential nature of war; they had also recast the shadow that weapon inventories traditionally projected on international politics. Still, arms controllers asserted that the resolution of tensions must precede a significant reduction in armaments. Arms control could not be the tail that wagged the dog.

Great powers have always been well armed. Now they were well armed and terribly vulnerable. The invention of nuclear weapons created an ahistorical and counterintuitive circumstance: vulnerability could not be alleviated by increases in weapon stockpiles. On the contrary, each side's collective sense of security seemed diminished with each successive lap of the strategic arms race. To make matters worse, each phase of the competition added political impediments to defusing and reversing the process.

No theme in the four decades of debate on arms control is more central than the call for political solutions rather than military initiatives. In 1945, James Franck, Leo Szilard and Eugene Rabinowitch implored Secretary of War Stimson not to use the A-bomb against Japan. Use of the new weapon "as a means of political pressure in peace and sudden destruction in war" would only breed mistrust, and the resulting tensions in international politics would heavily prejudice attempts to control this new menace to civilization. "It may be very difficult," wrote Franck and his colleagues at the University of Chicago's Metallurgical Lab, "to persuade the world that a nation which was capable of secretly preparing and suddenly releasing a new weapon, as indiscriminate as the rocket bomb and a thousand times more destructive, is to be trusted in its proclaimed desire of having such weapons abolished by international agreement."[22] For some in the scientific community, the Truman Administration's decision to end the war by means of the A-bomb compromised the peace. Their ranks were led by Einstein, who worried that "We are still making bombs and the bombs are making hate and suspicion."[23] Franck and Einstein weren't interested in managing an arms race; their goal was a political solution that would abolish A-bombs and the potential to make them.

The theme of political compromise was again prominent in the controversy over building the H-bomb in 1950. Truman's decision led Einstein to despair: "It is impossible to achieve peace as long as every single action is taken with a possible future conflict in view."[24] Einstein had a like-minded soul within the highest councils of government in David E. Lilienthal. Lilienthal, a former Director of the Tennessee Valley Authority, was in the awkward position of being the first Chairman of the new Atomic Energy Commission when the peaceful applications he placed such stock in were being eclipsed by military applications for which he had a growing sense of unease. Lilienthal couldn't help comparing the motivation behind the H-bomb effort to the A-bomb program before it: "Did it provide a sense of security to us, or much elbow room? What happened to the 'deterrent' — hadn't we seen how thin these arguments had proved in the past; why would it be different in the future?" For Lilienthal, as well as for the scientific advisers he relied on, "just as the A-bomb obscured our view and gave a false sense of security, we are in danger of falling into the same error again in discussion of 'Campbell' [Lilienthal's code word for the super-bomb] — some cheap, easy way out."[25]

The arguments for political solutions sharpened during subsequent debates, as the record grew of successful technical initiatives and failed attempts to reverse the arms competition. For the most part, however, these arguments were offered in losing causes; if a new nuclear weapon system did not run into deep technical difficulties, it stood a much better-than-even chance of being deployed.

For both wings of the arms control camp, nuclear weapon debates had still another damaging consequence: to help secure political support for new programs, their domestic opponents were continually bad-mouthing U.S. capabilities. This was an odd tack to take for those preoccupied with perceptions, worried about an emboldened Kremlin leadership, or concerned about alliance solidarity. It was, however, an effective one in domestic politics.

There has periodically been more political mileage in sounding the tocsin than in calming the waters. The first congressional exercise in broadcasting impending or actual nuclear weapons inferiority was the bomber gap hearings in 1956. The Stuart Symington who became known at the end of his Senate career as a deep skeptic of nuclear weapon programs was a far different man from the freshman Senator who directed these hearings with a megaphone instead of a gavel. Only one member of his investigating committee, Senator Leverett Saltonstall, offered a dissent from his colleagues' "unduly pessimistic findings."[26]

The shock and objective reality of the Soviet ICBM and Sputnik launches made it difficult for anyone to downplay Soviet strategic advantages. Those who took a fairly relaxed view of the overall state of U.S.-Soviet competition, like Deputy Secretary of Defense Donald A. Quarles, were savaged in the resulting political uproar. Earlier, as Secretary of the Air Force, Quarles made one of the first public statements by a ranking Defense Department official questioning the utility of strategic superiority. In the wake of Soviet advances, he was dubbed "Mr. Missile Gap" by columnist Joseph Alsop.[27]

Supporters of arms control treaties sought to combat assertions of inferiority during ratification hearings, but found it politically impossible to stop funding for a wide variety of safeguards which operationally-minded strategists considered essential for their consent. This did not prevent arms controllers from subsequently conducting spirited campaigns to block funding for such projects. During these debates, arms controllers rejected requirements for new weapon systems based on perceived inferiority. "Nuclear blackmail as well as nuclear attack is essentially ruled out," said Herbert Scoville, Jr., during one such debate, "unless we talk ourselves into being blackmailed by nuclear weapons."[28]

To men like Scoville, who held high positions in the Central Intelligence Agency and Arms Control and Disarmament Agency before becoming President of the Arms Control Association, the strategic arms race had long since lost any realistic or achievable political purpose, having become, in Kennan's phrase, "an institutionalized force of habit." McGeorge Bundy summed up the situation this way: "The neglected truth about the present strategic arms race between the United States and the Soviet Union is that in terms of international political behavior, that race has now become almost completely irrelevant. The new weapons systems which are being developed by each of the two great powers will provide neither protection nor opportunity in any serious political sense."[29]

5 The Military Utility of Nuclear Forces

The Atomic Battlefield

Ideologically- and operationally-minded nuclear weapon strategists part company over the military utility of nuclear weapons due to their different readings of Soviet motivation. Those who stress the ideological commitment of the Soviet state to expansion are more inclined to accept the Politburo's willingness to use conventional and nuclear weapons to accomplish their aims.

The notion of a surprise Soviet attack has been a constant and compelling theme for those who believe that the balance of terror is uncomfortably delicate and in constant need of significant reconstitution. The "window of vulnerability" that preoccupied many in the Carter and Reagan Administrations has been opened several times previously. In the late 1950s and early 1960s, nuclear weapon strategists expressed similar alarms over the vulnerability of Strategic Air Command bombers and land-based missiles. In this, they were joined by political figures of considerable standing.

Senator Stuart Symington's bomber gap hearings in 1956–57 picked up themes expressed earlier in private by President Eisenhower's Surprise Attack Panel, chaired by James R. Killian, Jr., and James B. Fisk. Symington's public exercise concluded that "the vulnerability of the United States to sudden attack has increased greatly during the past decade, and this vulnerability will continue to increase in the foreseeable future."[1] As Chairman of the Senate's Preparedness Investigating Subcommittee, Senator Lyndon B. Johnson led a strong chorus of wounded vulnerability after the satellite Sputnik launch, warning of dire consequences unless the United States adopted a national policy dedicated to winning control of outer space. Senator John F. Kennedy competed with both Symington and Johnson in making an issue of the missile gap in 1959, a gap which dealt not just with projected Soviet production rates, but with the vulnerability they foreshadowed for U.S. deterrent forces. This is not to say that there were no reasons for concern during this time. On the contrary, there were excellent reasons to press for dispersion of the bomber force, early warning systems, and upgraded command and control systems. But the concerns of ideologically-inclined analysts went far beyond these issues. In their reading of Soviet capabilities and intentions, a pre-emptive attack was a significant possibility.

One of those most concerned was William R. Kintner, who warned two years prior to the SALT negotiations that "the concept of the pre-emptive strike dominates the Soviets' strategic doctrine."[2] Kintner, a former instructor in atomic warfare tactics at the Army's Command and General Staff College, coauthored a book while a Lieutenant Colonel, *Atomic Weapons in Land Combat*, based on the premise that atomic weapons were an integral part of winning the next war—a war that the U.S. Army was ill-prepared for. He later became Strausz-Hupé's deputy and successor at the Foreign Policy Research Institute.

Many others shared Kintner's concerns. The Surprise Attack Panel concluded midway in Eisenhower's first term that "because of our vulnerability, [the] Soviets might be tempted to try a surprise attack. They might be so tempted in order to attack before we achieve a large multimegaton capability."[3] General Curtis LeMay's view during the bomber gap hearings was that, "The only thing I can say is that from 1958 on, he [the U.S.S.R.] is stronger in long-range air power than we are, and it naturally follows that if he is stronger, he may feel that he should attack."[4] The Gaither Report, sent to the National Security Council one month after the launch of Sputnik, warned of an imminent danger of Soviet attack that could virtually nullify the Strategic Air Command.[5] The missile gap controversy led to a paroxysm of political charges, with operationally-minded strategists joining their ideological brethren and a whole host of elected officials to protest the lax state of defense preparedness. As Senator Mike Monroney put it, "We will be in as much danger in a few months from the intercontinental ballistic missile as the people of France and Belgium who lived five miles from the Siegfried Line in World War II."[6] Henry Kissinger expressed the thought in his second book-length contribution to the debate that "the inferiority in missiles is not as worrisome as the vulnerability of the entire retaliatory force."[7]

The concern expressed by many over the first-strike potential of Soviet land-based missiles during the SALT II hearings was in one sense different from earlier episodes of anxiety: in this instance, the Soviets did possess the theoretical means to place a segment of U.S. strategic forces at risk. In other ways, this particular window of vulnerability was like its predecessors. Above all, it was vastly over-drawn, whether for reasons of political expediency or for fear that the Soviets would exploit their advantage if conditions were either favorable or desperate enough for them to do so. A majority of the Senate Armed Services Committee appeared inclined toward the latter view during the SALT II debate, when they concluded that "The United States now faces the near-certainty that a significant element of its strategic deterrent will be vulnerable to pre-emptive attack by the Soviet Union."[8]

In the view of strategists most attuned to the ideological dimensions of the conflict, the Soviet leadership took Clausewitz's dictum literally: even nuclear war was viewed as an extension of politics by other means. As Richard Pipes and others consistently pointed out, this meant that the Soviets didn't believe in the assumption commonly held in the West that nuclear war would have no winners. On the contrary, the Soviets believed (in Pipes' words), that "while all-out nuclear war would indeed prove extremely destructive to both parties, its outcome would not be mutual suicide; the country better prepared for it and in possession of a superior strategy could win and emerge a viable society."[9] For men like Pipes, the build-up of Soviet nuclear war-fighting capabilities — reloadable missiles, overheated production lines, and a considerable civil defense effort — provided incontrovertible evidence of Soviet offensive intent. The most effective response was to push for comparable U.S. programs. These, however, would be defensive in nature because they would block opportunities for Soviet political or military advances.

Members of President Ronald Reagan's national security team

made it a point to act on these predilections. The prescriptions offered, while not mimicking Soviet weapon programs and perceived strategy, bore a strong resemblance to them. These measures were deemed necessary not merely to ensure against a Soviet first strike, but to allow the United States to re-establish a degree of leverage in the event of a nuclear war between the two superpowers. "The important point to recognize," said Colin Gray, an adviser to the Reagan Administration, "is that the United States may have no practical alternative to waging a nuclear war."[10]

The pre-eminent instruments for carrying out nuclear strikes in the event deterrence failed were ICBMs. Only land-based missiles possessed the refined accuracy and secure, redundant, and timely command and control to carry out prompt and selective strikes against the full spectrum of Soviet targets. While upgraded Minuteman III missiles could provide some degree of "prompt hard-target-kill" capability against reinforced concrete missile silos, they alone were insufficient. The Soviets have continually hardened their silos to the point where a larger yield warhead than the Minuteman's best — 335 kilotons — was deemed necessary. (The bomb that destroyed the "soft" target of Hiroshima was 13.5 kilotons.)

Upgrading the Minuteman force wasn't sufficient because the Soviets possessed far more numerous and larger yield warheads on their land-based missiles, which were approaching the accuracies of their U.S. counterparts. In the view of American nuclear weapon strategists, the United States would be at a decided disadvantage in attempting to exert leverage on Soviet choices in the event of escalation without significantly improving its ICBM capabilities. Thus, deployment of the MX "Peacekeeper" missile in appreciable numbers was an absolute requirement. Without capabilities like those of the MX, the U.S. ability to deter the Kremlin or to control — let alone dominate — escalation would be seriously impaired.

Would, however, MX deployments in vulnerable silos serve as a magnet for a Soviet first strike? Not necessarily, in the view of its proponents. Some operationally-minded strategists expressed skepticism about the Soviets' delivering a bolt-out-of-the-blue attack. From their reading of Soviet capabilities and intentions, operationally-minded strategists tended to avoid apocalyptic warnings of Soviet surprise attacks, seeing instead a coherent design to gain political and military advantage. This was the analysis presented by the Chairman of the Joint Chiefs of Staff, General David Jones, during the SALT II hearings — a line of reasoning that clearly set him apart from his hawkish antagonists on the Armed Services Committee.[11]

Henry Kissinger and Paul Nitze both testified at the SALT II hearings that for all the dreaded possibilities of the agreement, a Soviet first strike was not one of them. These men did not discount the eventual use of nuclear weapons by the Soviet Union; they envisioned a situation of crossing the nuclear threshold only in extremis rather than as a calculated act to achieve political advantage. A natural corollary was that the military utility of nuclear weapons mattered most in confrontations at conventional levels. Nitze described the dynamics this way in one of his Committee on the Present Danger pamphlets:

> It is a copy book principle in strategy that, in actual war, advantage tends to go to the side in a better position to raise the stakes by expanding the scope, duration or destructive intensity of the conflict. By the same token, at junctures of high contention short of war, the side better able to cope with the potential consequences of raising the stakes has the advantage. The other side is the one under greater pressure to scramble for a peaceful way out. To have the advantage at the utmost level of violence helps at every lesser level.[12]

Similar intramural disputes over intentions and capabilities took place over Soviet ICBM modernization programs in the mid-to-late 1970s. In the view of ideologically-minded strategists, nothing could be more indicative of Soviet war-winnning intent. Not so, according to the Secretary of Defense at the time, James Schlesinger: "The Soviets built these massive missiles at one stage of their history. They then designed replacements for those missiles and made good use of the silo space they created."[13]

Despite differing diagnoses of Soviet capabilities and intentions, nuclear weapon strategists could usually agree on policy and program implications. In the above-mentioned case, Secretary of Defense Schlesinger yielded to no ideological hawk in the strength of his conviction that the United States should deploy similar warfighting capabilities. Those of the hawkish persuasion coalesced around the notion that, regardless of what Soviet intentions may be, Soviet war-fighting capabilities provided them with leverage that must be countered, and if possible, reversed in the event of nuclear war.

A War Without Winners

'When dealing with the absolute weapon, arguments based on relative advantage lose their point."[14] This thought, expressed by William T. R. Fox shortly after the A-bomb's shattering unveiling, has been an abiding theme for much of the arms control community ever since. While there might be intramural differences over questions of political utility, there were few disputes over the military value of nuclear weapons. How could military options make sense if they ultimately led to mutual destruction?

One strategist who thought long and hard about these questions was Bernard Brodie. Like others in the period after World War II, Brodie was working in the uncharted land of atomic weapon strategy, but he had a better compass than most due to his academic training and interests. Brodie was one of a handful of thinkers who attempted to master the obscure fields of military history, strategy, and politics. Before the A-bomb's appearance, he was already the author of two important books on naval strategy. His previous work and ability to write with grace and insight on even the most murky subjects lent special weight to his pronouncements. Less than three months after the first atomic bomb detonations, Brodie wrote a memorandum for the Yale Institute of International Studies entitled, "The Atomic Bomb and American Security." In it, he showed himself to be the first in a long line of arms control-oriented theorists to argue that as nuclear weapons were entirely different from previous instruments of war, success in preventing their future use depended on the ability of political leaders to maintain this distinction. "The atomic bomb," wrote Brodie, "is not just another and more destructive weapon to be added to an already long list. It is something which threatens to make the rest of the list relatively unimportant." Brodie went beyond this, however: "It is wholly vain to expect scientists or engineers to fashion any counter or 'answer' to the atomic bomb which will redress the present disequilibrium of offense versus defense to any degree worth mentioning."[15] This memorandum and others by Brodie's colleagues at Yale were pulled together into a short book which appeared the next year under the title *The Absolute Weapon*. The phrase became a catchword in the heated public debate that followed and intensified when the absolute weapon was eclipsed by hydrogen bombs. The H-bomb's development did not, understandably, detract from Brodie's propositions.

The judgments of strategists like Brodie were quickly seconded by members of the scientific community like Oppenheimer, who, in 1945, warned against any attempt ". . . to minimize the impact of atomic weapons, and thus to delay or to avert the inevitability in the radical changes in the world which their advent would seem to require. There are people who say they are not such very bad weapons. Before the New Mexico test, we sometimes said that too, writing down square miles and equivalent tonnages and looking at the pictures of a ravaged Europe. After the test we did not say it any more . . . I think that it will not help to avert such a war if we try to rub the edges off this new terror that we have helped bring to this world."[16]

The assumption that nuclear weapons were different from other weapons of war has been in dispute throughout the four nuclear decades. But for both wings of the arms control movement, it was an organizing premise. Their conclusion that nuclear weapons served no useful military purpose was a direct corollary to it. Perhaps the most commanding spokesman for this proposition at the outset of the debate was Albert Einstein, the scientist chosen by concerned colleagues in 1939 to warn President Roosevelt about the implications of atomic energy research in Hitler's Germany. The resulting letter eventually led to the Manhattan Project, in which Einstein had no part. Einstein's famous equation, $E = mc^2$, was confirmed by the two atomic explosions that ended World War II, and the sage of Princeton was much saddened by it; this form of energy release was not at all what he had in mind in his theorizing. After the war's end, there was no stronger proponent for banning nuclear weapons. "Rifle bullets kill men," said the new Chairman of the Emergency Committee of Atomic Scientists, "but atomic bombs kill cities. A tank is a defense against a bullet, but there is no defense in science against the weapon which can destroy civilization."[17]

Many scientists involved in the Manhattan Project joined with Einstein's campaign to ban the A-bomb, rejecting the notion that atomic might could be used to reform or control egregious Soviet behavior. These efforts were redoubled with President Truman's public directive to the Atomic Energy Commission to pursue the development of hydrogen weapons. This decision was criticized by some in the scientific community on a variety of grounds, one being the shortage of targets "suitable" to the H-bomb's scale of lethal effects.

Subsequent nuclear weapon developments elicited the same litany of opposing arguments. In his campaign against atmospheric testing in 1961, Hans Bethe based his case on the premise that "war simply no longer makes sense as an instrument of national policy."[18] When the subjects at hand were ABMs and MIRVs a decade later, Carl Kaysen, McGeorge Bundy's deputy at the National Security Council, lamented, "Our national security has been much diminished by these innovations and nothing we can do by adding more or better weapons can itself recover that loss of security."[19] A decade after that, Herbert Scoville, Jr., argued against the MX as a particularly pernicious development. For Scoville, the MX epitomized "all that is most dangerous and bad in nuclear weapons."[20] The dangers of the strategic arms race were growing because new weapons were being developed on precisely the grounds that Brodie warned against in 1945.

Another corollary to the principle of avoiding nuclear war was a declaratory policy of "no first use." Two early spokesmen on behalf of this policy were George Kennan and Hans Bethe. After Truman's decision to press ahead with the H-bomb, Bethe and eleven of his physicist colleagues petitioned the executive and legislative branches to "make a solemn declaration that we shall never use this bomb first. The only circumstance which might force us to use it would be if we or our allies were attacked by this bomb."[21] Kennan's internal memoranda and Bethe's public stand had little impact. The official U.S. defense posture was predicated on the use of nuclear weapons in defense of Western interests, whether during John Foster Dulles' blunderbuss strategy of strategic bombing or Robert McNamara's initiatives changing U.S. and NATO doctrine to one of flexible response.

In the abstract, the concept of flexibility was hard to argue with, but specific concerns focused on two areas. Did increased flexibility mean an increased likelihood that conventional military forces would be used? And once used, did the escalation ladder also ease the transition from conventional to limited nuclear war? The critical debates over MIRVs and nuclear war-fighting capabilities after McNamara's tenure revolved largely over the issue of "flexibility," with ex-Pentagon officials leading the opposition. To such individuals, "flexibility" was the problem, not the solution. Paul Warnke, McNamara's General Counsel and then Assistant Secretary for International Security Affairs, offered a different proposition: "Flexibility in nuclear weapons just means a greater chance that nuclear weapons will be used."[22] This critique had little practical effect during the SALT decade, but the demise of the SALT process and the ascendancy of severe critics of arms control to key government positions had an energizing effect. By 1981, McNamara joined with Kennan in asserting the wisdom of a "no first use" posture. Together with former National Security Adviser McGeorge Bundy and SALT I negotiator Gerard C. Smith they concluded that "in the age of massive thermonuclear overkill it no longer makes sense—if it ever did—to hold these weapons for any other purpose than the prevention of their use."[23] Their analysis was compelling not so much for the arguments presented, which were by no means original, but for the authors who were presenting them.

For the arms control community, the principal risk lay in the use of nuclear weapons—an eventuality all the more likely with the impulse for flexibility. Whatever were the risks involved in strategic arms control, they paled by comparison. Given the choice, how could opting for arms control initiatives rather than new refinements in nuclear weapons injure national security? Men like Oppenheimer and his colleagues on the AEC's General Advisory Committee wondered what added military utility hydrogen weapons would have over refinements to the A-bombs conceived in the Manhattan Project. Surely, the H-bomb would be exponentially more powerful, but to what military purpose? In a sense, proponents of a "bigger bang" in strategic weaponry eventually conceded this point when they dropped their quest for a one-hundred-megaton weapon in the early 1960s. While some, like General Curtis LeMay and Senator Henry Jackson, continued to see military advantages in such high-yield weapons—then pegged to greater area destructiveness and lethality against hardened underground targets—the quest for matching or exceeding Soviet high-yield capabilities died with ratification of the Limited Test Ban Treaty.[24]

Instead, subsequent strategic modernization efforts turned to downsizing the yields of hydrogen weapons and improving their "yield-to-weight" ratios. Laboratory work focused on generating the most bang for the smallest "physics package," and then packing them like commuters aboard a MIRVed "bus." In time, these developments merged with nuclear war-fighting strategies as the preferred means of securing deterrence for nuclear weapon strategists and, failing that, limiting destruction in the event a nuclear war should occur.

These initiatives sparked another full-scale debate in 1974 and 1975 when Secretary of Defense James Schlesinger proposed a series of programs to improve the accuracy and explosive power of U.S.

tercontinental ballistic missile warheads, thereby providing them
ith a limited counterforce capability against hardened Soviet miliary targets. To strategists like Schlesinger, the more options the
United States had to place Soviet forces at risk, the more deterrence
ould be strengthened. To opponents, Schlesinger's moves shifted
e emphasis of deterrence away from the existence of nuclear
eapons to their potential use.

At the outset, this debate was led by Senator Edward Brooke,
ho argued that "if such weapons were deployed in large numbers
nd were developed to levels of very high accuracy, they could seri-
usly threaten hardened missile silos and could undermine the stable
eterrence on which both countries depend . . . this could only in-
uce a larger arms race . . ." In other words, fine-tuning nuclear
eapon capabilities would not provide any military utility that
ould not be matched by the Soviet Union in the see-saw competi-
on that characterized the arms race.[25] At the time, the Nixon Ad-
inistration seemed to agree. Brooke and his colleagues secured
 pledge from the President that "we do not intend to develop
ounterforce capabilities which the Soviets could construe as hav-
g a first-strike potential."

In these rounds of the strategic debate, the case for arms con-
rol was strengthened by Senator Thomas McIntyre, Chairman of
he Senate Armed Services' Research and Development Subcom-
ittee. McIntyre initially wanted to block all funding for counter-
orce programs until the President certified that he was unable to
ake progress at SALT in controlling MIRVs. Later, he took
 more unequivocal postition: Counterforce programs should be
topped regardless of what happened at SALT, as they did nothing
o ensure the survivability of U.S. forces or provide an appropriate
ounter to the Soviet ICBM build-up. To McIntyre, counterforce
rograms placed a "hair trigger" on nuclear war. With each side
ncreasingly able to place its adversary's forces at risk, the incen-
ive to use nuclear weapons in a crisis rather than to risk losing them
ould increase.[26]

One of the most outspoken opponents of counterforce weapons
as Paul Warnke, who professed "difficulty with the idea that deter-
ence of nuclear war somehow is improved by increasing the ability
o fight a nuclear war." A commitment to counterforce, in Warnke's
iew, "inescapably would cause fears in the Soviet Union of an ef-
ort on our part to achieve a first strike capability which . . . could
rigger the onset of a new stage of the arms race."[27]

In 1980, a nuclear war-fighting doctrine of deterrence receive
another boost, this time from President Jimmy Carter. His Presi
dential Directive-59 was characterized by its backers as an evolu
tionary step, as indeed it was. But PD-59 was also seen as a mor
ominous development, perhaps because of its paternity by an ad
ministration that started out intensely committed to arms control
PD-59 also seemed a far cry from the notion of assured destruc
tion put forward by Secretary of Defense Robert McNamara.

In theory, strategic planning and requirements under assured
destruction could be relatively straightforward: U.S. forces had t
be of such size and composition as to ensure a devastating retaliator
blow. For those interested in curbing defense spending and new
weapon programs, assured destruction could provide a bulwar
against a variety of initiatives proposed by nuclear weapon strate
gists. To begin with, absolute levels of destruction and not relativ
advantage could be the yardstick used to gauge — and to reject –
strategic programs advocated by defense contractors or the militar
services. In addition, assured destruction left room for only the mos
narrow interpretations of the military utility of nuclear weapons

In actuality, these distinctions were more apparent than real
Critics of assured destruction tagged it with the acronym "MAD
(for Mutual Assured Destruction) and criticized it for all those con
cepts their domestic opponents hoped the new doctrine would em
brace. In truth, U.S. nuclear war planning proceeded along
straight path, marrying new strategic capabilities to long-standin
objectives, most notably successful attacks against military as wel
as industrial targets.

With PD-59, the United States affirmed a concept and declara
tory policy of denying the Soviet Union advantage in any nuclea
exchange. True, PD-59 also talked about assured destruction, bu
the reorientation of strategy away from this concept toward nuclea
war-fighting continued. Denying the Kremlin advantage required
of necessity, increasingly sophisticated ways to place an adversary
forces at risk.

From this juncture, it was only a short distance to the objectiv
of relative advantage in nuclear war-fighting, with its open-ende
requirements to exert leverage on Soviet choices in campaigns o
whatever duration and intensity. The Reagan Administration em
broidered PD-59 in precisely these ways in NSDD-13. Presiden
Reagan's advisers — to a man, ardent supporters of the nuclear war
fighting school of deterrence — believed that nuclear war could re

nain limited and that casualties could be kept to tolerable levels
vith sufficient preparations. The absolute weapon could be coun-
ered by new offensive forces and by protecting national leaders,
ndustrial lathes, and by relocating civilian populations during
rises. Although a natural extension of previous war plans, the
Reagan Administration's defense guidelines generated a torrent of
riticism. Most Americans felt uncomfortable on this slippery slope
f nuclear war-fighting plans and programs. Public concern was
rystallized over the unadorned language used to characterize U.S.
bjectives by ideologues. For weapon strategists in the Reagan Ad-
ninistration, the natural objective of war — even nuclear war — was
o prevail. For the general public, arms control appeared as an in-
reasingly attractive option.

At the outset of the SALT decade, chief U.S. negotiator Gerard
C. Smith worried privately in a letter to Secretary of State William
Rogers that "if either side is striving for or appears to be striving
or an effective counterforce first strike capability, then there is no
ope for strategic arms control."[28] As the decade proceeded, nuclear
veapon strategists succeeded in orienting U.S. strategy toward a
nore rigorous war-fighting approach to deterrence, much like the
ne they presumed Soviet leaders had accepted. For the arms con-
rol community, Gerard Smith's warning appeared increasingly
rophetic.

6 Arms Control

The Diaphanous Solution

The U.S.-Soviet competition was viewed by nuclear weapon strat
egists — moving rightward along the political spectrum — as an ideo
logical as well as geopolitical contest. At the far right, the idea
of arms control agreements with a committed adversary was a
contradiction in terms. Here, the competition was seen entirely
as a zero-sum game — one side advanced only at the other side's ex
pense.

Ideologically-minded strategists have long been reluctant to do
business with the Soviet Union in any way that suggested accommo
dation or common interests. As Strausz-Hupé said during negotiations over a Partial Test Ban Treaty, "The West cannot gamble
its security on a disarmament agreement until it faces across the
conference table men who represent an open political system, are
responsive to the popular will, and have foresworn aggression."
In this view, the pursuit of confrontation, rather than arms control, was the only appropriate means to engage an ideological foe.
Strausz-Hupé based his reservations on the Limited Test Ban Treaty
on moral and ethical grounds. "The treaty," he warned, "does not
bear upon the substantive issues which divide the United States and
the U.S.S.R. Thus the conclusion of the treaty signifies a symbolic
act which endows an existing condition with moral-legal sanction."

During most of his tenure as Secretary of State, John Foster Dulles fully agreed, asking at one point, "What is an agreement? An agreement is a meeting of minds. And so far I do not know of any agreement that the Soviet Union has made which has reflected a real meeting of minds."[3]

In the height of the Cold War, operationally-minded strategists often joined with their ideologically-inclined brethren in evaluating arms control agreements on these terms. In their view, nuclear weapons were merely the new currency of international power, used to advance political and conceivably even military objectives by the two great powers. Given the conflicting objectives of the two sides, how could arms control agreements reconcile them? As Senator Jackson was fond of saying, the problems of arms control were "indivisible from the Cold War,"[4] and hawks were not inclined to accept the notion of a stand-off as either the U.S. or Soviet objective in the Cold War.

In this sense, "linkage" — or the tying together of arms control with the resolution of outstanding political differences between the two parties — has deep roots, although the focus of geopolitical grievances has shifted over time.

The Baruch Plan to internationalize atomic energy was interred at a time when the division of Europe and the deeply competitive nature of U.S.-Soviet relations became unmistakably clear. Neither side could take seriously each other's hollow plans for general and complete disarmament, offered by both rivals as part of their intense competition. When the objectives of arms controllers finally narrowed, the impediments to agreement remained wide for most nuclear weapon strategists. In 1958, Paul Nitze testified before Senator Hubert Humphrey's Subcommittee on Disarmament that "it is hard for me to visualize the United States entering into any general and far-reaching agreement with the U.S.S.R. for the reduction and control of armaments which was not preceded by, or which did not provide for, a concurrent modification of Russian military interference in the internal affairs of Hungary."[5] Ten years later, Soviet intervention in Czechoslovakia derailed the start of the SALT I negotiations for a crucial year. Approximately another decade after that, the Soviet invasion of Afghanistan extinguished the fading hopes of SALT II supporters for ratification. In 1981, the Reagan Administration postponed the start of strategic arms reduction talks because of the imposition of martial law in Poland.

For many skeptics of arms control, linking progress in negotiations to favorable political resolutions elsewhere was mostly a one-way proposition. When asked by Senator J. William Fulbright if the Cambodian "incursion" would have any negative effect on the SALT negotiations, the Pentagon's Research and Development Chief, Dr. John Foster, replied in the negative, as the conclusion of a SALT agreement was "of such overriding importance."[6] Foster happened to be correct: the Soviets not only proceeded with the negotiations during the Cambodian extension of the war with hardly a mention of these hostilities, but also received President Nixon in Moscow shortly after the United States raised the stakes of the conflict by mining North Vietnamese ports.

Arms control talks could not be so insulated when it came to Soviet behavior in the Third World. Negotiations over Indian Ocean naval deployments quickly atrophied in the Carter Administration when the Soviets used their fleet and military advisers to gain ground in the Horn of Africa. As a result of this activity, the SALT negotiations were delayed, as well.[7] Third World linkage became even stronger during the extended SALT II debate, when first the "discovery" of a Soviet combat brigade in Cuba and then the invasion of Afghanistan dealt decisive blows to proponents of the agreement. Henry Kissinger, no friend of congressional encroachment on executive branch prerogatives, advised the Senate to make linkage a condition of SALT II ratification by establishing a set of congressionally-mandated principles of linkage, reporting provisions, and periodic Senate votes on Soviet compliance. That such proposals could be advanced seriously by Kissinger was a measure of concern within Republican circles over Soviet activities in Africa, Asia and Latin America in the late 1970s. A majority of the Republicans on the Senate Foreign Relations Committee ultimately concluded that "the failure [of the Carter Administration] to establish linkage was a mistake, and the Senate should not ratify that mistake."[8]

Whether the overriding political concern was Germany, China, or the Third World, the bottom line for hawks of all persuasions was that linkage should stand. The dividing line for operationally- and ideologically-inclined strategists was whether arms control agreements were simply weak, or totally inappropriate instruments to deal with the fundamental political issues that divided the United States and the Soviet Union. In the words of Richard Pipes, "Linkage means that until and unless the Soviet Union radically modifies its thinking and external policies, we cannot count on SALT nhancing our security and diminishing the probability of war. These ends can be better attained by building up our strength to he point where the Soviet leadership can no longer hope to attain ts global ambitions and is forced to turn inward."[9] For the ideologically-minded, negotiated settlements should not reflect power ealities as they exist, if those realities were deemed intolerable. The status quo must first be changed.

In a zero-sum competition, the Kremlin's interest in strategic arms control reflected mainly the political if not military advantages t had gained in the process. During the anti-SALT II campaign, hawks of all persuasions closed ranks on this score. As Paul Nitze wrote, "We wished for equal limitations designed to diminish the mpact of nuclear weapons upon world politics . . . the Soviet task was to achieve the right to that nuclear predominance which we appeared willing to relinquish."[10] For nuclear weapon strategists, a careful evaluation of agreements reached during the four nuclear decades confirmed the resulting penalties to the U.S. side. All but one member of the Senate Armed Services Permanent Investigating Subcommittee concluded that the Partial Test Ban Treaty "posed serious — perhaps even formidable — military and technical disadvantages to the United States."[11] For members of the Committee, such as Senators Stennis, Jackson, Thurmond, and Goldwater, the treaty meant ceding the edge to the Soviets in high-yield weapons and in understanding nuclear weapons effects, particularly as they applied to the potential deployment of anti-ballistic missile systems. One study, supported by the Georgetown Center for Strategic Studies and published four years after ratification, found these risks "even more serious than the excellent, but necessarily hasty, analysis" of the Armed Services Committee, concluding that the Treaty was "a serious mistake and a threat to the future security of the nation."[12]

Opposition to the Nonproliferation Treaty (NPT) was far more muted for a variety of reasons, one being the limited nature of the constraints placed by the treaty on U.S. actions. Still, some tied Soviet support for the NPT to the ill-defined safeguards that were to be devised to control proliferation, and to the constraints the treaty might place on relationships with allies of the United States. As Senator Thurmond said at the time, the NPT could hinder our ability to "arm our friends,"[13] — particularly the Germans — a situation that could only be exploited by the U.S.S.R. Senator Barry Goldwater warned that the NPT "would play right into the hands of Soviet strategic interests in Europe."[14]

The SALT I Interim Agreement, with the unequal launcher limits it codified, generated widespread skepticism among nuclear weapon strategists. (The Soviets were allowed one-third more missile launchers than the United States, offsetting U.S. advantages in other areas.) For defense-minded skeptics of the Interim Agreement, it didn't take too much prescience to see that the Kremlin could exploit the greater number of missiles and lifting power to secure a significant advantage in the number of warheads atop them.

In reaction, Senator Henry Jackson asked his colleagues, "What is wrong with parity?"[15] A large majority of his fellow Senators agreed with him as a matter of simple prudence, if not political expediency. When hawks voted en masse for the Jackson Amendment, requiring that a subsequent agreement not limit the United States to levels of intercontinental strategic forces inferior to the limits provided for the Soviet Union, they were, among other things, conducting a damage-limiting operation. In their view, the next SALT agreement would not be as injurious to U.S. interests as was the Interim Agreement.

Paradoxically, the zero-sum critique of SALT II which contained equal limits for various categories of U.S. and Soviet forces was more fierce than in the previous SALT debate, where the limits were superficially unequal. A majority of the Senate Armed Services Committee agreed with Senator Jackson that the SALT II Treaty did not meet their standards of equality set previously. They concluded the agreement was "unequal in favor of the Soviet Union," and would certify "general military superiority" to the Soviets in the early or mid-1980s.[16] Of particular concern was the leverage provided the Soviets by their sole possession of "heavy" missiles with approximately twice the throw-weight of any other missile in the U.S. inventory, an advantage the Soviets were busily proceeding to convert into extraordinary numbers of accurate warheads. Additionally, the SALT II agreement did not constrain Soviet weapon systems of less than intercontinental range with strategic potential, such as the Backfire bomber. In contrast, the agreement's protocol placed constraints on intermediate-range U.S. systems, such as the cruise missile. There were, of course, countering arguments to all of these contentions, but none dissuaded hawks from the view that Soviet enthusiasm for the SALT II Treaty was well founded.

The relative strategic balance had a great deal to do with how nuclear weapon strategists viewed arms control agreements on Capitol Hill. The Partial Test Ban Treaty was ratified overwhelmingly by a vote of 80–19 during a period of dramatic U.S. superiority. SALT I was also considered during a period of U.S. superiority, but with troubling trends beginning to emerge. Even so, with passage of the Jackson Amendment, the Interim Agreement limiting offensive systems sailed through the Senate with only two dissenting votes, as was the case with the ABM Treaty, as well. Only four members of the House of Representatives voted against the Interim Agreement. In contrast, the SALT II debate took place in troubling circumstances, with a parade of witnesses, including the Joint Chiefs of Staff, stating that the strategic balance would shift against the United States in the early 1980s, if it had not already done so. Against this chorus, it was not particularly comforting or convincing to hear the Secretary of Defense assert that the balance was "adequate," that it would be "less favorable in the early 1980s to us than it is now, and that it would improve after 1985.[17] It was ironic, then, that SALT II foundered during a time of rough strategic parity, supposedly one of the preconditions of successful arms control. Instead, the loss of superiority and transition to uncertain parity loosened the floodgates of anxiety.

It was no wonder that the SALT II Treaty became for nuclear weapon strategists of many different shades a symbol of retrenchment — not just to Soviet military gains, but to the political system benefiting from them. The heart of Paul Nitze's opposition to the treaty can be summed up in the question he raised before the Senate Foreign Relations Committee: "Is unequal and one-sided accommodation by us the best way to assure the cooperation of the Soviet leadership toward world progress and toward peace?" In times of increasing danger, Nitze asked one audience after another, "is it wise to let down our guard?"[18] In keeping with this theme, Eugene Rostow testified that Senate ratification of the SALT II Treaty "would be an act of submission on our part."[19] For Senator Henry Jackson, the issue was largely one of "retreat and appeasement."[20]

During the four nuclear decades, skeptics argued that arms control agreements had not fundamentally altered long-term Soviet ambitions; instead they had placed limitations on U.S. strategic capabilities essential to foil Soviet objectives. Ideologues thus argued that arms control agreements were a hindrance to U.S. interests, becoming instead "a device," in the analysis of Richard Pipes, "to inhibit the United States response to Soviet long-term strategic programs."[21] Like so many others in the strategic debate, this belief was largely intuitive. It rested on a deep skepticism that arms con-

trol agreements with an inveterate ideological or geopolitical foe
could be anything but the most diaphanous instruments of accord.
At best, such agreements reflected tactical retrenchments of long-
term Soviet objectives; at worst, a means to manipulate public opinion and lull the West.

The theme of Soviet manipulation of the peace movement has
deep roots which Kremlinologists can trace back to Lenin's pronouncements. Without doubt, Soviet arms control proposals have
always been geared to a wide audience. It was not unusual in the
early negotiating rounds after World War II to expect Soviet proposals to be delivered over the heads of the U.S. negotiators, aimed
exclusively for the general public. In this, the Soviets were not alone.
U.S. negotiators also offered shopworn and unrealistic disarmament
plans in multinational negotiating forums. A body of literature on
negotiations grew in the United States about how to capture the
high ground in the battle for public support. With the advent of
the Kennedy Administration, both sides began to talk more seriously
about realistic arms control outcomes, and, coincidentally or not,
the theme of the lulling effect of arms control took on new force.

The Partial Test Ban Treaty raised considerable concern from
troubled members of Congress on these grounds. Senator Carl Curtis wondered aloud if the treaty "might have an adverse effect on
our national will to resist communist aggression and our national
will to win the cold war."[22] Senator Bourke Hickenlooper, speaking
for a number of his colleagues most wary of long-term Soviet objectives, concurred: "The unfortunate part is that the psychology
of the people of this country is being fed by the idea that this is a
great step toward a reliable peace, toward the guarantee of peace,
and the cessation of atomic warfare."[23] Lewis Strauss, formerly head
of the Atomic Energy Commission, reminded Senators of historical
lessons ("too often, however, and too late, a pact hailed by a hope-
ful majority as signalling 'peace in our time' actually turns out to
be a first step on the path of disaster"),[24] while Strausz-Hupé warned
that "one of the greatest dangers arising from the treaty, therefore,
is the psychological atmosphere it has generated: the notion that
we are now somehow moving, step by step, into a new period of
détente."[25]

Consideration of the SALT I agreements was, of course, inseparable from considerations of détente. But détente did not mean
a lowering of one's guard. As Secretary of Defense Melvin Laird
said at the time, "peace cannot be bought cheaply,"[26] and his sup-

ort for the SALT I agreements was predicated on funding for a broad range of strategic initiatives to ensure that subsequent negotiations would have a satisfactory result.

The theme of the lulling consequences of arms control resurfaced strongly during the SALT II hearings, as might be expected in a period when the Soviet appetite for geopolitical advantage appeared whetted, and the U.S. defense effort lagging. Paul Nitze warned that accepting SALT II as written would "incapacitate our minds for doing the things that are necessary,"[27] while Edward Teller expressed the judgment that Senate ratification would contribute to a most dangerous cover up. It will have helped to lull the American public into a sense of security which is not based on reality and which is itself our greatest danger."[28] The concern of General David Jones, that SALT II must not be allowed to become a "tranquilizer" to the American people, was echoed by one Senator after another during the hearings.[29] The parallel between Jones' admonition, and that of his predecessor during the Limited Test Ban Treaty debate sixteen years earlier could not have been more striking. At that time, General Maxwell D. Taylor said, "The most serious reservations of the Joint Chiefs of Staff with regard to the treaty are more directly linked with the fear of a euphoria in the West which will eventually reduce our vigilance and the willingness of our country and of our allies to expand continued effort on our collective security."[30]

Taylor's point about the impact of the Partial Test Ban Treaty on allied relations has also surfaced at every arms control debate. For those of the hawkish persuasion, a strong alliance system required shared defense burdens as well as shared perceptions of threatening Soviet capabilities and intentions. Arms control agreements therefore posed the risk of weakening these bonds by lulling the West into a collective and false sense of security. Skeptics of arms control repeatedly made the case that negotiated agreements affected allied perceptions of Soviet intentions far more than the Kremlin's military capabilities—a dangerous trend that made détente such a troubling policy.

Expressions of concern over the impact of arms control on alliance relations were quite evident in the Limited Test Ban Treaty debate, where Edward Teller, Robert Strausz-Hupé, and others argued that the treaty was supported by our allies "with scarcely concealed misgivings," in Strausz-Hupé's words.[31] Strausz-Hupé was even more emphatic five years later during the Nonproliferation Treaty ratification hearings, saying that, "The present Treaty, if

ratified, will nail down the lid on the coffin of NATO."[32] In thi
view, U.S.-German relations would be particularly hard hit, be
cause the NPT would prevent the Federal Republic from acquir
ing nuclear weapons. "How do the Germans feel?" asked Senato
John Tower during debate over ratification. "They feel that we are
standing over them with a bludgeon, with a blackjack, and that they
are being blackmailed into ratification of a treaty which they con
sider to be contrary to their national interest."[33]

As the military balance shifted in the Soviets' favor, reaching arm
control agreements with the Russians was hardly the hawkish pre
scription for stiffening allied resolve. Nor could the United State
take comfort in expressions of allied support for the SALT process
Ostensible European interest in SALT II, in the words of Admira
Thomas Moorer, could be understood in the light that they "do no
want to see any action taken which would encourage the Soviets to
be even more aggressive in the pursuit of world paramountcy."[34]
Alexander Haig, Eugene Rostow, and Paul Nitze all suggested tha
allied support for SALT II not be taken at face value, given thei
misgivings over strategic trends and the domestic political con
straints under which European leaders operated. In this view, the
false sense of security engendered by arms control was, by the time
of the SALT II Treaty, more than ever an alliance-wide concern.
For these strategists, SALT II epitomized a problem in alliance
relations that had been brewing for twenty years. From the Par
tial Test Ban Treaty to SALT II, arms control posed more of a risk
than a remedy to collective security. As the Foreign Policy Research
Institute authors said in 1961, "Our own strength is the most con
vincing pledge of our loyalty to friends and allies."[35]

An Act of Political Imagination

When Niels Bohr tried to convince Franklin Delano Roosevelt and
Winston Churchill during World War II that the West's advantages
accruing from atomic weapons would be "outweighed by a perpetual
menace to human security,"[36] he was considered a man who needed
to be watched carefully. Later, James Franck attempted to reach
Secretary of War Stimson before the first A-bomb test with essen
tially the same warning: "The race for nuclear armaments will be
on in earnest not later than the morning after our first demonstra
tion of the existence of nuclear weapons."[37] Franck's concerns were

considered, then set aside. Again, after the war, J. Robert Oppenheimer said aloud what most knowledgeable government officials knew at heart but tried not to think about: "our atomic monopoly is like a cake of ice standing in the sun and melting every hour."[38]

What would the United States do when its nuclear weapons' lead had completely melted? Then, as later, the arms control community saw stark options reduced to political accommodation or fruitless and dangerous attempts to achieve military advantage. The clear preference for these men of science was to pursue political initiatives; otherwise, the United States would continue to be the driving force behind the strategic competition. What James Franck and others of a like mind wanted instead of an A-bomb strike was an act of "political imagination." They assumed that "only lack of trust, and not lack of desire for agreement, can stand in the way of an efficient agreement for the prevention of nuclear warfare."[39] Arms control-oriented scientists stood foursquare behind the Acheson-Lilienthal Report of 1946 as a creative step toward effective international control of atomic energy. They had the backing of a group of elected officials completely committed to an internationalist view. One first-term Senator, J. William Fulbright, welcomed the plan as precisely the sort of courageous political initiative needed to halt the arms race in its tracks: "If we can once make a breach in the hard crust of suspicion and jealousy which has always enveloped the question of sovereign armed might, we will have opened the door, at least a small crack, to the settlement of all questions by reason."[40]

When the Soviets joined the atomic club, these individuals saw development of hydrogen weapons as precisely the wrong initiative to pursue. But by 1950, when the decision was taken, negotiations over international control at the United Nations had lapsed into a comatose state. Oppenheimer, Kennan and others failed in their attempt to steer the decision away from a new generation of nuclear weapons. In Oppenheimer's case, the attempt extracted a particularly heavy price. By the mid-1950s, advocacy of a soft line toward the Soviet Union was cause for suspicion. Oppenheimer's position against building the H-bomb was a key part in the bill of particulars raised by those who succeeded in suspending his security clearances. The Atomic Energy Commission, by then firmly oriented toward the atom's military applications, decided to do so just two days before the clearances would have expired in any event. In retrospect, the most telling finding of the Personnel Security Board which sat in judgment of Oppenheimer was that a man of

his views and widespread influence within the scientific community "could have serious implications for the security interests of the
country."[41]

In the wake of the AEC's findings in the Oppenheimer case, advocacy of political accommodation with the Soviet Union was rare
in the scientific community and rarer still in the government. At
least until the Cuban missile crisis, attempts to enhance security
by means other than the continued accumulation of nuclear weapons
had little serious chance of success. The likelihood of political accommodation was quite slim, in any event. The Cold War was then
at its height, with U.S. forces committed to block an overt attempt
at Communist aggression in Korea. Channels of communication
between the two sides hardly existed. Reflecting on this state of affairs at the outset of the Kennedy Administration, Jerome Wiesner
concluded that the United States and the Soviet Union were forced
"to work harder and harder in the effort to maintain a given degree
of security. Thus we create twin spirals of invention and production, which, because of the nature of the weapons involved, appear
to lessen, rather than enhance, the possibility of that security."[42]

The twin spirals of invention and production could only be
dampened by political compacts. Wiesner and others entered the
Kennedy Administration with this goal in mind, but their successes
fell far short of their aspirations. The Limited Test Ban Treaty was
a significant achievement, but it did not appear to make much of
a dent in halting and reversing the arms race. When these men left
government, they were at the forefront of those calling for a freeze
on ABM and MIRV activity at the outset of the SALT process—
much to the chagrin of a new set of government officials who were
looking for leverage with which to negotiate successfully. Proponents
of a freeze in 1969 and 1970 found these arguments unconvincing
since deploying MIRVs and ABMs would make, in the words of
the Federation of American Scientists, "another spiral in weapons
deployment . . . inevitable."[43]

The arguments for and against a nuclear weapons freeze at the
outset of the START talks were little different from those raised
a decade earlier at the beginning of the SALT negotiations. Again,
administration officials asserted that a freeze would damage U.S.
security interests and a positive outcome in the negotiations. Their
opponents in the domestic debate stressed the need to block yet another spiral in the nuclear arms competition.

The arms control community did not always present a united

front in freeze debates. The farther left one moved along the political spectrum, the more intense opposition became to modernization programs across the board. This position followed logically from the disarmament wing's assumptions about the nature of the Soviet challenge and the near-absolute lack of political or military value for nuclear weapons. The operational wing of the arms control camp, more concerned with questions of credibility and military balances, generally viewed modernization programs on a case-by-case basis. At the same time, operationalists were wary of the negotiating objectives of sitting presidents, thereby acknowledging the political value of broadly-based freeze campaigns. Faced with the prospect of ABM and MIRV deployments, operationalists drafted and strongly supported the "Stop Where We Are" proposal in the Nixon Administration. In contrast, the freeze campaign at the outset of the Reagan Administration had the wholehearted support of one wing of the arms control movement and the reserved support of the other.

Despite these differences, nuclear weapon strategists usually lumped together both wings as inveterately hostile to a strong military posture. In response, arms control strategists argued that the way to enhance national security was to integrate fully rather than subordinate arms control to defense planning. This was the message carried by the Subcommittee on Disarmament in the 1950s, whose leader, Senator Hubert Humphrey, called arms control and defense programs the "inseparable twins of national security policy."[44] Humphrey's philosophy was written into the statute creating the Arms Control and Disarmament Agency (ACDA), and it has been a guiding principle of arms controllers ever since. Arthur Dean, who helped negotiate the Test Ban Treaty, once maintained that "Disarmament is as much a function of national security as is armament."[45] Dean's ardor over arms control later cooled. His successor several arms control negotiations later, Paul Warnke, remained convinced about the utility of his craft. During the struggle over his nomination to be director of ACDA and SALT II negotiator, Warnke defended his record with the credo, "sound measures of arms limitation may do more to protect this country than new armament programs."[46]

Arms control could be integrated with defense planning because advocates of this course continually rejected the premise that arms control was a zero-sum game. It was difficult to argue this point during the first fifteen years of the strategic debate, when attempts to deal with the Red Russians prompted considerable ridicule or scorn. George Kennan was, in a very real sense, still breaking ground in 1958 when he asserted that "I do not think that they practice deceit just for the sake of practicing it."[47]

Arms controllers defended every negotiated agreement before the Congress and the American public as being in the superpowers' mutual interest. The Partial Test Ban Treaty was justified on the basis that it would slow the spiral of the nuclear arms race, help contain the spread of nuclear weapons to other countries, and reduce radioactive fallout. The Non-Proliferation Treaty was advanced as a means to help curb the spread of nuclear weapons, thereby bolstering the security of all nations. The SALT I accords — the ABM Treaty and the Interim Agreement — were presented to the public as freezing the number of offensive launchers permitted to either side, and drastically curtailing anti-ballistic missile defenses. According to Nixon Administration officials, these accords could promote strategic stability and help defuse the action-reaction phenomenon of the arms race. The SALT II agreement was justified as a means to preserve a stable military balance, learn more of Soviet military capabilities and programs, and strengthen alliances and U.S. leadership.

With the exception of the ABM Treaty, arms control supporters would be among the first to criticize these benefits as being entirely too modest for the time and effort spent in their pursuit. The benefits could have been far greater if the accords had been more far-reaching and comprehensive. That they were not, only confirmed the doves' lament that there continued to be too little official willingness anywhere to make a success of arms control. In particular, the Partial Test Ban Treaty, the SALT I Interim Agreement, and the SALT II agreement reflected the failure of political leaders to summon the will to overcome short-term political concerns for long-term security benefits. "The fault lies," wrote Marshall Shulman, "in the absence of an effective political leadership in either Russia or America capable of presiding with common sense over the pressures of military services and new war technologies . . . the absence of a political judgment to cry enough. . . ."[48]

The lulling impact of arms limitation agreements did not particularly bother the arms control community. The American political system seemed an all-too-efficient regulator for arms control to have much of a tranquilizer effect: agreements reached were too modest, and the price or "safeguards" required to secure their passage were far too exorbitant. The American public would hardly be lulled into a false sense of complacency when there periodically appeared to be a full tank of political mileage in directing attention to the Soviet threat. Advocates of arms control and disarmament have long been concerned with a tranquilizer effect of a very different sort — a built-up immunity to the horrors of nuclear war and the dangers of a business-as-usual arms race. As Richard Barnet wrote, "The mindless accumulation of weaponry is sapping the spirit of our people."[49]

Another bogus issue from the standpoint of arms controllers was the damaging impact of negotiated agreements on alliance resolve. Arms controllers of all persuasions rejected this argument, in part because they repudiated the notion that U.S. alliances could be led very effectively or very long by the animus of fear. For men like George Kennan, alliances in the West were sustained on the basis of common values and ideals; attempts to overmilitarize the relationship could very well corrode those values and ideals. In contrast, arms control agreements that promoted deep-seated and popular goals on both sides of the Atlantic could only strengthen alliances and U.S. leadership. Certainly, the troubling repercussions on alliance ties feared by opponents of the Partial Test Ban Treaty, Non-Proliferation Treaty and the SALT I accords did not come to pass. In their view, the negative impact on alliance relations associated with the SALT II agreements resulted not so much from its terms, but from the U.S. failure to ratify them. When the SALT II agreement was placed in limbo, it became the third successive agreement negotiated by American presidents which was not ratified. A similar fate befell the Threshold Test Ban Treaty, signed by President Nixon, and the Peaceful Nuclear Explosions Treaty, signed by President Ford. When entrusted again with the responsibilities of alliance leadership, operationally-minded nuclear weapon strategists in the Reagan Administration accepted that the pursuit, if not the practice, of arms control was a necessary component for an alliance torn over the impending deployment of intermediate-range nuclear forces. "The purpose of this whole exercise is maximum political advantage," said Assistant Secretary of State Richard Burt. "It's not arms control we're engaged in, it's alliance management."[50] Ideologically-minded strategists within the Reagan Administration preferred other management tools.

The linkage of most concern to the arms control community was that between arms races and the prospect of war. This was the basis for the treatises on general and complete disarmament prepared by men like Grenville Clark and Louis Sohn. Clark acknowledged that the risk of cataclysm might actually diminish in the short-term because of increased understanding about the destructive consequences of a nuclear war, but over time that risk would increase due to "the rapidly mounting potentialities for destruction."[51] Clark and Sohn's conclusion was seconded by Richard Barnet, then about to enter the Kennedy Administration. In his first book on the subject, Barnet wrote that disarmament ultimately required an act of faith on the part of both superpowers. But this act of faith was also tied to separate and common national interests because the arms race meant "a high risk of catastrophe, for intensive rivalries in arms have usually led to disaster."[52]

Operationally-minded arms control strategists were more equivocal on this point, but they, too, have been animated by the same nightmare. In 1961, Jerome Wiesner warned, "there is an ever-increasing likelihood of a war so disastrous that civilization, if not man himself, will be eradicated."[53] In this view, nuclear weapon developments that threatened opposing forces inexorably increased the possibility of confrontation. Developments in missile accuracy prompted concerns over each side's intentions, not relief over revised calculations of collateral damage in the event of "surgical" nuclear strikes. Instead, the growth of counterforce capabilities increased tensions between the superpowers across a broad spectrum.

For arms controllers, trying to link progress in negotiations to proper Soviet behavior on secondary issues was self-defeating, since negotiated agreements improved U.S. security. In retrospect, did holding SALT II negotiations hostage to Soviet activities in the Horn of Africa improve U.S. security over the long run? True, progress in arms control could not be isolated from unrelated activities, as was evident in the SALT II agreement's state of suspension after the Soviet invasion of Afghanistan. Political impediments of this kind had to be grudgingly acknowledged, but only as a source of temporary delays.

In the past, every significant arms control agreement was delayed due to linkage. Some delays were crucial; others were not. When the SALT I negotiations were delayed because of the Soviet invasion of Czechoslovakia, MIRVs moved closer to deployment, although whether MIRVs could have been stopped is an unanswerable question. When the 90th Congress chose not to take up the Non-Proliferation Treaty, awaiting the incoming Nixon Administration's reaction to it, the delay proved entirely inconsequential. The new administration promptly resubmitted the treaty despite the Czech invasion as part of its broader strategy of moving from an era of confrontation to an era of negotiation. The failure of the 96th Congress to consent to the ratification of the SALT II Treaty clearly resulted in short-term damages, at least in the view of operationally-minded arms controllers committed to its passage. Provisions calling for the Soviets to dismantle missile launchers were not implemented, and further progress in arms reductions, alliance relations, and U.S. leadership in this field suffered immediate setbacks. Longer-term losses appeared dependent on achievement of a subsequent accord between the Reagan Administration and the Kremlin.

The disarmament wing of the arms control community had far less invested in the ratification of the SALT II Treaty. For them, the price tag linked to Senate consent was difficult to meet in view of the agreement's marginal accomplishments. In the absence of ratification, both the U.S. and the Soviet Union agreed to take no actions contravening SALT II provisions. The Reagan Administration's position was that it would not "undercut" SALT as long as the Soviets acted in a similar fashion. The concept of linkage, then, took on a curious reverse twist: Soviet behavior was too egregious to consent to ratification, but satisfactory enough to warrant informal consent.

A form of reverse linkage was often advocated by the left wing of the political spectrum. "Once tensions caused by the arms race have been diminished," wrote Louis Sohn and David H. Frisch in 1961, "it may be hoped that it would become easier to find an adequate solution for various problems of a political and economic nature which appear insoluble in the present dangerous atmosphere."[54] Grenville Clark was even more emphatic on this score, arguing that "it is impossible to arrive at any important political settlements in the absence of an agreement for comprehensive disarmament."[55]

This was a transcendental view of arms control over international politics: disarmament efforts had to and could succeed in spite of the traditional dynamics of great power competition. The notion has been given unusual force by literary figures, scientists, grassroots leaders, and others outside the political mainstream. Unlike most political leaders, they believed the nature of nuclear weapons made extraordinary solutions both necessary and possible. The most

distinguished figure among them after World War II was Albert
Einstein, who warned that "the construction of the atom bomb has
brought about the effect that all people living in cities are threatened,
everywhere and constantly, with sudden destruction." Einstein's
words appeared in a special paperback publication, *One World or
None*. Collected within its covers were contributions from some of
the leading scientific figures of the day, offered to the American
public around a unifying theme: "The atomic age challenges every
one of us to wake up and adjust our thinking, our laws, our ways
of life so that we may make the best possible use of this new force
that has been put into our hands."[56]

The A-bomb's impact prompted calls for drastic revisions of the
international system. Norman Cousins wrote an impassioned es-
say, *Modern Man is Obsolete*, based on the "flat truth that the greatest
obsolescence of all in the Atomic Age is national sovereignty." To
his audience of readers in *Saturday Review*, Cousins editorialized that
"there is no need to discuss the historical reasons pointing to and
arguing for world government. There is no need to talk of the difficulties in the way of world government. There is need only to ask
whether we can afford to do without it."[57] Arthur H. Compton, one
of Secretary of War Stimson's science advisers and a key figure in
the Manhattan Project, pushed the idea that "world government
has become inevitable. The choice before us is whether this government will be agreed upon or whether we shall elect to fight a catastrophic Third World War to determine who shall be master."[58]

A rich literature began to appear on methods and approaches
to disarmament. One of the most prominent texts was Clark &
Sohn's *World Peace Through World Law*. Clark played a central role
in armed forces recruitment efforts during both World Wars — he
is, for example, largely credited with conceiving and writing the
Selective Service Act of 1940. But he is best known for his crusad-
ing efforts for some form of world federation in the aftermath of
Hiroshima and Nagasaki. He and Sohn, a Polish-educated legal
scholar who participated in the San Francisco Conference establishing the United Nations, worked tirelessly in advancing their objective of a peaceful world order. *World Peace Through World Law*
provided detailed blueprints on what that world government might
look like. It was based on the premise, according to Clark, that the
accumulation of nuclear weapons presented a "real risk," which
would, "in the absence of universal and complete disarmament under effective world law, be a steadily mounting one."[59]

In reflecting on this period, J. Robert Oppenheimer said,

The control of atomic weapons always appeared possible only on the basis of an intensive and working collaboration between peoples of many nationalities, on the creation . . . of supra-national patterns of communication, of work, and of development. . . . Thus, the problem as it appeared in the summer of 1945 was to use our understanding of atomic energy, and the developments that we had carried out, with their implied hope and implied threat, to see whether in this area international barriers might not be broken down, and patterns of candor and cooperation established which would make the peace of the world.[60]

The clamor created by an aroused public and scientific community had two immediate effects. First, the newly-created Atomic Energy Commission was a civilian rather than a military-controlled operation, holding custody over our stock of A-bombs. Second, an official effort was made to internationalize control over atomic energy.

Secretary of War Stimson was instrumental in convincing President Truman to undertake this act of political imagination. In a memorandum to the President dated 11 September 1945, Stimson wrote:

If the atomic bomb were merely another though more devastating military weapon to be assimilated into our pattern of international relations, it would be one thing. We could then follow the old custom of secrecy and nationalistic military superiority, relying on international caution to prescribe the future use of the weapon as we did with gas. But I think the bomb instead constitutes merely a first step in a new control by man over the forces of nature too revolutionary and dangerous to fit into the old concepts. I think it really caps the climax of the race between man's growing technical power for destructiveness and his psychological power of self-control and group control — his moral power. If so, our method of approach to the Russians is a question of the most vital importance in the evaluation of human progress.[61]

The official U.S. government response in 1946 embraced the concept of nuclear disarmament. The Acheson-Lilienthal Report, written largely by Oppenheimer and a group of scientific advisers, attempted to provide a conceptual plan for effective international control of atomic energy. Under this proposal, the dangerous aspects of atomic energy — identified as prospecting, mining, refining and enriching fissile materials — would be taken out of national hands.

When the Acheson-Lilienthal blueprint was revised by Bernard M. Baruch, President Truman's representative for the ensuing United Nations debate, Stimson's suggestion of a private arms control initiative among great powers gave way to a public, international effort. The Baruch Plan required punishment of violators and suspension of the Security Council veto power in such cases. The Soviet response, presented by Deputy Foreign Minister Andrei Gromyko, was predictably negative. Whereas the United States wanted an international agency to be formed and functioning before nuclear disarmament would occur, the Soviets demanded that the sequence should proceed in the reverse order. Moreover, annulment of the veto power in the Security Council was unacceptable to the Soviets. The impasse over when and how to achieve significant nuclear disarmament has stymied Gromyko and a long succession of U.S. counterparts ever since.

The Baruch Plan has subsequently been criticized by the arms control community as constituting an offer the Soviets couldn't possibly accept. Yet the Baruch initiative was also animated, in large part, by the same transcendental spirit that could be found in the writings of men like Grenville Clark and Norman Cousins. In Robert Oppenheimer's words, the Baruch Plan seemed "an opportunity to cause a decisive change in the whole trend of Soviet policy, without which the prospects of an assured peace were indeed rather gloomy, and which might well be, if accomplished, the turning point in the pattern of international relations."[62] After the war's end, neither Stimson nor Oppenheimer could be labeled the most fluttery of doves. Both advocated a variety of military preparedness programs, including nuclear weapons development. But their response in the summer and fall of 1945 epitomized the internationalist view. With the advent of the A-bomb, international politics-as-usual was simply not the preferred option.

The necessity to transcend traditional approaches and concerns of statecraft was an organizing principle for many atomic scientists after V-J Day, leading to the formation of groups like the Federation of American Scientists.[63] That the transcendental potential of arms control be realized required an almost visionary effort on the part of those caught up in the thrall of nuclear weapons. As Richard Barnet explained, "There has been no disarmament because the as-

sumptions of the arms race have been almost universally accepted."[64]
There could be disarmament only with the wholesale rejection of
our "psychological dependence" on nuclear weapons as a security
crutch, and acceptance of the counter-intuitive proposition that
more weapons meant less security.

In the past, operationalists within the arms control community
usually held different assumptions concerning the transcendental possibilities of their craft. While Clark and Sohn were advocating
one sequence of action, George Kennan was suggesting the reverse.
"It is true," Kennan wrote, "that armaments can and do constitute
a source of tension in themselves. But they are not self-engendering.
No one maintains them just for the love of it. They are conditioned
at bottom by political differences and rivalries. To attempt to remove the armaments before removing these substantive conflicts
of interest is to put the cart before the horse."[65] The final report
of Senator Hubert Humphrey's Subcommittee on Disarmament,
written in 1958, came to the same conclusion: "Although the subcommittee does not believe that a start on disarmament should await
the settlement of outstanding political issues between the Communist bloc and the Western Powers, it perceives the link that exists
between the resolution of important political problems and a large-
scale reduction of armaments."[66]

Although the disarmament wing of the arms control community
constitutes the primary practitioners of transcendental politics, it
does not have a copyright on blueprints for implausible reduction
proposals. Other factions participating in these protracted debates
have tabled ambitious negotiating proposals with no realistic prospects for success. What often appeared as romantic exercises by
the disarmament wing took on the coloring of tactical maneuvers
by operationally-minded arms controllers. When tabled by nuclear
weapon strategists, transcendental offers appeared more like exercises in cynicism.

In March 1977, President Carter proposed deep cuts in strategic
forces that would result in significant reductions in Soviet ICBMs,
the main arm of their strategic forces and the main concern of U.S.
planners. In November 1981, President Reagan proposed the complete dismantling of the primary arm of Soviet theater nuclear forces
in return for cancelling two U.S. weapon programs then in development—the Pershing II and the ground-launched cruise missile. In
May 1982, President Reagan proposed a formula for strategic arms
reductions that would reduce by two-thirds the most threatening

Soviet land-based missiles while increasing U.S. capabilities by proceeding with every U.S. strategic modernization program.

In all cases, the U.S. negotiating initiatives were supported by a curious alliance of enthusiastic nuclear weapon strategists and cautious arms controllers. For their separate reasons, both domestic camps chose to pursue the transcendent possibilities of arms control. The Reagan Administration succeeded in reorienting the terms of debate from arms control to arms reduction — and how could the arms control community be against that? But politics is the art of the possible, and arms control is a political exercise. These negotiating objectives could not be realized because great powers radically revamp their military forces in response to technological change and lessons learned in war, not from an adversary's negotiating proposals.

Moreover, in these cases, U.S. initiatives were not accompanied or preceded by signs of political accommodation between the two countries. On the contrary, the March 1977 proposal was preceded by growing tensions over human rights in the first months of the Carter Administration; the November 1981 initiative was preceded by eleven months of staunch anti-Soviet rhetoric by President Reagan and his national security team; the Reagan START offer was crafted amid the duress in Poland and conflict over East-West trade. It was not surprising then that, whether or not the Soviets shared U.S. concerns about strategic stability, they rejected the sort of transcendental solutions that Presidents Carter and Reagan initially had in mind. Whatever the skills that U.S. negotiators could bring to the bargaining table, those skills did not include pulling rabbits out of hats.

7 The Art of Negotiation

Negotiating with the Enemy

In 1961, many nuclear weapon strategists were reluctant to create
the Arms Control and Disarmament Agency. For those strategists
who placed particular stress on the dichotomous nature of the competition, negotiations with the Soviets made little sense. As Senator
Strom Thurmond said during oversight hearings one year after AC-
DA's creation, "We will make a great mistake to attempt to bring
about any disarmament arrangement with the Communists until
they have abandoned their goal of world Communism and domination and enslavement, and proved it by deeds as well as by words."[1]
Twenty years later, Colin Gray raised the same question when he
asked, "whether, or perhaps how, the United States can conduct
serious arms control business with the Soviet Union, which shows
no evidence of endorsing a recognizable or attractive concept of
strategic stability."[2]

For many operationally-minded hawks, such a "no negotiation"
stance made little sense, if for no other reason than negotiations
themselves could be an integral part of engaging the Communist threat. This was the view taken in NSC-68, which declared
that "a sound negotiating position is . . . an essential element in
the ideological conflict."[3] Senator Henry Jackson expressed the same
thought in the Senate Armed Services Committee's initial oversight

hearings of the Arms Control and Disarmament Agency: "We ought to keep talking to the Soviets . . . you always keep contact with the enemy . . . the thing that concerns me, however, is that we have to realize that talking to the Soviets is another weapon in the cold war. Conferences and discussions are one great arena of combat and conflict."[4] Then again, the political penalties of a "no negotiation" stance have become considerable, for the same reasons why endorsing the goal of strategic superiority carries domestic and international political costs. Offensive forces needed for escalation and protracted nuclear war are particularly troubling, one reason why weapon strategists have begun to show more interest in defenses against nuclear attack. Defensive systems have less of a stigma than nuclear war-fighting strategies and forces, but their object is the same: political and military leverage over the Soviet Union, including leverage for favorable outcomes in negotiations.

Almost all nuclear weapon strategists expressed allegiance to the concept of "genuine" arms control and reductions, and a readiness to sit down and negotiate with the Russians toward these ends. The difficulty arose in figuring out how to operationalize this stance. How could the United States maintain adequate positions of strength and the public vigilance deemed necessary to counter long-term Soviet objectives within a negotiating context that called for equality between the two sides? Nuclear weapon strategists have traditionally responded to this dilemma with the nostrum "negotiation from strength." While this impulse is as old as statecraft itself, the phrase gained fresh currency in the political lexicon in 1950, after highly publicized speeches by Dean Acheson and Winston Churchill.[5]

The concept of negotiation from strength was politically unassailable. Who, after all, could argue the opposite case? Moreover, a strategic build-up for the purposes of negotiation could at least limit the amount of damage that any resulting agreement could impose upon U.S. forces. At the same time, a strong negotiating hand increased leverage for positive outcomes. As Senator Stuart Symington said as he opened the celebrated hearings on the bomber gap, U.S. arms control goals would have little chance of success unless they were "conducted from a basis of relative strength instead of from one of relative weakness, because history shows that the Communist leaders . . . respect only power."[6] The Eisenhower Administration didn't need lessons from the Congress on this score. John Foster Dulles considered negotiations with the Soviets from precisely the same perspective: "experience has taught . . . that those who are weak do not achieve very successful results in dealing with the Soviet Union." The natural corollary was that "we should have in all essential respects positions of strength from which to negotiate."[7]

One of the general concerns raised by the establishment of ACDA was that those who would run and staff the new agency would not believe in the wisdom of negotiating from strength. Former Secretary of Defense Robert A. Lovett worried out loud that ACDA would become "a Mecca for a wide variety of screwballs. . . . It would be a great pity to have this Agency launched and shortly become known as a sort of bureau of beatniks."[8] At the hearings that led to ACDA's creation, General Lyman Lemnitzer, then-Chairman of the Joint Chiefs of Staff, spoke on behalf of orthodoxy when he said, "We can hope for progress [in disarmament] only if we maintain such clear military strength that others will also be made to hope for progress."[9]

Until the SALT decade, negotiation from strength was viewed as the means to codify U.S. superiority. As Dulles told the Humphrey Subcommittee on Disarmament in 1956, "we believe that without giving up positions of strength . . . that there can and should be a balanced reduction."[10] Supporters and opponents of the Partial Test Ban Treaty both agreed that one reason for Soviet interest in the agreement was the strength of the U.S. weapon program, even as they disagreed as to the military implications that would result from ratification.

The testimony of Administration witnesses on the question of superiority changed markedly during the SALT hearings. Nixon Administration officials readily commiserated with skeptics of the SALT I Interim Agreement over its unequal limits, citing the unequal level of effort in missile launcher construction that was reflected in the agreement's terms. The refrain that "things could be worse," which was used repeatedly by proponents of both the SALT I and II agreements, was hardly the glue to stiffen support for these compacts on Capitol Hill. This line of defense had precisely the opposite effect on those who believed strongly in the need to negotiate from strength. In their view, the only way to compensate for past agreements was to tie them to conditions that assured a proper degree of preparedness and a more positive outcome in future negotiations.

After the Limited Test Ban, SALT I and SALT II agreements were negotiated, skeptics in the Congress elicited support from the executive branch on appropriate "safeguards" in view of the risks associated with treaty ratification. The Test Ban Treaty produced four such safeguards: a vigorous underground test program, maintenance of modern and active weapons laboratories, facilities and resources necessary to conduct atmospheric tests if the Soviets abrogated the treaty, and improved capabilities to monitor compliance.

The assurances sought during the SALT I ratification debate were of an entirely different order of magnitude. Here, Secretary of Defense Laird and Admiral Moorer were both noticeably lacking in enthusiasm for the agreements reached. They predicated their support on a series of strategic modernization programs then in research and development, such as the B-1, Trident, ABM activity permissible under the treaty, sea-launched cruise missiles, and other miscellaneous items. The next round of negotiations looked bleak indeed, in the view of Administration spokesmen, unless the United States retained its technological edge through deployment of these systems.

Many within the Carter Administration saw their only hope for ratification of the SALT II agreement in linking its passage to a steady, long-term program to modernize all three legs of the triad and a multiyear commitment to increase funding for the defense budget. Included in this package were the deployment of weapon systems such as the MX and Trident II missiles. The decision by the Carter Administration to build the MX with a 92-inch diameter — thus precluding its placement in existing ballistic missile-carrying submarines — could be traced to the imperative of negotiation from strength. Every Cabinet-level participant in the Carter Administration knew that the selection of an MX missile of this size would limit U.S. strategic flexibility. But in the words of one, "you can't get to SALT III unless you have SALT II." In this case, as with preceding preparedness programs linked to arms control agreements, the negotiations were as much with the legislative branch as they were with the Soviets.

The farther rightward one traveled along the political spectrum, the more strategists were inclined to align negotiating proposals to unilateral strategic and political objectives. An early example of this approach was found in NSC-68. As drafted by Paul Nitze and others, NSC-68 postulated negotiating objectives

> consistent with a positive program for peace — in harmony with the United Nations Charter and providing, at a minimum, for the effective control of all armaments by the United Nations . . . The terms must not require more of the Soviet Union than such

behavior and such participation in a world organization. The fact that such conduct by the Soviet Union is impossible without such a radical change in Soviet policies as to constitute a change in the Soviet system would then emerge as a result of the Kremlin's unwillingness to accept such terms or of its bad faith in observing them.[11]

Tying negotiating strategies to the transformation of the Soviet state is, of course, the ultimate form of linkage. While not postulated in such an extreme form, the echoes of NSC-68 were subsequently heard three decades later in the Reagan Administration. Eugene V. Rostow, Reagan's first Director of the Arms Control and Disarmament Agency, suggested an approach to negotiations 'which would link arms control to the effective revival of the Truman Doctrine and the acceptance by the Soviet Union of the rules of the Charter of the United Nations regarding the international use of force."[12] Another proponent of using negotiating proposals to smoke out Soviet objectives and to clarify their unwillingness to accommodate to Western objectives has been Richard Pipes. At the start of the SALT decade, Pipes, then a Harvard professor of Russian history, was questioned by Senator Daniel Inouye about how negotiation from strength would work in the SALT context:

Senator Inouye: What would you think Russian reaction would be?

Dr. Pipes: I think under these conditions the Russian reaction would be either to continue the arms race or to come to terms.

Senator Inouye: Then what is the use of going to Vienna?

Dr. Pipes: Because there we can find out if they are willing to come to terms. You can approach them by accepting from the beginning a position of parity which would place us at a disadvantage, because we would have nothing to bargain with; or you can approach them with the assumption that unless an agreement of some kind is reached in a reasonable time, we will press for superiority. I should think this is a better contingency. I also think that once the Russians conclude for their own reasons that agreement is desirable, they will promptly accept realistic terms, and not insist on perfect parity.[13]

In political terms, it was relatively easy to table a one-sided proposal at the outset of negotiations. But in democratic societies, difficulties arose when considering fallback positions, especially for an arms control-oriented president susceptible to pressures from his right flank. There is a natural tendency for any initial offer in arms negotiations to protect one's own force structure while placing clamps on the most disturbing aspects of an adversary's. For example, hawks of all persuasions didn't find too much fault with the Carter Administration's March 1977 SALT proposal. This comprehensive, deep-cut proposal sought to bring about the reconfiguration of Soviet strategic forces through sharp reductions in Soviet ICBMs. Even assuming that the political basis existed for significant reductions in strategic forces, the Soviets were not offered much by way of compensating reductions or concessions to see the wisdom of the U.S. proposal. Among other things, the March 1977 offer required a 50 percent cut in Soviet heavy missiles and a 58 percent cut in MIRVed ICBMs below levels previously allowed under the Vladivostok formulas negotiated by President Ford and Leonid Brezhnev. In return, the Soviets were primarily offered the cancellation of the MX missile then in advanced development. One high-ranking U.S. official was quoted as saying, "We would be giving up future draft choices in exchange for cuts in their starting line-up."[14]

"Concessions" from an opening negotiating position often raised hackles among nuclear weapon strategists because of their definitions of equity — definitions that invariably made successful settlements extremely difficult to achieve. Critics of the SALT II agreement eventually negotiated by the Carter Administration such as Paul Nitze, Lt. Gen. Edward Rowny, and Senator Henry Jackson felt that the March 1977 proposal still conferred significant advantages to the Soviets. The sensible negotiating solution, in Rowny's view, was "for the Soviets to scrap those systems which give them strategic superiority. Should they elect not to do so, then we have no choice but to enter into a vigorous program to restore parity." Rowny felt that the March 1977 proposal could have been negotiable if we had stuck with it.[15] Paul Nitze expressed the view that the March 1977 proposal conferred "guaranteed superiority" to the Soviets, and that U.S. concessions were "significantly larger" than those requested of the Kremlin.[16]

The concept of utilizing negotiating proposals as a lever in the political and strategic competition with the Soviets gained a new lease on life in the Reagan Administration, with several key appointees subscribing to this general approach. Most important among them were Paul Nitze, who became chief U.S. negotiator at the Geneva talks on intermediate-range nuclear forces (INF), and General Rowny, who became chief negotiator at the strategic arms reduction talks, or START (as SALT was renamed). In both negotiating forums, President Reagan authorized "deep cut" solutions. The brunt of reductions were to be on land-based forces, where the Soviets had directed most of their effort. Sea-based and air-launched weapons, where the United States had long held the strongest hand, were not the focus of the initial U.S. negotiating proposals. The Reagan Administration's opening START proposal actually allowed a net increase in U.S. strategic forces.

The choices of Nitze and Rowny to lead U.S. delegations in the Reagan Administration were significant, as both had criticized previous U.S. negotiators for being too eager to reach agreement. Such tactics, in the view of many nuclear weapon strategists, were self-defeating because the United States tended to forget that the negotiations themselves were part of the geopolitical competition. That's the way the Soviets played ball: their negotiating proposals were tightly bound to strategic and political objectives. As Paul Nitze said in one of his Committee on the Present Danger pamphlets, "the purposes of the two sides were discrepant from the outset. We wished for equal limitations designed to diminish the impact of nuclear weapons upon world politics. The Soviet side viewed the negotiations as an engagement between adversaries."[17]

In other words, while the United States was concerned with problem solving, the Soviets were seeking to assure their strategic objectives. When dealing with an adversary who played a zero-sum game, the search for negotiated settlement meant giving up ground. Twenty years ago, Senator Henry Jackson expressed this concern during negotiations over the Limited Test Ban Treaty:

. . . we sometimes create the impression we are too anxious. We are somehow no longer good Yankee traders: we have the attitude we must reach an agreement. I think we need to realize that maybe we are making great progress when we don't reach an agreement. They keep talking, we keep talking, but we recede from one position to another; and the world gets the impression we are afraid.[18]

Jackson countered the executive branch's case for the SALT I and SALT II agreements by preparing charts of the distance between initial U.S. negotiating positions and the final terms of the agreements reached—the distance being his measure of U.S. retreat from sound negotiating positions. As a result, he alleged, the Soviet Union had succeeded in pulling off a series of negotiating coups. In SALT I, they managed to stem U.S. momentum on defensive systems via the ABM Treaty, while the progression of Soviet offensive programs continued. In SALT II, the Soviets managed to have their emerging strategic superiority codified, because the United States agreed to insufficient reductions on Soviet ICBMs and failed to include weapon systems like the Backfire bomber in the agreement. Those who disagreed with Senator Jackson could point to U.S. weapon systems that were similarly unconstrained by SALT, or the distance between initial and final Soviet negotiating positions, but these arguments were unconvincing to skeptics. Since the Soviets did not share our basic premises and objectives behind the negotiations—something our negotiators failed to appreciate adequately—there was no reason to expect that the Soviets could be held to equivalent constraints.

Paul Nitze is part pamphleteer part shrewd negotiator. Given negotiating responsibilities, his operational orientation stood out amid the ideologues of the Reagan Administration. With Yuli Kvitsinski, his negotiating partner in the INF talks, Nitze attempted a bureaucratic end-run in July 1982, despite his negotiating instructions. The two negotiators' famous "walk in the woods" formula was later disavowed in both Washington and Moscow, and an early chance for a diplomatic solution to INF deployments was cast aside.

In contrast, Nitze's counterpart in the START negotiations, Lt. Gen. Edward Rowny, continued to advocate a hard line. Rowny had become a vocal critic of SALT II and the U.S. negotiating style at the conclusion of the negotiations. As Rowny lamented before the Senate Foreign Relations Committee, "I wish the other [U.S.] negotiators shared my conviction that if we had negotiated tougher we could have achieved a better treaty." In his view, the United States went into the negotiations "having negotiated away most of our negotiating leverage" through internecine debates and lowest common denominator bureaucratic positions.[19] Combined with the urge to break negotiating deadlocks with new proposals, this led to unfortunate end results. The folly of this negotiating approach, as Rowny told the Senate during his confirmation hearings to become the new START negotiator, was magnified because the reverse was actually the case. "They need it, in my opinion, more than we do . . . I think it is as simple as establishing the willpower o bring the situation to fruition."[20] Willpower, however, was not sufficient to prompt Soviet interest in the terms the Reagan Administration was offering at START. Major modifications in the Administration's position came as a result of Congressional pressure, over Gen. Rowny's opposition.

In essence, the strategic debate has revolved around alternative choices of risk. Throughout the four nuclear decades, ideologically-minded hawks found no remedy in negotiated agreements worth their risk. The Foreign Policy Research Institute analysts believed that "the greatest hope for progress toward mutual arms security lies in the technological-military competition itself, and in mutual, informal arrangements for the unveiling of military secrets."[21] In other words, the arms race itself would provide stabilizing checks and balances, as long as both sides had a clear understanding of the military measures and countermeasures underway. In this view, political differences were the basis of tension between the superpowers—differences that were unlikely to be narrowed by arms control agreements. "Armaments," said Strausz-Hupé, "are not the causes but the symptoms of conflict."[22]

Arms control, then, did not simply pose the risk of dealing with the Soviet Union on particulars when basic issues of contention were unresolved; negotiations meant entrusting to political dialogue the strategic concerns that properly should be handled unilaterally. In Strausz-Hupé's words, "The danger of armed conflict is proportionate to the intensity of unresolved political conflicts and not to the quantity of arms possessed by the parties to those unresolved conflicts."[23]

Moving rightward along the political spectrum, strategic modernization programs and arms control agreements become increasingly conflictual rather than complementary. A former head of the Strategic Air Command, General Thomas S. Power, characterized the tension between the two by asking, "How can we dress and undress at the same time?"[24] Given their view of the utility of military power and the nature of Soviet intentions, ideologically-minded strategists concluded that arms control was at best only a marginal solution to the real conflicts of the international system. Prudence and geopolitical realities dictated that the United States rest its security on more tangible instruments of persuasion. The world was full of risks; it was better to face them heavily armed.

In order to do so, arms control objectives had to be subordinated to nuclear weapon requirements. As General Rowny said between his military and civilian negotiating appointments, "attempts within the United States to have arms control go hand in hand with defense planning have only harmed the latter. If there is a case for integrating the two, it is to be increasingly vigilant that we do not make decisions in defense planning in the expectation that some particular limitation or control of arms will result in a verifiable and enforceable agreement with the U.S.S.R." Failure to adopt this stance would place the U.S. at a disadvantage both at the bargaining table and on the battlefield. Again, Rowny articulated the hawk's lament:

> The Soviets have their priorities straight. First, they determine their national objectives and foreign policy goals. Then they develop and deploy the forces needed to carry out these objectives and goals. Finally, and only in third priority, they see where and if controls or limitations of arms can be accepted which fit into this scheme . . .
>
> In the U.S. we have tried to stand this pyramid on its head. First we examine what arms might be controlled or limited. Then we plan and tailor our forces accordingly. Finally, we look around to see what objectives and goals we might be able to achieve with the forces that are left.[25]

Nuclear weapon strategists are acutely aware of the notion of risk-taking because defense planning essentially begins with risk assessment and the best apportionment of limited forces to cover a wide range of unsettling contingencies. For such individuals — whether of an operational or ideological bent — arms control piled additional risks onto a burgeoning mound. Negotiated agreements were unlikely to make strategic problems that much less complicated to compensate for the limits placed on U.S. military forces.

For one-fifth of the Senate, the advantages of the Partial Test Ban Treaty did not outweigh the risks it posed to our nuclear weapon programs and retaliatory forces. The ban on atmospheric tests would, in the view of all but one senator on the Senate Armed Services Preparedness Investigating Subcommittee, foreclose critical weapon effects tests, and the development of optimum U.S. nuclear warheads. An additional risk resulting from the treaty would be to deny us a valuable source of information on Soviet nuclear weapon capabilities, as the United States collected nuclear debris after Soviet atmospheric tests.[26] As Senator Thurmond lamented, the question boiled down to "whether political or military considerations are of more importance to our Nation."[27] With public opinion running four-to-one in favor of the treaty, there was no doubt about the outcome of the ratification vote on the morning of September 24, 1963. But that afternoon, the Senate also voted 77–0 for the then largest peacetime defense budget in history.

Many of the arguments over risk have hinged on the difficulties of verification and the likelihood of Soviet cheating. The Senate voted for a Partial Nuclear Test Ban Treaty instead of a comprehensive one largely because of this concern. It was difficult enough to monitor weapon tests in deep space or in remote ocean areas. (The Foreign Policy Research Institute analysts, as well as other critics of the treaty, worried that "outer space tests would be particularly difficult to detect if the testing nation would shield them behind the moon and thus reduce the intensity of telltale X-rays from the explosion.")[28] There was a far greater likelihood that weapon tests could be muffled underground, although the considerable effort involved in attempting to do so would leave a good many telltale signs. On-site inspections were needed to provide confidence on these matters. Kennedy eventually decided that six or seven inspections per year was a "rock bottom" requirement, and Khrushchev at one time agreed to three, but neither man felt he could compromise further on the issue.[29]

Five years later, Senators such as Richard Russell, John Tower, Barry Goldwater, John Stennis and Strom Thurmond found the risks of the Nonproliferation Treaty too great to warrant ratification: there were no assurances that the proposed international safeguard system would be adequate, and the treaty could complicate alliance relations. Still later, nuclear weapon strategists argued against a MIRV ban or MIRV limits, partly on grounds that monitoring flight tests of multiple independently targetable re-entry vehicles would be difficult. In this instance, Defense Department officials argued that MIRV testing could be disguised as space launches, and that the absence of MIRV flight testing did not provide adequate confidence that MIRVs wouldn't be deployed covertly.[30] In the case of MIRVs, verification arguments were of secondary importance, but they added to the burden of those wishing to block deployment.

For Henry Jackson, the SALT I agreements constituted "enor-

mous risks," going to the heart of the U.S. ability to field a credi
ble deterrent.[31] As a result, another round of new strategic weapon
programs was needed as safeguards to the Interim Agreement
Secretary of Defense Laird and every military witness before the
Senate Foreign Relations and Armed Services Committees condi
tioned approval of the SALT I accords on improvements in al
phases of our nuclear weapons program. Congress dutifully
authorized funding for these initiatives initially, but much of the
steam behind them soon evaporated. The Trident program could
not support an accelerated building rate of three boats per year
the B-1 bomber was canceled on the verge of its deployment by
President Carter, and the ABM site around Washington was fore
closed by a 1974 Protocol to the ABM Treaty, limiting both side
to a single ABM complex. The remaining U.S. ABM site at Grand
Forks, North Dakota, was deactivated.

Meanwhile, none of the steam seemed to be going out of the
Soviet strategic build-up. Of particular concern was the extent to
which the Soviets were modernizing ICBMs, one of the loose nego
tiating ends that could not be tied in the frenetic days of the 1972
Moscow Summit. At issue was the possibility that the Soviets could
replace existing ICBMs with newer versions appreciably larger, thu
having far greater throw-weight and military potential. Both side
agreed that "in the process of modernization and replacement . .
dimensions of land-based ICBM silo launchers will not be signifi
cantly increased," but there was no common definition of just what
was meant by this phrase. All that could be agreed upon was that
the term "significantly increased" meant the increase would not be
greater than 10 to 15 percent of the dimensions of land-based ICBM
silos then in being. But "significant" increases calculated on the basis
of silo diameter as well as depth translated into an increase in
missile volume of slightly over 50 percent. The negotiating record
both in Moscow and before, indicated no agreed interpretation or
how the term "significant" was to be defined. The issue came up
only once in Senate Foreign Relations Committee hearings, but be
came a source of contention in the House and Senate Armed Serv
ices Committees, where members were more critical of the agree
ments reached.

As might be expected, every official witness offered the narrow
interpretation of this key provision, when asked: increases in silo
volume were to be calculated on the basis of one dimension, no
both. Chief SALT negotiator Gerard Smith said that if the Soviet

proceeded otherwise, "we would consider that as incompatible with the Interim Agreement." Admiral Moorer stated that an increase in both dimensions "would constitute a violation, in my opinion, of the agreement." Defense Department negotiator Paul Nitze concurred: "By and large," he told skeptical members of Congress, "I think the agreements are very precise." With respect to the provision in question, "only one of the two dimensions, depth or diameter, could be increased as much as 15 percent."[32]

The Soviets did not accept this unilateral U.S. interpretation, and the next generation of new Soviet ICBMs, which shortly began to appear, did not conform to it. To the U.S. SALT negotiators, this explained why no tightly phrased common definition had ever been agreeable to Moscow. To Senators like Henry Jackson it was proof positive of their worst fears about placing reliance on arms control instead of strategic modernization programs.

When it came time for the Senate to consider ratification of the SALT II agreements, Senator Jackson and others were more reluctant than ever to rely on executive branch promises that remedies would be forthcoming to offset the risks inherent in the treaty. In their view, if arms control was a political imperative, it was essential to link the process to strategic modernization programs. The resultant alliance might be fraught with tension, but it was far better than arms control alone. Bargaining chips and arms control negotiations were necessarily bedfellows. As Admiral Moorer testified during the SALT I hearings, "I do not feel that we will ever get a suitable treaty . . . unless we have this leverage . . . If we stand fast and do nothing, then I do not think there is any incentive whatever for the Soviets to negotiate any further."[33]

For nuclear weapon strategists, any military program that provided leverage against the Soviet Union and Soviet objectives had very direct utility. One of the reasons why hawks were so concerned over many of President Carter's appointments was that his nominees did not seem to share their views on negotiating leverage. Paul Nitze's stand against the selection of Paul Warnke to head ACDA and the SALT II negotiations was based, in part, on Warnke's periodic advocacy of restraint instead of leverage. "I don't know what negotiation is about," said Nitze, "unless it has something to do with bargaining chips . . . you are not going to get something unless your position is one from which you can effectively negotiate."[34] In this view, critics like Senator J. William Fulbright who feared that bargaining chips would undercut SALT had their concerns mis-

placed. As National Security Adviser Henry Kissinger said at th
time of the SALT I debate, "Our experience has been that an on
going program is no obstacle to an agreement and, on the contrary
may accelerate it."[35]

At a later point, Kissinger excluded the decision to MIRV U.S
ballistic missiles from this rule of thumb, and with good reason
More than any single event in the four nuclear decades, the deci
sions by the United States and the Soviet Union to deploy MIRV
fueled the arms competition and mocked attempts at significant con
trols. It was a decision the United States government made first

During the critical period of 1969–71, the Nixon Administra
tion proceeded to flight test and deploy MIRVs rather than to seel
in a serious way their limitation in SALT I. Recommendations b
some participants to slow down or to halt the MIRV test program
while negotiations were underway were rejected by the White House
The U.S. negotiating proposal was to link a ban on MIRV de
ployment to on-site inspection, a linkage that was both unnecessar
in a technical sense and unacceptable to the Soviet Union, thu
assuring its rejection at the negotiating table. On-site inspectio
was unnecessary because a ban on MIRV flight tests could provid
assurance that MIRVs could not fulfill their military function: re
peated developmental and operational flight tests were required fo
minimal assurance that warheads could be directed accurately agains
separate targets. Such flight tests could not be concealed from U.S
intelligence sources and methods for very long, despite the qualm
expressed on this score by some Nixon Administration officials

For their part, the Soviets were also reluctant to ban MIRVs dur
ing SALT I. At the time, the United States had already begun
developmental flight tests; they had not. Moreover, at the outse
of the SALT negotiations, the Soviet Union was lagging far behind
in numbers of overall launchers, as well as warheads. The Kremli
therefore proposed that MIRV flight testing be permitted, but de
ployment prohibited—a proposition that couldn't be verified witl
high confidence except by on-site inspection, which, of course, th
Soviets adamantly refused to permit.

As chief SALT I negotiator Gerard Smith later recounted, th
MIRV proposals tabled by both sides were an ingenious and dis
ingenuous mismatch. The prospects for a MIRV ban or for sever
limitations therefore hinged on the most intensive negotiating ef
forts, which many in and out of Congress advocated. The prospect
for success were slim, but in view of the consequences anticipated

by many, seemingly worth the effort. In retrospect, it is possible
to patch together the rationale for agreement. Although the United
States had already begun to flight test MIRVs in the summer of
1968, not enough tests had been conducted during SALT's early
rounds to provide for a necessary degree of operational confidence.
As a practical matter, the Soviet Union could rely on the American
press to verify that the United States was not deploying MIRVs
that were only partially flight tested. While the Soviets undoubtedly
would feel uncomfortable with this asymmetry in flight testing, they
had good reason to block MIRV deployments by the United States
in 1971: it would take them the better part of a decade to match
the pace and scope of the U.S. program.

For key officials in the Nixon Administration, there seemed at
the time to be compelling reasons to go ahead with MIRVs. Henry
Kissinger was keenly aware that while the Pentagon was lukewarm
toward the ABM, powerful figures were "passionately in favor of
MIRV." The Soviets were excavating two hundred new missile silos
per year; the U.S. was standing pat. To the White House, MIRV
was "crucial"; it was "our counterweight to the growing Soviet
numbers."[36] No Administration has ever feared that an arms control agreement it negotiated would be savaged from the left; but the
right flank has to be protected vigilantly, sometimes at considerable
cost. In this instance, the right flank within both the executive and
legislative branches was extremely restive. The President's adviser
most strongly in support of a MIRV ban, SALT negotiator Gerard
Smith, sadly concluded that "the President may have calculated that
ABM limitation was all the traffic would bear, the 'traffic' in this
case being the Secretary of Defense, the Joint Chiefs, their supporters in Congress, and their constituencies around the country."[37]
The U.S. decision to link a MIRV ban to on-site inspection was
final; such a ban would be offered up in the early rounds at SALT
to conciliate arms controllers on Capitol Hill and in the bureaucracy
(otherwise, Kissinger explained, "all hell would have broken loose").[38]
Then it would be supplanted by more serious negotiating proposals.

It was left to Deputy Secretary of Defense David Packard to explain on Capitol Hill the Administration's insistence on continued
MIRV flight testing as a matter of simple prudence, as well as sound
negotiating tactics. Packard told unsympathetic members of the
Senate Foreign Relations Committee that, "Until we actually do
get an arms limitation agreement, it is inappropriate for us to stop
our ongoing programs." Since the fall of 1968, the Soviets had

deployed 450 new ICBMs and 19 Yankee-class submarines (the approximate equal to our older Polaris boats.) Given the breadth of the Soviet strategic build-up, Packard asked, "Do you mean to tell me you think it would be appropriate for us to stop everything we had programmed, when they are doing these things? I don't think that would have been advisable."[39]

Key figures in the State Department and ACDA disagreed, but Packard had support for his view in the White House and in the congressional offices where it mattered most. The Pentagon had made a conscious decision to depend on qualitative, rather than quantitative increments in U.S. forces, a judgment accepted and expected to be implemented by key Congressional leaders. This meant MIRVing U.S. systems. The MIRV decision was presented to the Congress by Secretary Packard as "a very important bargaining chip, if you want to put it that way. If we are going to make progress, it has to be done in tough, hard bargaining."[40] Moreover, the original MIRV deployment decisions were characterized by Packard and others as restrained — the United States was not proposing warheads with such yield and accuracy as to pose a threat to Soviet ICBMs. According to Packard, "The building up of a counterforce capability is destabilizing . . . That is precisely what we don't want to do."[41]

Three years later, the strategic debate revolved around just such ICBM improvements, with the Schlesinger initiatives to increase the yield and accuracy of MIRVed land-based missiles. Nuclear weapon strategists had surmised a similar effort on the part of the Soviet Union and stressed the requirement to maintain our technological edge and bargaining leverage in the face of a continuing Soviet strategic build-up. Proponents of this course argued that U.S. restraint would not be reciprocated and that, in the words of Senator John Stennis, "accuracy is always desired in weaponry."[42] In 1975, Senator Henry Jackson spoke for three-fifths of the Senate when he asked, "Does it make any sense for us to deny our Government unilaterally the opportunity to improve our own ICBM systems? . . . Should we throw away a source of leverage here?"[43] From the H-bomb decision in 1950 through the debates over MIRVs and counterforce in the 1970s, to the contests over the Reagan strategic program in the 1980s, the imperative for negotiating leverage arising from U.S. nuclear weapon developments has remained constant for those of the hawkish persuasion.

It would not be correct to assert that nuclear weapon strategists failed to foresee the implications of the bargaining chip approach o arms control. In the case of MIRVs, the Senate Armed Services Preparedness Investigating Subcommittee certainly did. The Subcommittee held a series of hearings in 1968 to vent its concern that not enough was being done to maintain a strategic edge over the Soviets, and perhaps too much reliance was being placed on MIRVs as the means to ensure that edge. The Committee report warned:

> If this [MIRVing] is within our technological capability and resources, then prudence surely dictates that we assume that it is also within the technological capability and resources of the Soviets. In addition, we must recognize that the greater throwweight which many of their missiles possess gives them greater flexibility to proceed with such warhead improvements as MIRVing . . . It may be dangerously misleading to credit our forces with as yet unattained technological advances while denying the Soviets such credit. The hard fact is that, if the Soviets . . . MIRV, . . . it is entirely possible that in the future, they can put on a larger number of more accurate, separately targetable . . . warheads.[44]

Characteristically, the Committee's response to this analysis was not to urge arms control measures to foreclose MIRV deployment. Consistent with their assumptions of the utility of nuclear weapons and disutility of arms control, the Senators on the Preparedness Investigating Subcommittee concluded that MIRVs were necessary, but not sufficient, to provide for an adequate defense.

Negotiating Partners

Surprisingly little has been written by the arms control community on how to secure their objectives through negotiations. The disarmament wing has been almost entirely silent on this score since the Acheson-Lilienthal Report was published in 1946. Given their basic premises, advocates of disarmament naturally tend to see the negotiating process as less important than its end result. To some, the process is suspect because it has led to unacceptable results. Preferred negotiating tactics usually were tied to unilateral or reciprocal initiatives leading toward disarmament. How one got there was usually based on the application of some mechanistic formula for reductions.

For the operational wing of the arms control community, the pro-

cess of negotiation was far more important and complex. While
there have been few "how to" manuals on successful arms control
negotiations, there has been no shortage of explanations why pre
vious attempts to reverse the arms race have ended badly. Failure
is usually traced to the impulse by nuclear weapon strategists to use
negotiations as a means to secure positions of strength or to test the
bona fides of our negotiating partner. For arms controllers of all
persuasions, the negotiating process would not work if it was used
as one instrument in the overall political and military struggle with
a sworn foe or as a means to secure superiority. Negotiations would
work if adversaries secured their common interests through business
like bargaining. Although the goal of superiority was formally
abandoned in 1969, arms controllers have continued to sense its
presence at the negotiating table, the "margin of safety" proposed
by the Reagan Administration being one of many manifestations.

The impetus to negotiate from strength led naturally to a reliance
on bargaining chips; and bargaining chips, in the view of Paul
Warnke, "lead to agreements to arm rather than agreements or
arms control."[45] Those who supported negotiated agreements noted
that the distinction between nuclear weapon programs that were
essential and those that were required for bargaining purposes
tended to erode over time. "Perhaps the 'bargaining chip' theory
may be sound diplomacy under some circumstances," warned Marshall Shulman at a time when MIRVs and ABMs were the current bargaining chips, "but it is clear in the strategic weapons field
it provides dynamism for the arms race."[46]

Virtually all of the strategic modernization programs initiated
during the SALT decade were characterized, at one time or another,
as bargaining chips. The only major strategic program not deployed
over this period (the B-1 bomber was canceled and then resurrected)
was ballistic missile defense. In this instance, a direct corollary could
be noted between lack of domestic support and the absence of ABM
deployments. As Ralph Earle II, Warnke's replacement as chief
SALT II negotiator, observed, "in the only case where a bargaining chip was cashed, there was extraordinarily strong opposition
to spending cash for the program in question."[47] Other weapon programs were protected by a Catch-22 provision: The United States
needed bargaining chips to negotiate from strength, but it could
not bargain away any position of advantage.

Since the debate over the A-bomb, the arms control community
has consistently argued that the negotiating process could only bear

ruit as a result of concrete actions by the United States, whether
n the form of exemplary behavior, specific initiatives, or conspicu-
ous restraint. This was the central theme of the Franck Report in
945, which recommended a demonstration A-bomb explosion
before international representatives on a desert or barren island.
The report's authors felt that the demonstration shot, tied to a public
declaration of readiness to renounce the A-bomb, would both end
the war and protect the peace. They acknowledged that such recommendations in the midst of a war against a brutal adversary sounded
fantastic," but defended them on the grounds that A-bombs changed
the stakes of international conflict in such a fundamental way that
new and imaginative methods" were required.[48]

The debate over proceeding with the H-bomb again accented
the theme of restraint. In an appendix to the General Advisory
Committee's report which recommended against a crash effort to
produce hydrogen bombs, Oppenheimer, James Conant, Lee Du-
bridge and others said, "we see a unique opportunity of providing
by example some limitations on the totality of war and thus of limit-
ng the fear and arousing the hopes of mankind." For these limits
to be realized, the United States had to take the initiative by ab-
staining from the production of thermonuclear weapons. Committee
members Enrico Fermi and Isadore I. Rabi took a more unequivocal stance, based on moral and ethical principles. They proposed
that the United States "invite the nations of the world to join us in
a solemn pledge not to proceed in the development or construction
of weapons in this category." Renunciation or circumvention of this
pledge could be met with the U.S. stockpile of atomic weapons, and
thus this country would not run a military risk.[49]

The arguments for restraint and exemplary behavior were raised
with similar intensity over an atmospheric test ban during the
Eisenhower Administration. President Kennedy took a more active interest in trying to achieve a negotiated agreement than his
immediate predecessor. Toward this end, Kennedy made several
initiatives — twice postponing a series of nuclear weapon tests, and
offering a pledge of reciprocal restraint on atmospheric testing in
a speech at American University that led to the final round of
negotiations.

The debates over impending MIRV and ABM deployments a
decade later elicited numerous calls for restraint from the arms control community. Here were two programs with profound consequences for strategic stability and arms control that were maturing

at the very onset of the SALT process. The intensity of opposition was due also to the profound skepticism of some members of Congress about the Nixon Administration's negotiating objectives. Here, too, was a parade of distinguished citizens and former government officials more than willing to help arms control-oriented Senators make their case. Marshall Shulman advised against pursuing MIRV deployments as "a clear indication of the seriousness of our intentions to achieve stability, leveling off and where possible, reductions" in strategic offensive forces. For Shulman and others, "one essential mark of our seriousness would be a clear indication of our willingness to exercise restraint . . . there are also risks to this course, but if our security is best advanced at this stage by a stable deterrent balance at a moderate level, the risks are neither disproportionate nor irretrievable."[50] Arguing on behalf of the same causes, Paul Warnke added that, "we can afford to exercise greater restraint . . . in fact, we cannot afford not to."[51]

Calls for restraint continued throughout the SALT decade. Senator J. William Fulbright opened the Senate Foreign Relations Committee's review of the SALT I accords with the warning that the entire panoply of "safeguards" favored by the Administration led to the "danger of having our actions belie our words" and risked undercutting the agreements.[52] When Secretary of Defense James Schlesinger originally proposed improving U.S. counterforce capabilities in 1974, opposition again mounted on the grounds that such programs were contrary to the spirit and purposes of SALT. Most arms controllers strongly opposed these initiatives on other grounds as well. In their view, deterrence based on quick-strike, accurate forces would only fuel the arms race and send the wrong signals to Moscow about U.S. intentions. At that time, the nature of similar Soviet programs was only dimly apparent, and Pentagon critics still believed that the power of example could influence the extent of Soviet ICBM modernization programs. Congressman Les Aspin berated Fred Iklé, the ACDA Director at the time, on precisely these grounds: "I think by doing this we are going for competition and we are encouraging them to go into competition . . . if we start now with a counterforce capability, it is certain they will go for a counterforce capability with that increased capability they are building. You are fueling the arms race . . ."[53] By the late 1970s, the emergence of Soviet counterforce capabilities was difficult to contest. Three new types of Soviet ICBMs (the SS-17, SS-18, and SS-19) provided the Kremlin with quick-strike, accurate warheads far in excess of

hose residing in U.S. missile silos, and the United States had
nothing comparable to a new Soviet intermediate-range missile,
he SS-20.

Still, most people in the arms control community urged restraint.
Rather than compound the problems created by Soviet ICBMs by
matching their deployment, arms controllers suggested compensating actions. In operational terms, this meant placing greater
reliance on sea-based forces that would be highly survivable and
therefore stabilizing.

Calls for restraint came easily to those who regretted previous
activism, and some of the most powerful voices on behalf of moderation belonged to men intimately familiar with the innards of nuclear
weapons. A case in point was Herbert York, who served as the Pentagon's top research official two decades before becoming ACDA's
chief negotiator for a comprehensive test ban. In York's view, "The
United States has taken most of the initiatives in building up the
present fantastic arsenals of nuclear arms, so why don't we take some
small initiatives in reducing them?"[54] York, who once directed a
nuclear weapons laboratory, believed that technological imperatives
fueled the arms race. This necessarily placed the United States in
the role of being the chief miscreant, given our pre-eminent position in most of the key applications of military science. The MIRV
and ABM deployment decisions symbolized the dangers of the
technological impulse. Technical fixes couldn't solve these problems;
political solutions were needed.

Since the United States was more enlightened than the Soviet
Union on these matters, the arms race wouldn't be reversed unless
we led the way. Arms controllers could cite several examples of concepts generated in the United States which were adopted by the
Soviet leadership after initial and sometimes prolonged resistance.
One notable example was the evolution of Soviet views toward
verification.

For years the Soviets had rejected photo-reconnaissance satellites
and other "national technical means" of monitoring arms control
agreements as intrusions upon state sovereignty. The Kremlin has
subsequently accepted "national technical means" as an integral part
of the arms control process. For the first time, in the text of the
SALT II agreement, the Soviets agreed to exchange data on their
strategic forces—information that was previously considered state
secrets closely held from even civilian officials. The Kremlin also
agreed to data exchanges in the Threshold Test Ban agreement to

assist the United States in calibrating Soviet underground nuclear tests. In the Peaceful Nuclear Explosions agreement, the Soviets agreed to allow foreign nationals access to the sites of nuclear explosions for peaceful purposes. And in the Comprehensive Test Ban negotiations during the Carter Administration, Russian negotiators agreed to the placement of "black boxes" on their territory along with on-site inspection procedures to assist in verification. As none of these agreements were ratified, their provisions moderating centuries of Russian xenophobia were not realized. Still, in the view of the arms control community, they were proof that U.S. initiatives and persistence could make a difference in changing the Kremlin's attitudes.

Arms controllers were, as a group, diplomatic risk-takers. Why not take risks that paled in comparison to the risks of an unconstrained arms race? In the words of McGeorge Bundy, "we can take the lead in practical steps for the simple and persuasive reason that even without agreement some such steps are in our own best interest."[55] Taking risks meant accepting the fact that some restraints would be placed on U.S. forces, but comparable restraints would be levied on Soviet forces. Trade-offs wouldn't be harmful because the United States could compromise with the Russians in this domain without compromising our security.

The Acheson-Lilienthal Report of 1946 freely admitted the risk it proposed to accept: "inherent in any plan of international control is a probable acceleration of the rate at which our present monopoly will disappear."[56] This was a risk worth taking, however, given the indisputable fact that at some point the Soviets would join the atomic club.

The same calculus of benefits and risks was evident during deliberations over the H-bomb. Lilienthal argued "not [to] threaten by a decision now what might be the last chance to adopt a less certain course of danger,"[57] but his plea for a review of overall U.S. national security policies led directly to NSC-68 instead of a more conciliatory course.

When the Soviets showed that they, too, could run the race, calls for restraint received less of a hearing from skeptics; exemplary behavior seemed safer when the United States held a commanding lead in the competition. Still, pleas for restraint continued. Even in the uproar over Sputnik, George Kennan cautioned that "certain risks must be assumed in order that greater ones may be avoided."[58] He was talking about arms control, not an increased defense ef-

'ort. Hans Bethe offered the same refrain during the nuclear test
ban debate: "Sometimes insistence on 100 percent security actually
.mpairs our security, while the bold decision, which at the time
seems to involve some risk, will give us more security in the long
run."[59] Bethe lost this debate, as did Oppenheimer, Lilienthal, and
Kennan before him.

The notion of pursuing a policy of restraint toward the Kremlin
was usually anathema to nuclear weapon strategists who felt that
proper Soviet conduct could best be assured by demonstrating to
the Kremlin the risks of misbehavior. It was therefore not surprising that the issue of restraint, dressed in the garb of unilateralism,
figured prominently in Paul Warnke's divisive confirmation hearings in 1977. Warnke was one of the most outspoken proponents
of taking initiatives to defuse the arms race, most prominently in
an article entitled "Apes on a Treadmill." In it, he urged "a policy
of restraint, while calling for matching restraint from the Soviet
Union." Warnke felt that "highly advertised" restraints would be
reciprocated, once the Soviets had attained a position of rough parity
with the United States in strategic forces.[60] Warnke's harsh ex-
periences before Congressional committees did not bode well for the
success of future arms control negotiators who have not adopted
a bullish posture on strategic weaponry. Indeed, a comparison of
the treatment received by Warnke and his successor in the Reagan
Administration, Lt. General Edward Rowny, was striking. Rowny's
confirmation hearings were the epitome of decorum and bipartisanship. For arms controllers, it seemed ironic that strong congressional
support was accorded a negotiator who was an ardent proponent
of new nuclear weapons and a skeptic of arms control. The con-
verse of these predispositions, however, could make a man unfit
for the job.

8 Stalemate

In military terminology, uniformed services and commands have defined roles and missions. The same can be said for key individuals in the extended debate over arms control and nuclear weapons. The views expressed over time by men like George Kennan and Paul Nitze demonstrate a pattern of discourse that has led to a domestic condition of political stalemate.

Both Kennan and Nitze were present at the creation of the post-World War II world, manning important positions in Dean Acheson's State Department. Each man had come to Acheson's Policy Planning Staff from different training grounds. Kennan was a career Foreign Service officer with first-hand experience in the Soviet Union, where his dispatches had laid the groundwork for the containment policy. Nitze carved out a successful career as a New York investment banker who later held a series of government posts during World War II, including a tour as Vice Chairman of the United States Strategic Bombing Survey.

When Kennan stepped down as head of the Policy Planning Staff in 1949, his position was taken by Nitze. In the first few weeks of 1950, Kennan submitted to higher authorities his first, in-depth analysis of the problems and prospects for arms control; Nitze began to prepare NSC-68, which served as manifesto and planning document for the intense phase of U.S.-Soviet rivalry which followed

he outbreak of war in Korea. Kennan's dissent from this document
had little effect.

Their paths crossed many times in subsequent years. Both were
often called to testify on Capitol Hill to stress the themes that mattered most to them: for Kennan, the "overmilitarization" of foreign
policy in general and U.S.-Soviet relations in particular; for Nitze
the requirements of vigilance and strength. Over the years, they
differed on virtually every nuclear weapons issue, but those differences became increasingly pronounced after the SALT I debate.
Nitze worked ardently for a revitalized U.S. nuclear force posture,
and was rewarded with a position of great responsibility by an
administration that appreciated his talents. Meanwhile, Kennan's
divorce from the prevailing politics of arms control and nuclear
weaponry became complete. In a series of highly publicized pronouncements, he proceeded to call for complete nuclear disarmament through a series of sweeping and mutually reciprocated initiatives.

The increased distance between men like Kennan and Nitze was
symptomatic of a larger problem. The gulf between the two had
long existed, but the penalties associated with it somehow seemed
more manageable in the past. Until the Nixon Administration, partisans from opposing camps could draw solace from certain achievements of no little consequence. Nuclear weapon strategists could
point to a bipartisan goal of strategic superiority and an array of
military hardware that matched rhetoric with muscle. Arms controllers could see hope for the future in the Partial Nuclear Test
Ban and the Non-Proliferation Treaties. To be sure, both camps
were restive with the state of affairs that existed in 1969. Conser-
vatives were dissatisfied with U.S. force levels, and arms controllers
knew that previous achievements were in the nature of limited victories: the Test Ban Treaty still permitted nuclear testing underground and the Non-Proliferation Treaty wasn't embraced by all
nuclear or nonnuclear states. Nevertheless, these were important
and useful first steps.

The Nixon years represented a paradoxical turn in the strategic
debate. Significant accomplishments were achieved in strategic arms
control and in nuclear weapon developments, but in the process,
it became a good deal more difficult for both camps to be sanguine
about fulfilling their respective agendas. Debates over these issues
consequently took a far more severe turn. Perhaps both camps realized that the stakes of their domestic as well as the international

competition were rising precipitously, and resolved that compromise was not a likely route to secure their objectives. More likely, the natural tensions arising from decisions reached during the Nixon years became increasingly apparent and irreconcilable.

For nuclear weapon strategists, a clear warning signal lay in President Nixon's acceptance of the goal of "sufficiency" rather than superiority in nuclear forces. How could parity — dressed in whatever fancy term was then in vogue — offset Soviet military advantages in other areas or create incentives needed to convince the Kremlin of the wisdom of our negotiating positions? Or worse, was parity the forerunner to still more unsettling changes in the strategic balance, changes that could also be clouded by rhetorical flourishes? Conservative strategists began to mobilize in 1976, when President Ford and Secretary of State Kissinger explored the possibility of an early SALT II agreement based on the Vladivostok accord. This idea was shelved after ACDA Director Fred Iklé and Secretary of Defense Donald Rumsfeld initiated blocking action. Instead, President Ford deleted the word "détente" from his vocabulary and prepared to defend against a challenge from the right, led by Governor Ronald Reagan.

The warning signals of most concern to the arms control community emanated from a procession of new military technologies their opponents wished to queue up for flight testing and deployment in the late 1960s. The pressures to proceed with anti-ballistic missile defenses and multiple independently-targetable re-entry vehicles reached critical decision points during the first Nixon term. ABMs were stopped in their tracks in the SALT I accords, but when MIRVs were left unconstrained, the SALT process largely became an exercise in trying to limit the resulting damage.

Congressional opposition to the SALT I accords was mollified somewhat by a purge of government officials associated with the negotiations. In retrospect, the Nixon White House's action was not simply a major departure from previous practice, but also a harbinger of things to come. For nearly three decades, presidents attempted to shield operationally-minded strategists holding such positions from political pressures. When President Nixon decided to sacrifice them, the immediate consequences of this action were clear: henceforth, public servants working on the nuclear question would necessarily be less protected from political pressures, however unreasonable. A natural consequence — although one that wasn't immediately apparent — was that these positions would be open to individuals with a wider range of views, depending on the vicissitudes of the public mood. One precedent was set in the Carter Administration, when key Cabinet and subcabinet positions were assumed by dedicated arms controllers, while their political opposition girded for battle. Then, in the Reagan Administration, a group of ideologically-inclined strategists were similarly favored with key government positions—another precedent.

After the SALT I debate, the political center on the nuclear question became increasingly hard to find. Succeeding debates became not merely bruising, but debilitating. The result of these debates has been a condition of domestic political stalemate to go with the stalemated arms competition between the United States and the Soviet Union. The nuclear arms race continues, despite the widespread recognition that neither side can "win" the race or usefully exploit whatever marginal or temporary advantages to be derived from it. At home, a different kind of stalemate has resulted: the two estranged camps have established a pattern of conflict that resolves issues of great national importance in ways that leave both deeply unsatisfied, and the nation weaker as a result.

There is some comfort in the power of neutralization when it means blocking initiatives that are based on ardent beliefs rather than sound analysis. The problems associated with our current stalemate run far deeper, however. Coalition-building over nuclear weapon and arms control questions has become highly tenuous, at best. The political standing of recent administrations has been repeatedly undercut at home and questioned abroad by one jarring domestic debate after the other. A two-camp environment leaves both camps with Pyrrhic victories and sound defeats. Each camp can effectively block or, at the very least, exact heavy political penalties against the fondest objectives of the domestic opposition.

President Jimmy Carter, who began his administration with ambitious goals for disarmament, left a far different legacy to his successor. His top lieutenants who were firmly committed to arms control began to depart as, one by one, the President's negotiating initiatives came to naught.

The Reagan Administration felt the sting of strategic stalemate no less than the Carter Administration before it. Support for major increases in defense spending plummeted while a grass roots movement to halt the nuclear arms race took hold. Both were linked to extraordinary official pronouncements on nuclear strategy (such as allusions to "prevailing" in a protracted nuclear war) that proved incapable of a coherent public defense, although they were central to the Reagan team's conception of security.

In an odd way, the Reagan Administration's fortunes became a mirror image of the Carter Administration's. President Carter attempted to carry out campaign pledges to cut back defense spending and make dramatic progress in arms control. The first objective was quickly reversed while the second was whittled down and ultimately sidetracked by a determined opposition at home and disturbing Soviet activity abroad. President Reagan and his national security advisers also suffered reverses: their attempts to increase the nation's sense of security by building up our nuclear arsenal while treating arms control as a strategic afterthought failed to provide much public comfort. In the dialectics of national security policy, two succeeding administrations managed at one and the same time to undermine their own agenda and boost that of the domestic opposition. In the first instance, President Carter and his advisers helped to create a consensus for higher defense spending, a far different objective than that for which they were entrusted with public office. President Reagan and his national security team generated skepticism over defense spending and broad public insistence for arms control, contrary to their campaign slogans.

There were few individuals able to moderate these destructive tendencies. In earlier periods, men like John J. McCloy could act as a bridge between the camps. McCloy, a former Assistant Secretary of War and High Commissioner of Germany, could hardly be deemed soft on national security issues. Yet he was the driving force behind the creation of the U.S. Arms Control and Disarmament Agency. One of McCloy's tasks as President Kennedy's disarmament adviser was to investigate ways in which the U.S. government might become better prepared to deal with the subject of arms control. Insistent Senators like Hubert Humphrey and Joseph Clark were calling for the creation of an independent agency to pursue arms control, but after sounding out legislative leaders, Kennedy reluctantly came to the conclusion that a bill to create such an agency had to have a lower priority; the opposition was too strongly felt to push this initiative and to expend political capital on it early in his administration. What Kennedy hadn't counted on was the persuasiveness of John McCloy, who believed in the purposes of the legislation, and who found more than a few distinguished retired military officers who could be similarly convinced.

The new agency was created by overwhelming Congressional

majorities eight months after Kennedy was inaugurated. McCloy's interest in ACDA continued as the first Chairman of its General Advisory Committee, a position he held for thirteen years. Under McCloy's leadership, the GAC took its advisory role seriously, recommending at the end of his tenure a complete ban on ABMs and a suspension of MIRV flight tests, much to the discomfiture of the Nixon White House and the Pentagon. Here, it seems, was one veteran of the Cold War who had no qualms about relying on arms control to help provide for the common defense.

McCloy's example of bridging the two camps wasn't unique. Until the divisive debate over the SALT I accords, collegiality and bipartisanship were the general rule. The Limited Test Ban Treaty was negotiated in good measure through the efforts of Arthur A. Dean, a Republican and former law partner of John Foster Dulles, and Averell Harriman, the renaissance man of Democratic politics. Later, President Nixon drew on the talents of a Republican, Gerard Smith, and Paul Nitze, a veteran of previous Democratic Administrations, to negotiate SALT I.

After two gruelling SALT debates, these men no longer provided much bipartisan ballast to the ship of state. Some became associated with or victims of centrifugal political forces. Gerard Smith's services to the Republic were deemed suspect in some quarters after having led the U.S. SALT I delegation. Nitze and Arthur Dean became founding members and board directors of the Committee on the Present Danger, where Nitze's activities as Chairman of its Policy Studies were instrumental in critically wounding the SALT II Treaty. Averell Harriman, in contrast, continued to combine appeals for détente with efforts aimed at the electoral successes of Democratic candidates.

The internationalist wing of the Republican Party was too emaciated to counter these centrifugal tendencies. In New York State alone, the party that produced Teddy Roosevelt, Elihu Root, Charles Evans Hughes, Henry L. Stimson and Nelson Rockefeller was utterly transformed. The remaining tall tree of the species, Senator Jacob Javits, lost his party's endorsement for re-election in 1980 to a Town Supervisor from Long Island.

The vacuum of bipartisanship left by this generation of elder statesmen was not filled during the SALT II debate, despite Javits' best efforts. Most witnesses talked of the need to upgrade U.S. forces significantly as well as the necessity for arms control, but few felt compelled to seal such a bargain or to rally around the executive branch in support of what the Joint Chiefs' characterized as a "modest but useful" treaty.

When they were most needed, there were no key figures within the legislative branch able and willing to engineer a compromise that included prompt ratification of the SALT II agreement. Howard Baker, the Senate's Minority Leader at the time, had aspirations for the presidency and wounds from his previous support for the Panama Canal Treaties. Faced with a growing irreconcilable wing within his own party and a difficult president to deal with, this Republican leader, like his predecessor during the League of Nations debate, felt compelled to bridge the gap within his own party rather than with the treaty's proponents. The failure of the Senate to ratify SALT II was not simply a matter of the breakdown of bipartisanship, however. A clearly defined segment of the Democratic Party was also unalterably opposed to the treaty's terms.

The SALT II ratification debate symbolized the politics of strategic stalemate. Lacking enthusiastic supporters or powerful brokers, the prospects for SALT II ratification collapsed completely in 1979 after the Soviet invasion of Afghanistan. Subsequently, critics of SALT II swallowed the bargain they had previously rejected: The hue and cry over ratification essentially boiled down to a somewhat larger boost in defense spending and informal, rather than treaty-clad, adherence to the terms of the agreement.

The SALT II debate graphically demonstrated the functional veto power over arms control agreements held by those most skeptical of their worth. It has always been more difficult to build a working majority behind meaningful arms control than for continued arms build-ups, if only because arms control agreements require a vote of at least three-fifths of the Senate to invoke cloture or two-thirds to consent to ratification. Defense build-ups, on the other hand, require simple majorities. Arms control supporters have been reluctant to employ their opponents' parliamentary tactics, such as filibustering to oppose specific weapon programs.

In addition, the political burdens associated with negotiated agreements can be quite heavy. Arms controllers must convince large majorities of the rightness — not just the righteousness — of their view. This is more easily done in the abstract than on behalf of specific agreements. Advocacy of arms control is cost-free; on the other hand, responsibility for negotiated agreements can be costly if the agreements in question fail to live up to popular expectations.

The chances of satisfying expectations are remote since compre-

hensive agreements are difficult to achieve and since the resulting
"interim" agreements are usually oversold in order to obtain needed public and congressional support. The greater the compromises
reached to secure agreement, the larger the failures of omission.
To make matters worse, the Soviets have a habit of exploiting ambiguities in negotiated agreements, leaving arms control supporters
with the unenviable choices of defending Soviet behavior in legalis-
tic terms or joining the cacophony questioning Soviet compliance.

Nuclear weapon strategists are in an easier position because, politically, the burden of proof isn't on them; it's on the Kremlin. It's
much easier to make the case of malevolent behavior on the part
of an adversary than it is to call for some necessary accommodation
with him, particularly when that adversary periodically behaves
egregiously. In the shorthand of political debate, if the choice is between trusting one's adversary or being wary of him, it's not too
difficult to understand who captures the high ground. As long as
the implications of a continuing arms race appear diffuse and remote, there are few political costs involved in pressing for increased
defense spending or new weapon programs. If boosting defense
spending fails to achieve results by inducing the Soviets to be com-
pliant, the remedy is then precisely what one has advocated all
along—increased defense spending for still more strategic programs.

This is not to say that a strong chief executive is without the
powers to push for arms control agreements negotiated under his
auspices. The SALT I accords, and before that, the Limited Test
Ban Treaty and the Non-Proliferation Treaty received overwhelming support in the Congress. Yet each of these agreements (with
the exception of the ABM Treaty) was far from comprehensive in
scope. Their limited nature attests to perceptions of political vulnerability in attempting to do more, quite apart from whatever military risks may have been involved. At the very least, the combination of potential political and military risks has provided skeptics
with a virtual veto power over comprehensive and dramatic strategic
arms control agreements. At most, they have provided a functional
veto power over agreements that simply moderate and regulate the
competition, as was the case with SALT II and a Comprehensive
Test Ban Treaty banning all nuclear weapons tests. The latter has
yet to be concluded despite a quarter of a century of sporadic effort.

Only in the last decade of the strategic debate have arms controllers gained a similar means of wounding their adversaries. The arms
control community still does not have the strength to block new "big

ticket" items consistently, but it does have the power to make their purchase politically costly. In doing so, the symbolic or negotiating leverage nuclear strategists might hope to gain from deployment is significantly dissipated in the resulting controversy.

The debates over anti-ballistic missile defenses in the Johnson and Nixon Administrations provided the first case study of how this power could be wielded. Opposition to the nationwide ABM program proposed by President Johnson took hold as the Department of Defense approached the stage of site preparation when it became clear to many elected officials that their constituents around the proposed sites didn't wish to be defended that way. The Nixon Administration narrowed the program's objectives, but still found itself in the awkward position of seeing its negotiating leverage being used up at home rather than in SALT parlays in Vienna and Helsinki.

Two additional examples of the functional veto power of arms controllers could be found by following the fortunes of enhanced radiation and binary chemical weapons. Both were attempts to improve upon existing munitions that were clearly deficient from the perspective of weapon strategists. Stockpiled nuclear artillery shells were, for example, too indiscriminate in their effects and poorly matched against more modern means of delivery. Enhanced radiation weapons (or "neutron bombs") were designed to produce less damage to structures while having an increased lethal range against personnel. Stockpiled nerve gas munitions were difficult to maintain and transport. In binary munitions, nerve gas would be produced only in the flight of the projectile when a membrane separating its components is broken, thereby providing for safer handling and storage.

After a series of fits and starts (the Congress having repeatedly expressed reservations about production), the Reagan Administration decided to push ahead on both fronts, but wisely refrained from asking our allies about storage facilities for them. For the near term at least, the political penalties of storing these weapons on European soil appeared to most NATO leaders to outweigh the military advantages in doing so. As a result, the military utility or negotiating leverage these weapons could provide have been heavily mortgaged by factors over which their proponents had little or no control.

The arms control community has far more leverage on programs to flight test and deploy ABM systems, because of ABM treaty constraints. For this reason, arms controllers will be in a position to exact heavy political penalties on any president who wishes to alter or abrogate an existing treaty in order to pursue "Star Wars" programs.

Prospective debates over futuristic defenses against nuclear weapons will graphically demonstrate the political dynamics of strategic stalemate. Partisans of space-based defenses and the ABM Treaty both have powerful political arguments on their side, but neither side can "win" these debates, politically or programmatically. Politically, one side's imperative to defend the American public has great appeal (particularly when the Soviets are also pursuing these options), as does the other's imperative to protect arms control agreements already in force. Programmatically, nuclear weapon strategists can progressively undermine the ABM Treaty by defining treaty constraints in increasingly permissive ways, but arms controllers can continue to make abrogation or selective nonobservance of treaty constraints politically unattractive. Repeated and bitter debates over this issue will undercut presidents and U.S. negotiators, while sowing confusion abroad—especially in Europe—over American strategy and steadiness.

The ups and downs of U.S. strategic modernization programs are another indicator of the politics of strategic stalemate. Individual nuclear weapon programs have become the subject of semiannual knock-down, drag-out debates during military authorization and appropriation bills. The B-1 bomber has been a source of contention in two presidential campaigns; it has been developed, then canceled, then produced. A new Stealth bomber will likely face similar turbulence, given budgetary pressures and competing programs. The MX missile program has generated more controversy than any other strategic program initiative in the SALT decade. A new, single-warhead missile, the Midgetman, seems certain to become vulnerable in the political arena as cost estimates and program definitions mature. Matters of strategy are also open to continuous debate, as the arms control community continues to take strong exception to the evolution of U.S. strategic doctrine. Any weapon programs that suggest nuclear war-fighting doctrines of deterrence or the slightest revision of the ABM Treaty will face determined opposition.

Of course, the turbulence surrounding nuclear weapon programs can also be directed against arms control proposals or agreements; strategic stalemate works both ways. Removed from positions of official responsibility, nuclear weapon strategists can expect to wage a spirited war of attrition against any president who endorses an ambitious arms control agenda or who fails to pursue actively strategic modernization programs. In the dialectics of national security politics, the more ambitious the agenda, the more intense the potential opposition. The campaign against the SALT II Treaty provided a model of how questions of equity, stability and verifiability could be raised over time to undermine a president's position. These have been powerful arguments when orchestrated skillfully, the kind that have stymied arms control initiatives in the past, and that could well stalemate significant progress in the future. The record of arms control agreements speaks for itself: the last time the United States Senate consented to ratification of a strategic arms limitation agreement was in 1972.

Absent specific agreements to defend or attack, the focus of controversy has shifted to the arms control proposals formulated by the executive branch. Congressional arbiters have increasingly challenged executive authority, as deal-making with the legislative branch has become as much a preoccupation for American presidents as negotiations with the Soviets. With good reason, chief executives have wondered aloud how they can get their best deal with the Kremlin after bargaining first with the Congress.

After bargaining with what remained of the political center in both the House and the Senate, President Reagan agreed to revise his START position. The Reagan Administration was in an extremely poor position to defend executive authority, however. The Administration's personnel, public statements, and initial negotiating positions did not inspire confidence on Capitol Hill. On the contrary, key moderates in both the House and the Senate became convinced that only an interventionist posture could move the Reagan Administration toward agreements with the Kremlin.

The political dynamics facing an arms control-oriented president are far different. The more future presidents are inclined to take risks for arms control benefits, the more vulnerable they will be in the political arena if they are perceived as unsteady in handling U.S.-Soviet relations. These difficulties with the legislative branch or with the domestic opposition can be surmounted if a president has a great deal to show for his negotiating efforts. But the constraints associated with a two-camp domestic environment make significant accomplishments difficult to achieve. Each camp continues to talk bravely about sweeping aside these difficulties with "political will." Political will, however, is not enough, nor is it a substitute for a broad political base. The latter is no less important than the former, particularly when the electorate is so ambivalent and the experts so divided over what course to pursue.

Intense and bitter debates over nuclear weaponry and arms control seem assured, then, for the foreseeable future. During the Reagan Administration, there has been a steady erosion of the political center. Nuclear weapon strategists continue to seek more credibility and effectiveness for nuclear forces as the best way to enhance deterrence, while arms control strategists become increasingly convinced that nuclear weapons can serve no useful military purpose. Earlier debates provide models for those that lie ahead. Without mechanisms to bridge deep disagreements over what will best promote deterrence and stability, each camp will remain locked into antagonistic agendas. The agenda for much of the arms control and disarmament community will be "freezing" the arms race and blocking the means to implement nuclear war-fighting or space warfare strategies. The agenda for many nuclear weapon strategists will be acquiring counterforce weapons and the eventual deployment of anti-ballistic missile defenses.

These agendas will galvanize the faithful, trouble the uncommitted, and mobilize the opposition. The intense debates they will generate do serve certain purposes: they satisfy the confrontational instincts of some of the participants and much of the media, and they advance someone's policy preferences and political interests in the short term. Over the long run, however, it is hard to see what useful purpose is served by established patterns of debate. The record of the past decade clearly shows the penalties in persisting to believe that the right answers can be found if only the domestic opposition can be routed. The opposition can't be routed; domestic divisions reflect enduring values on both sides, values which must be assimilated in an integrated policy if it is to enjoy enduring support.

The executive branch's freedom of action, already weakened through the deep wounds of Vietnam and Watergate, is weakened further by failing to bridge the differences between the two camps. Instead, successful national political campaigns are increasingly based on accentuating them. The tone is set by assertive members of the legislative branch who assume strong postures on both sides of the issue at hand, under the intense, if fleeting scrutiny of the media. Debates turn and the spotlight focuses on subsidiary issues rather than on a broader set of concerns. Political penalties arise as goals are set that are extremely difficult to achieve in a two-camp political environment, where partial implementation becomes more a yardstick of failure than success. Positions are mortgaged to powerful political interest groups, which subsequently narrows room to maneuver on current and future issues.

None of this is particularly shocking. It happens all the time, and is part and parcel of the balancing act that democratic societies continually perform. But balancing acts need some sort of fulcrum, and in the politics of nuclear weapons and arms control, that fulcrum is decidedly off-center and variable. The current impasse means that each camp has the power to rein in effectively the other's most threatening initiatives, but neither has the power fully to consummate its own. Tactical victories are still possible, but strategic objectives cannot be realized. The two-camp environment leaves us ultimately with problems that continually worsen and marginal solutions that are increasingly unsatisfactory. What seems to have evolved from our procession of national debates—from MIRVs and ABMs to war-fighting strategies and SALT—is a jury-rigged combination of strategic weapon programs and arms control agreements that coexist uneasily at best. Certainly, neither camp claims great satisfaction with the current state of affairs. Nuclear weapon strategists are deeply concerned about the status of U.S. strategic forces, while the arms control community bemoans the lack of progress in reversing the arms race.

In the past, we have taken pride in our often bitter national debates over these and other issues as symbols of our democratic strength and vitality. We have warned others not to misrepresent our resolve, nor to equate debate with weakness or lack of firm national purpose. We can no longer take refuge in comforting homilies. Our procession of debilitating national security debates has left a far different impression. The messages the United States has increasingly broadcast are ones of drift and unpredictability, despite the steady growth of our strategic nuclear power. No matter who's in charge, solutions to our current impasse will remain illusive as long as we remain a house divided.

9 Consensus Bargaining

A wise chronicler of nuclear strategy has observed that "much of what is offered today as a profound and new insight was said yesterday; and usually in a more concise and literate manner."[1] The same could be said for imaginative solutions to the domestic condition of strategic stalemate. After all, each camp has long had its own list of preferences for arms control and nuclear weapon developments over which battles have been waged for almost four decades. Those of a more reflective or less partisan nature have offered conciliatory ideas in the past, but lasting coalitions haven't been able to form. The essence of the problem is not so much discovering the grounds for consensus as it is working out the bargains needed to make sound positions sustainable.

The prospects for reconstituting a deeply rooted, bipartisan national security policy are slim, as the possibility of regaining the degree of leadership and followership necessary to cement coalitions is too remote. The executive branch doesn't have the authority to command a consensus view; nor does the legislative branch, with all its different voices, have the inclination to join forces over the long haul. Everyone still offers lip service to bipartisanship; but it's bipartisanship on one's own terms.

Moreover, on a popular level, definitions of the problem have become too disparate to expect a lasting consensus to be reformed. The more hawkish the partisan's persuasion, the more the Soviets become the essence of the problem. To the operationally-minded, the Kremlin is looking for any edge it can prudently achieve. For those more ideologically-inclined, the Soviets are prepared to take greater risks because they are seeking more far-reaching victories.

Within the arms control and disarmament community, the more one moves toward the left fringe of the political spectrum, the more the United States becomes the essence of the problem. Those in the United States who are most inclined to take a nonthreatening view of Soviet behavior see U.S. initiatives as fueling the arms race; the Kremlin is primarily reacting to continued American attempts to extract political, if not military, leverage from new nuclear weapon programs.

Among the far left, to raise questions on subjects like Soviet noncompliance with arms control agreements is to ensure a heated discussion. The evidence of improper Soviet behavior is dismissed as being insubstantial or no different than U.S. activities. To accept evidence that the Soviets are undermining existing agreements contradicts a bedrock assumption that U.S. actions constitute the problems that must be solved if arms control is to succeed.

Popular divisions over the nature of the national security dilemma haven't been bridged by a recognized foreign policy elite that in previous eras served as a stabilizing, if suspect, force. The foreign policy "establishment" remains suspect by both wings of the political spectrum, and is itself divided as a result of the punishing national security debates during the past two decades.

For these reasons and others, a long-term consensus approach to arms control and nuclear weapon questions would be difficult to achieve. Nevertheless, a series of shorter-term political coalitions can be built around principles to which working majorities have already sworn allegiance, and which can be readily operationalized. Three such principles are parity, reductions, and survivability. Decisions relating to new nuclear weapon programs or arms control agreements can merit broad support of operationally-minded strategists if they lead directly to overall parity, survivability, and reductions in forces. They will be opposed by strong coalitions if they do not.

While political consensus requires world views that are fundamentally compatible, bargains do not necessarily require a similarity of views among constituencies. All that is needed is an appreciation of the desirability of compromise and a willingness to settle for partial achievements. The result will be a process of consensus bargaining, which is probably all that can be expected in the fractious arena in which national security decisions are debated.

The prescriptions offered by the ideological wings of both domestic camps do not provide a basis for consensus bargaining. Both wings assume that conflict is pervasive in the international political system and, for this reason, that nuclear weapons must either be superior to our opponent's, or eliminated entirely. These positions have internal consistency if one accepts either of two wholly irrational basic premises — that wars involving nuclear weapons will be won and lost by the same calculus of factors that mattered previously, or that nuclear weapons can be abolished and that suitable restraints can be devised to prevent mankind from reassembling them and resuming the competition.

Taking issue with these basic assumptions means parting company with the ranks of the true believers or, for that matter, the pursuit of logical consistency. For, once the human mind conceived of nuclear weapons and human hands crafted them, the logic of a stable international political system turned several degrees off-axis. Henceforth, security must somehow be reconciled with the twin realities that nuclear weapons will always be in our midst, and that protection of the planet requires that they never be used repeatedly.

Finding the middle ground between ideological truths can be a slippery and, at times, contradictory business. Those whose goal is disarmament can be brought in under this tent, but only if the results of negotiated agreements demonstrably help achieve broader objectives. The disarmament wing of the arms control community will continue to play an indispensable role in the national debate. It reorients that debate away from subsidiary issues back to first principles, providing a counterbalance to the skewed proposals of ideologically-inclined adversaries, and keeping their arms control-oriented brethren honest. Arms controllers, after all, have tended to become mired in the operational formulas and abstract concepts of their craft. The disarmament wing reminds them that tactical maneuvers to maintain a stable strategic balance are necessary and important, but not sufficient: reductions in weapon inventories are also necessary.

Ideologically-inclined hawks are unlikely to participate in a bargaining process on any terms but their own. Their exclusionary mind-set toward arms control is best summed up by Phyllis Schlafly's reaction to the Partial Test Ban Treaty: "What does disarmament mean if it doesn't mean dismantling our military strength?"[2]

There is no way this mind-set can be enlisted in support of the kind of consensus bargaining advocated here. The burden of striking bargains between the two domestic camps will fall on the operationally-minded factions of both.

The operationalist wing from each camp must be included if only because neither can solve current problems unilaterally. As long as each camp tries to exclude the other, it will face a functional veto power whenever the domestic opposition feels policy objectives to be fundamentally at odds with its basic assumptions. The success of initiatives from either camp will continue to depend on where the power lies between them at any one point of time. But since the locus of power is as variable as the vicissitudes of national security politics, the weaker side's agenda is never completely erased — it has merely been tabled for another day.

Consensus bargaining is the best alternative at present to reconstituting a domestic consensus on national security issues. Shorter-term bargains can lead to working coalitions between the executive and legislative branches on narrow arms control and nuclear weapon questions, providing American presidents with the leeway needed in negotiations with the Soviets. Bargains based on the principles of parity, survivability and reductions will also demonstrably improve U.S. security, unlike the outcomes of recent debates.

There is reason to hope that less ideologically-inclined partisans of each camp can agree to political compromises on common objectives. The incentives for success, after all, are directly tied to a mutual recognition of the penalties of failure. For in a condition of stalemate, neither camp "wins": Far-reaching arms control initiatives die on the vine, as do ambitious nuclear weapon modernization plans. The strategic arms race continues at increasing levels of sophistication without the positive effects intended by nuclear weapon strategists but with the negative effects feared by arms controllers. As the political pendulum continues to swing between the two camps, the Soviets become more and more confused by the vagaries of U.S. politics, while our allies become increasingly estranged by the variability of U.S. objectives. Surely, as the penalties of the two-camp approach become increasingly apparent, more people will search for common ground. One test of our political sophistication and maturity will be to move sooner rather than later to mend the necessary fences.

In pursuit of common objectives in consensus bargaining, the two operational wings must narrow differences over the nature of

he superpower competition. Otherwise, there will be no respite
rom contentious, no-win debates over Soviet intentions. For nu-
lear weapon strategists, the heavy Soviet reliance on accurate, land-
ased missiles is compelling evidence of the Kremlin's search for
dvantage. In this view, Soviet ICBMs mock Western concepts of
trategic stability and indicate a seriousness about waging nuclear
var that most devotees of arms control would rather overlook.

Arms control and reductions would be far simpler if the Kremlin
greed to common definitions of strategic stability and rearranged
ts force structure to mirror our own. Near commonality on these
ssues is unlikely, however, given differences in history, military
ulture, geography, and domestic bureaucratic politics. For these
easons and others, the Soviets will always rely to a far greater de-
ree on land-based missiles than the United States does. As long
s one rejects the ideological premise that arms control is a zero-
um game, negotiations need not await nor produce common doc-
rines and symmetrical forces. To conduct arms control business
vith the Kremlin, it is sufficient that the two political leaderships
rrive at a compatible calculus of benefit and risk, each from their
wn perspective: that the benefits of agreements to avoid nuclear
var and to contain the nuclear arms competition outweigh their
isks.

Soviet behavior has clearly been problematical in many areas,
ut the lack of progress in arms control and reductions cannot be
aid solely at the Kremlin's door. After all, there are concrete rea-
ons why it is in the Politburo's interest, no less than the White
House's, to arrive at negotiated agreements. The strategic arms
ompetition doesn't help the Kremlin decrease the likelihood of nu-
lear war, help the sorry state of the Russian economy, solve a wide
variety of security concerns of a more prosaic nature, or gain po-
itical benefits associated with the arms control process.

A benign interpretation of Soviet intentions is just as unsatisfactory as a devil theory of the Kremlin's activities. After all, Soviet
nuclear weapon programs can hardly be characterized as benevolent. For most of the SALT decade, actions by the Kremlin and
not the White House defined the nature and extent of the strategic
competition. The United States continued to MIRV one-half of its
land-based missiles during this period, and initiated improvements
in their accuracy, as well. But these actions paled before Soviet deployment of over 5,000 accurate warheads atop their new missiles.
Together with the command and control and training exercises asso-

ciated with them, Soviet ICBMs set the standards for counterforc
missiles which Presidents Carter and Reagan decided to follow

The development and deployment of SS-20 intermediate-rang
ballistic missiles set a similar standard for theater weapons, alter
ing a balance that had been relatively static for two decades an
making it appear essential politically to counter such deployment
in kind. (To measure just how unsettling SS-20 deployments were
one might ask under what other circumstances the U.S. Air Forc
could be expected to operate ground-launched cruise missiles, o
the German Federal Republic and four other NATO countrie
might initially agree to host them.)

Soviet testing of anti-satellite (ASAT) weapons during the SAL
decade revived a dormant phase of the competition and added an
other, extraordinarily destabilizing dimension to the strategic arm
race. One might argue in the case of Soviet missile programs men
tioned above that the Kremlin was anticipating or responding t
similar U.S. weapon programs. But there was no way for Sovie
planners to anticipate a U.S. anti-satellite program in the earl
1970s because the Pentagon had phased out its earlier efforts

As the arms control community asserts, there are a variety c
plausible and nonsinister explanations for Soviet defense efforts sinc
the Cuban missile crisis. These explanations certainly attest to th
bureaucratic power of the Soviet military, and within that comple:
of competing interests, the strength of the Strategic Rocket Forces
They probably connote a belief that the best way to deter the Unite
States is with convincing nuclear war-fighting capabilities. Th
steady expansion of Soviet nuclear capabilities may also reflect ex
aggerated security concerns that are deeply rooted from past mili
tary campaigns fought on Russian soil.

All of these explanations provide some insight into the Soviet mil
itary build-up, but they do not fully explain its size and the con
current growth in strategic, theater, and conventional forces. Surely
the totality of the Soviet military effort says a great deal about th
state of inferiority the Soviets were coming from, but its constan
cy necessarily raises questions about where the Kremlin is headed

This does not mean to suggest that the Politburo harbors illu
sions about the military utility of nuclear weapons. The evidenc
at hand strongly suggests that Communist Party elders are nothing
if not pragmatic about risk-taking, whether involving nuclear o
conventional forces. Even if one rejects this assumption of prag
matism, believing that the Kremlin's global maneuvering is ideolog
ically motivated, no sane Politburo member is about to risk pur

oosely the fruits of the Russian Revolution in the rubble of World
War III.

What the Soviet defense effort does suggest is a strong belief in
the political utility of military capabilities, broadly defined. The
growth of Soviet forces across-the-board can be interpreted as the
best means to prevent World War III and to promote Soviet political objectives at the same time. If a position of advantage can be
gained as a result of the Soviet military build-up (whether via negotiations or in the absence of them), the Kremlin isn't going to
pass it by. Soviet leaders appear to subscribe, no less than their
American counterparts, to the notion that relative military capabilities can affect the way the superpowers relate to one another,
and the way that third countries relate to them. In this context, nuclear weapons, no less and perhaps more than other military forces,
are perceived to be convertible currency in the international political system.

Ideologues presume either Moscow or Washington is responsible for the nuclear arms competition. Operationalists presume a
measure of complicity in both capitals, although the camps differ
in their apportionment of blame. Each nation has driven the arms
race at certain stages and felt impelled to react at others. It was easy
enough to castigate Washington for the H-bomb and MIRV decisions, and to censure Moscow for the first ICBM launch and its
preoccupation with MIRVed land-based missiles. In the 1980s, the
apportionment of blame was more difficult: the Reagan Administration talked brashly, but the Soviet Union's strategic weapon programs continued their cyclical progression. During those periods
when the United States was in the driver's seat, the arms control
community charged their domestic adversaries with attempting to
gain illusory political and military advantages from new nuclear
weapon programs. Why haven't those same factors applied at times
when the Kremlin forced the pace?

This perspective of the superpower competition offers the opportunity for coalition-building among operationally-minded strategists. Even though operationalists differ in their apportionment of
blame, they are able to see the strategic arms race in a geopolitical
context: each great power is motivated by a constant search for advantage and by a concurrent fear of potential disadvantage. The
actions of both nations must be modified if the security of both —
as well as of mankind — is to be improved.

Nuclear weapons are therefore not the essence of the problem,
as advocates of disarmament assert. If this were the case, solving

the problem would be as simple as reducing nuclear weapon stock-piles. Reductions remain difficult to achieve, however, because nuclear weapons are a manifestation of a more intractable problem: political dynamics that lead both sides to compete for at least marginal gains out of fear of consequential losses.

Nuclear weapons obviously constitute a serious threat to mankind and to the planet we live on. New refinements in weapon capabilities have increased vulnerabilities and tensions, providing still more impetus to the strategic competition. But nuclear weapons don't detonate by themselves. Technology is an important driver in the arms race, but there is human intelligence behind the wheel. Any explanation of the strategic competition that relegates U.S. and Soviet leaders to the role of accomplices is as unsatisfying as attempts to single out either party for blame, and just as unlikely to lead to coalition-building. Decisions to develop and deploy new weapon programs are made as a matter of conscious choice from a variety of motives. The arms race is at its core, a political engagement, and political events aren't driven by inanimate objects.

The action-reaction theory of the arms race is similarly unsatisfying, although several initiatives by one nation could be traced in part to earlier events by the other. For example, once the United States built an A-bomb, there was no doubt that Soviet leaders would have to follow suit. And after the Kremlin launched Sputnik, the U.S. Army, Navy, and Air Force fell over one another to match this feat.

Notwithstanding these and other examples, defining the problem as the action-reaction phenomenon fails for a variety of reasons. Most events in the arms race, like the H-bomb, were pursued concurrently. Some developments impelled a quite different set of reactions. For example, the emergence of the Strategic Air Command's fleet of intercontinental bombers generated an expensive Soviet air defense network, not a matching force of aircraft. The competition has been driven by internal forces as well as external ones: both political leaderships have powerful political constituencies and bureaucratic interests that must be served.

In domestic as well as international politics, the pursuit of gain and the fear of loss that propelled the strategic arms competition were inextricably linked. U.S. and Soviet leaders have been both culprits and victims of this complex political dynamic. The most powerful testament to these twin generators is the continued growth in strategic forces on both sides. When the atomic and hydrogen bombs were conceived, who could have predicted that weapon in-

entories would reach the tens of thousands? Or that at such levels,
he competition would still be going full bore?

The arms race continues as both a natural and unnatural out-
rowth of domestic and international politics because neither of the
reat powers has been willing—or able politically—to drop out of
he contest on the grounds that it has lost meaning. The illogical
et inescapable conclusion for both countries is that the order of
attle still matters, no less today than in previous eras when the
alance was measured in terms of battleships or horse cavalry. To
ail to compete (i.e., not to maintain a strategic balance) can there-
ore be disabling in a domestic political context and injurious in
he international arena, even though the weapons themselves have
nly the most questionable utility on the battlefield. At the hazy
ntersection of political and military affairs, the search for national
dvantage and risk avoidance continues, with nuclear weapons no
ess than with other instruments of war. Both nations are locked
nto the competition since failure to compete confers too many po-
itical, if not military, penalties.

For operationalists in both domestic camps, this definition of the
roblem yields certain benefits, since effective solutions are possi-
le only when both sides are fully engaged. Nuclear weapon mod-
rnization programs are required to convince the Kremlin of our
villingness to deny advantage and of the desirability of compromise.
Arms control agreements are essential to set bounds on the com-
etition and to curtail its most negative effects.

By implication, this interpretation of Soviet intentions—like
thers of a nonideological bent—reaffirms the need for operation-
lists within the two camps to close ranks behind the objectives of
urvivability and parity in nuclear forces as well as reductions in
heir deployment. Survivability and parity should suffice in dissuad-
ng the Soviets that advantages could accrue from their continued
veapon refinements. Mutual and verifiable reductions in nuclear
veapon launchers should diminish the political significance attached
o these weapons.

Parity

n the strategic arms competition, only mutual acceptance of pari-
y can defuse the twin generators of potential gain and fear of loss.
Parity, as codified in arms control agreements, allows each super-
ower to allay its anxieties and confirm its standing. Parity has yet

another benefit: "We have witnessed," wrote Bernard Brodie, "for what is surely the first time in history, a huge development and growth of outlandishly powerful weapons systems which are sealed off from use but not yet from utility."[3] To seal these weapons off from political utility requires rough balances in U.S. and Soviet nuclear forces.

The issue of parity is not as abstract as it sounds because it has important meaning in both the political and negotiating contexts. If either the United States or the Soviet Union attempted to codify a position of superiority in negotiations, the negotiations would fail. Neither side can concede inferiority at the negotiating table, just as neither can accept such a result at home. In a political context, many Americans are not about to accept a position of being second best to the Soviet Union in nuclear forces, even if, in a military sense, disparities in numbers have long since lost their meaning. Attempts to reach an agreement over their heads won't work. For better or for worse, the principle of rough parity between U.S. and Soviet nuclear forces has been a prerequisite for arms control to date, and will remain so for the foreseeable future.

The quest for parity can, however, become an exercise in futility if it means matching detailed weapon system characteristics rather than aggregate force levels. Before concerns over the disparity of U.S. and Soviet missile throw-weight became a pressing issue, statesmen wrestled with earlier problems of defining parity in naval forces. Britain's Ramsey MacDonald remarked during the preliminaries to the London Naval Treaty in 1929 that, "This parity business is of Satan himself. I am sure it has struck the President as it has me as being an attempt to clothe unreality in the garb of mathematical reality."[4]

The yardstick of parity will not work if it becomes a surrogate to the objective of drastically reconfiguring opposing forces to one's liking. The objective of parity will work in a domestic and in a negotiating context if it is applied to aggregate units of account which counterbalance advantages on each side. This is what the SALT process was supposed to be about. One reason for its failure can be traced to agreed rules of competition — SALT-permitted modernization programs — that were so lax that each nation began to question the other's long-term objectives when both exercised virtually all of the military options available to them.

The primary failure was not so much one of conception, but of political choice. Had both nations been willing to forgo threaten-ng new weapon systems, questions about long-term objectives would not have arisen with such force. For the United States, unwillingness to forgo MIRVs dealt a severe blow to the SALT process and to prospects for effective arms control. For the Soviet Union, unwillingness to forgo a fourth generation of land-based missiles with silo-busting characteristics had the same grievous consequences.

In the United States, operationally-minded arms controllers and nuclear weapon strategists tentatively signed onto the concept of parity at the outset of the SALT process, but agreement broke down almost immediately over competing definitions. The tenuous consensus for SALT could not hold before the political pressures that were brought to bear upon it. In SALT II, a defense build-up which included the MX missile and several varieties of cruise missiles became the price of an agreement. Before that, the failure to ban MIRVs, or at least to limit them severely, was critical. The SALT I Interim Agreement with its disparity of launchers (in favor of the U.S.S.R.) and warheads (in favor of the U.S.) collected no debts and payed out all dues: It was attacked as promoting a condition of "subparity" by critics,[5] while ensuring limited results in the future by allowing MIRVs to run free.

The preoccupation with numbers by much of the public and the media has made numerical equality and equal rights to weapon systems a political imperative under most circumstances. At the same time, strategic debates that focus on unequal subunits of account that have questionable operational significance will no doubt continue. Whatever the intent of those raising such issues, their practical effect can be to scuttle the arms control agreement under review or to shore up requests for new nuclear weapon programs demanded in compensation.

For many, such controversies imply that the concept of parity is not one that lends itself well to operational formulas. But the SALT II agreement faltered not so much on the question of parity as on unrelated Soviet activity and the absence of many committed supporters. Would parity have been a prominent issue had the agreement been championed by a strong President who had much to show for his negotiating efforts? If a President slows down the nuclear arms competition and achieves a more stable balance of forces at lower levels, concerns over particular components of the resulting balance are unlikely to resonate in the political arena. Put another way, if the benefits of an agreement are attractive enough, the electorate and the Congress will be willing to take the risks for it, particularly when a strong President is at the helm, and when the Kremlin is seen as behaving properly elsewhere. With these conditions even partially met, parity is a far easier standard around which to build the necessary degree of political support. It merely requires equal levels in subaccounts that cannot be symmetrical because both sides have consciously chosen to accentuate different components of their forces.

Reductions

Debates over arms control agreements do not focus on the goal of strategic stability but on the requirements for it. In the catechism of arms control, strategic stability will result from a stable balance of deterrent forces. But agreement breaks down over what forces strengthen deterrence. For weapon strategists, nuclear forces that place at risk that which the Kremlin leadership holds dear will make war less likely. For the arms control community, nuclear threats make war more likely.

It is also clear from post-SALT domestic debates that strategic stability, however defined, is not a sufficient outcome of negotiations; decreasing force levels must also result. Professed allegiance to the concept of reductions now cuts across the political spectrum — a relatively recent phenomenon in domestic debates over arms control. In the past, ideologically-inclined weapon strategists argued that U.S. interests could best be served by larger and more diversified stockpiles, not by smaller ones. Agreements that constrained U.S. nuclear forces not only limited our ability to block Soviet expansionism, but also generated concerns over vulnerability to a surprise attack.

During the missile gap controversy, Robert Strausz-Hupé and his colleagues asked, "Can a balanced security for both sides be achieved best at a high or low level of deterrent forces? It takes little imagination to see that acceptance of a low force level plays into the hands of a potential aggressor." The Foreign Policy Research Institute analysts concluded that "moves to bring about drastic reductions may plunge us into a situation in which the deterrent will break down and large-scale war will once again seem profitable to an aggressor."[6] Such thoughts were not atypical for those most wary of Soviet intentions. The Reagan Administration altered this criique of arms control. Their opposition to the SALT process was based in large part on its failure to accomplish enough. Henceforth, "real" reductions would be a central objective for both ideological wings in domestic debates.

This curious alliance underscored the difficulties in operationalizing the objective of reductions. The disarmament wing generally took the position that reductions were a positive development, regardless of the weapon launchers that were deactivated and destroyed. Other factions in domestic debates took issue with this proposition, fearing that a stable balance of forces wouldn't necessarily follow from reductions unless they were targeted in some fashion. When left with complete freedom of choice, both sides could actually reduce their forces in such a way as to generate mutual insecurity: both could hold onto their most threatening forces if those forces were valued most highly. The resulting balance would then be more unstable, since each side would have smaller, yet more threatening forces.

For arms controllers, reductions had to be tied to a concept of strategic stability that allowed some latitude in the forces to be cut as long as both nations felt more secure as a result. One way to do so was to lower the ratios of accurate missile warheads on one side to opposing missile silos on the other. For nuclear weapon strategists of all persuasions, drastic cuts had to be focused specifically on Soviet forces and military potential of most concern — MIRVed land-based missiles. Otherwise, the resulting agreement might not be worthy of their support, particularly if it was negotiated by a president in whom they lacked confidence.

No consensus bargaining is possible without general agreement over a framework for reductions. Ironically, an agreed formula was reached between U.S. and Soviet negotiators, but not between the U.S. domestic camps.

SALT II placed limits on five categories of strategic forces: land- and sea-based missile launchers and intercontinental-range bombers; MIRVed missiles and bombers carrying cruise missiles; MIRVed missiles; MIRVed land-based missiles only; and "heavy" missiles. By progressively lowering these limits, particularly those singling out MIRVed ICBMs and "heavy" ICBMs of the greatest military potential, the wishes of nuclear weapon strategists could have been respected, although not as quickly or as dramatically as they would have liked. Percentage reductions from SALT II categories would have forced appreciable cuts in Soviet ICBMs of most concern: a

20 percent reduction from SALT II baselines would have resulted in equivalent reductions in the Soviet SS-18 force and a comparable cut in missile throw-weight; 30 percent reductions from SALT II categories would have required 30 percent cuts in Soviet missile forces, and so on. By following through on these reductions, many of the earlier criticisms of the SALT II Treaty would have become inconsequential. The question for discussion would have been how deep each side was prepared to reduce from an already agreed framework.[7]

One negative consequence of our failure to ratify SALT II was that the framework for reductions embodied in that agreement was not put into effect. Critics found the achievements of SALT II wanting, but every year that passed without a better agreement was a reminder of reductions that were declined from an already negotiated baseline — reductions that could have met the standards for strategic stability set by operationalists from both camps.

Instead, U.S. and Soviet officials argued over an alternative framework for reductions in the START negotiations. Since the Reagan Administration rejected the previously agreed framework, both sides were free to propose completely new formulas for reductions. U.S. and Soviet preferences were predictably far apart. The resulting impasse generated bold new concepts for reducing each side's forces; their merit had to be weighed against the extended negotiations and uncertain results associated with proposals that departed significantly from previous agreements.

One such proposal — the "guaranteed build-down" — demonstrated the possibilities and pitfalls of the post-SALT consensus-bargaining process. This concept allowed modernization programs to proceed as long as both nations were willing to deactivate a larger number of warheads on operational forces. The U.S. preference was to penalize most heavily those forces of greatest concern — new MIRVed land-based missiles. Variable ratios could be devised to exact lesser penalties on the deployment of less-threatening nuclear weapon systems.

The build-down concept had several attractive features, most notably its solid bipartisan sponsorship in the Senate, led by Armed Services Committee members William Cohen and Sam Nunn. It therefore offered the prospect of muting controversies over the framework for arms reductions if contending parties could agree to reduction formulas. Questions over equity could then be defused because it would be up to each nation how to achieve reductions to equal levels.

This still left a great deal of potential controversy over new weapon and deactivation choices since there was no provision in the build-down to guarantee wise choices. Indeed, in order to interest the Reagan Administration in the build-down proposal, its key backers linked it to their support for MX production, a missile they conceded to be at variance with the philosophy behind their actions. The build-down's prime sponsors recognized that building weapons that were both threatening and vulnerable to opposing forces would not lead to a stable balance of forces at lower levels. Nevertheless, they were willing to strike a bargain with the executive branch because they saw no better way to break the impasse over the MX while limiting its numbers.

The Reagan Administration incorporated the build-down concept into the U.S. position at the Strategic Arms Reduction Talks in 1983. Still, questions persisted as to whether this modified stance reflected changes in the Administration's basic negotiating objectives or its priorities for new weapons. The overriding objective of many within the Administration continued to be deep cuts selectively applied to Soviet land-based missiles and a build-up in comparable U.S. capabilities.

The build-down plan was promoted by President Reagan's Commission on Strategic Forces, another post-SALT experience in consensus bargaining. This panel, chaired by former National Security Adviser Brent Scowcroft, was formed to help lead the Reagan Administration and the Congress out of the dilemma over MX basing. Panel members and senior counselors were drawn mostly from the ranks of operationally-minded nuclear weapon strategists. They concluded that the MX was needed, and that one hundred of them should be placed in fixed silos. In addition, the panel strongly endorsed arms control, dismissed alarms over the "window of vulnerability," and recommended eventually moving away from MIRVed ICBMs toward single warhead missiles.

Critics of the Scowcroft Commission pointed to the inconsistency of the report's finding that "stability should be the primary objective" and its recommendation that MX missiles posing a direct threat to their opposite numbers be made inviting targets in fixed silos.[8] The Commission's rationale for doing so seemed a reprise of the annual posture statements forwarded to Congress by the four Secretaries of Defense who participated in its deliberations: MX deployments would provide leverage in negotiations, demonstrate "national will and cohesion," and redress a "serious imbalance" in prompt silo-busting capabilities. "Our ability to assure our allies

that we have the capability and will to stand with them," the re
port warned, " . . . is in question as long as this imbalance exists."
Several arms control strategists in the House of Representative
were willing to take the Scowcroft Commission's findings as a pack
age. Congressmen Les Aspin, Albert Gore, Jr., and Norman Dick:
led the consensus bargaining which traded MX missile productior
for modifications in the Administration's arms reduction proposal;
and commitments to a single-warhead missile.

The compromises reached on the MX and build-down by opera
tionally-minded strategists in the executive and legislative branche:
would have been difficult to overturn during earlier internecine de
bates. But the conditions of strategic stalemate have advanced con
siderably since then. By the time the Reagan Administration wa:
inclined to revise its strategic modernization and negotiating pro
posals, it was extraordinarily difficult to sustain the bargains struck

One reason for the fragility of the agreements reached relatec
to the unique mix of operationally- and ideologically-minded weap
on strategists in the Reagan Administration. Because of this mix
initiatives to revise the President's positions had to come from out
side the executive branch. While operationally-minded strategist:
in the Congress or elsewhere could occasionally tip the scales to
ward problem-solving approaches, they could not execute these pol
icy preferences: this responsibility remained delegated to those whc
were deeply divided over whether or how to implement the trade
offs authorized by President Reagan. When the power of the Pres
ident is not felt in either the initiation or the execution of consen
sus bargaining, it will be difficult to sustain coalitions on behalf of
the agreements reached.

The coalitions engineered on behalf of the MX and the build
down were quite narrow to begin with, since consensus bargain
ing with an Administration populated by ideologues made those
bargains suspect to most arms controllers. For them, the bona fide:
and judgment of the Reagan Administration remained in question,
thereby undermining the rationale for the bargains struck.

In the aftermath of the SALT II debate, most arms controllers
felt consensus bargaining that included funding MX production
mandated their opposition, as the MX would make adequate con
trols and subsequent reductions much more difficult to achieve. The
SALT II agreement, which arms controllers were willing to sup
port, permitted MX. Indeed, the Carter Administration wished to
deploy two hundred missiles, twice that proposed by the Scowcroft

Commission. But when nuclear weapon strategists chose not to support SALT II ratification, all deals regarding the MX were off.

In the future, the essence of domestic bargaining over a framework for reductions will necessarily have to address one domestic camp's concerns over Soviet ICBMs and the other's difficulties with the MX. The concerns of nuclear weapon strategists over the Kremlin's MIRVed ICBMs cannot be dismissed. One need not accept anxiety-ridden scenarios of Soviet escalation dominance to concede a variety of difficulties associated with the Kremlin's accent on quick-strike, accurate missile forces. The Soviet emphasis on speed and accuracy has made the maintenance of a stable strategic balance far more difficult. Reductions in forces won't necessarily help matters unless those missiles posing the greatest risk to opposing forces are at least reduced proportionally.

The concerns raised by the arms control community over the MX cannot be dismissed, either. The strategic rationale for choosing to respond in kind to Soviet MIRVed ICBMs has long been suspect. Why is the combination of speed and accuracy in nuclear forces so supremely important? Does the possession of a nuclear weapon that assuredly arrives slowly and accurately somehow convey a lack of resolve? Does a weapon that assuredly arrives quickly but is withheld from immediate use place the United States at a military disadvantage? Do these forces prove any less of a deterrent to rational leaders?

For arms control strategists, nuclear forces must be sufficient to deny advantage to the attacker. In this view, ornate theories of deterrence and war termination emphasizing the value of counterforce weapons make little sense: arms controllers are a good deal less interested in ending a nuclear war on favorable terms than on preventing such a war from starting in the first place. For them, no improvements in nuclear war-fighting capabilities could be as useful as open lines of political communication between heads of state, particularly in the event of nuclear weapons' use. Weapon systems like the MX which are both vulnerable and extremely threatening to opposing forces do nothing to advance this objective.

In moving rightward along the spectrum of deterrence strategy and strategists, the objective becomes achieving "favorable" outcomes in nuclear exchanges. From this perspective, MX missiles are essential—favorable outcomes are unlikely without accurate missiles. At present, only ICBMs can selectively place at risk the military forces and means of domestic control so dear to the Kremlin.

in so doing, U.S. counterforce capabilities can strengthen deterrence and provide U.S. leaders with essential military capabilities in the event deterrence fails. Bomber forces can deliver weapons accurately and selectively, but only after many intervening hours. Submarine-launched weapons can be delivered quickly, but not accurately. While this problem is being addressed, the command and control difficulties of delivering instructions quickly and safely to commanders at sea seem more intractable. In sum, only ICBMs — at least through the 1980s — appear to have the requisite nuclear warfighting capabilities deemed essential by weapon strategists. When faced with the choice of having vulnerable missiles with these capabilities or more survivable weapon systems without them, most weapon strategists opted for vulnerable missiles.

Both domestic camps have leverage in these debates. Arms controllers will continue to argue the common sense propositions that nuclear warfare will result in unfavorable outcomes, and that the deployment of lucrative and threatening targets should be avoided. Nuclear weapon strategists will continue to counter these arguments by asserting that current Soviet advantages in such forces are unacceptable and that the United States should not give away a source of leverage in negotiations.

To restate these arguments is to suggest the nature of future domestic bargaining between operationalists from both camps, trade-offs that are very much compatible with feasible negotiating outcomes between the two superpowers. The Kremlin expects new programs like the MX to be deployed, despite controversy between the executive and legislative branches. Traditionally, the Congress merely wounds big-ticket nuclear programs; it doesn't kill them. Because MIRVed land-based missiles pose problems for the Soviets, they have an interest in seeing deployments blocked or severely limited. The trade-off Kremlin negotiators offered during SALT II was no new MIRVed ICBMs for either side. The Carter Administration was then unwilling to accept such a trade over the inevitable protests of the Pentagon and the Congress: the MX was seen as a political, if not a military, counterweight to the Kremlin's forces of SS-18s and SS-19s. Subsequently, with yet another generation of Soviet ICBMs undergoing flight tests, the trade-off previously spurned appears increasingly attractive — but only, as nuclear weapon strategists would no doubt insist, if it is linked to progressive reductions in the Kremlin's force of existing MIRVed ICBMs. The resulting agreement would still confer advantages to the Kremlin n MIRVed land-based missiles. But there is no need to equalize those capabilities as long as the United States maintains rough balances in overall forces and assured retaliatory capabilities sufficient to deny the Kremlin gain in the event of a first strike.

Survivability

Parity and reductions in U.S. and Soviet nuclear forces are necessary but not sufficient conditions to defuse domestic debates over new arms control agreements and nuclear weapon programs. These debates will continue to be heated unless negotiated reductions are linked to an acquisition strategy that directly results in more survivable, retaliatory forces. Survivability is no less important than parity and reductions for consensus bargaining at home and successful negotiations with the Soviet Union.

In the past, operationally-minded strategists from both domestic camps supported the goal of survivability, but with important qualifications. For nuclear weapon strategists, survivability was essential. But so, too, were highly accurate, quick-strike forces. Arms controllers also stressed the need for survivability, but they, too, expressed an important qualification: survivable nuclear forces that also placed Soviet military targets at greatest risk were to be avoided if at all possible.

At the outset of the Reagan Administration, the nuclear weapons freeze campaign generated spirited support at one end of the political spectrum and opposition at the other because both wings recognized that a comprehensive freeze would dramatically curtail counterforce capabilities. Operationally-minded weapon strategists tended to support new counterforce systems, particularly as adjuncts to limited MX deployments, while arms controllers were predisposed against new counterforce systems, especially with MX deployments.

In the resulting impasse, the focus of debate has gravitated away from the objective of survivability, turning instead to nuclear warfighting capabilities and strategies. The goal of survivable nuclear forces — both U.S. and Soviet — thereby becomes an indirect objective. For proponents, the acquisition of accurate, quick-strike forces will eventually force the Kremlin to reconfigure its forces in a more stable fashion. For opponents, survivability requires the defeat of counterforce initiatives.

Survivability cannot, however, be a derivative objective — whether in pursuing counterforce weapons or new technologies for defensive systems. Instead, survivability must be linked directly to the process of reductions. Reductions, in turn, cannot be achieved in the absence of reasonably good bilateral relations between the superpowers and mutual perceptions of military security. Both of these conditions are jeopardized unless counterforce capabilities are offset by improvements in survivability. If the growth of counterforce capabilities outdistances improvements in survivability, each nation's leaders will find it increasingly difficult to insulate political problems from the military dimension of the competition. Neither side will be willing to conclude arms reduction agreements with an adversary who is succeeding in placing his strategic forces in jeopardy. Seeking to achieve "deep cuts" in nuclear forces under these circumstances is, at best, a contradiction.

Large increments in counterforce capabilities pose difficult negotiating problems. Current capabilities on both sides are both substantial and asymmetrical: most Soviet counterforce warheads are carried by ICBMs, while U.S. counterforce capabilities reside mostly on bombers. Moreover, counterforce weapons are central to prevailing calculations of risk avoidance and competitive advantage in both nations. While reductions in some counterforce capabilities can be achieved through negotiations, other increments can be expected. Some of these additions are not strongly opposed by the arms control community. The deployment of air-launched cruise missiles (ALCMs) on strategic bombers, for example, is almost never contested. ALCMs have greater accuracy than ICBMs, but they take several hours to reach their targets from U.S. bases, during which time the aircraft carrying them can be recalled. Because verifiable limits can be placed on their launch platforms, ALCMs need not pose difficult problems for achieving a stable balance of forces at lower levels.

Arms controllers are more ambivalent toward the Midgetman missile, which will carry one accurate and powerful warhead. Midgetman is clearly preferable to the MX, but concerns over vulnerability, cost, and missile accuracy are likely to increase as deployment nears in the early 1990s.

Operationally-minded arms control strategists are more concerned over the development of counterforce sea-based missiles that can be launched from close to Soviet borders, like the Trident II submarine-launched ballistic missile (SLBM). The development of counterforce SLBMs will be difficult to stop without a complete freeze on missile flight-testing, something Soviet and U.S. weapon strategists are likely to resist fiercely. Even if decisions are made in both Washington and Moscow to forgo new counterforce SLBMs like the Trident II, existing missiles can be upgraded to achieve greater accuracies. Improvements can continually be expected in guidance systems both on board the missile itself and from locations external to it, developments that cannot be foreclosed even with a freeze on flight tests.

Of still greater concern to the arms control community are sea-launched cruise missiles, which, although slow-flying, can destroy military targets with great precision. They can also be launched from an endless number of sea-going platforms. In this view, the accumulation of counterforce missiles at sea will make successful negotiations far more difficult. Both sides are likely to feel less accommodating and more threatened by these developments. Moreover, SLCM deployments pose extraordinarily difficult verification problems.

Deployed ground-launched cruise missiles, Pershing II and SS-20 missiles are not difficult to count under existing practices, but continued deployments of these intermediate-range counterforce missiles in Europe is a sure formula for alliance and East-West tension. The political case for responding to Soviet SS-20 missiles in Europe has always been strong; the military rationale for countering with land-based missiles has always been weak. While Pershing II and ground-launched cruise missiles are mobile, they are not necessarily survivable. Their movements beyond base perimeters will draw considerable attention, as they must be accompanied by support and security vehicles which have the appearance of a long circus train when in transit. As a result, mobile land-based missiles on the Continent are likely to remain a good deal more vulnerable than submarine-launched missiles, whether SLBMs or SLCMs.

Sea-based missiles were considered and rejected for the roles assumed by Pershings and ground-launched cruise missiles for doctrinal and perceptual reasons so central to the calculations of nuclear weapon strategists. Land-based missiles would most visibly demonstrate alliance resolve and shore up the biggest "gap" in a ladder of deterrence ranging from battlefield nuclear weapons to intercontinental forces. Whatever credence these arguments had in 1979, when the decision was made to deploy land-based missiles in Europe, has now faded with initial deployments.

Nuclear weapon strategists are loathe to cede significant advantages to the Soviet Union in land-based missile forces, with their nuclear war-fighting potential. Whatever is lost in this regard by moving toward increased reliance on sea-based and bomber forces is more than offset by having more survivable forces. These arguments were advanced and rejected before NATO decided to deploy ground-based nuclear forces. They have gained far more credence with the passage of time. Continued attempts by weapon strategists to emulate Soviet land-based missiles will only make the realization of arms reduction agreements and stable force balances extremely difficult to achieve.

For consensus bargaining to work on the issue of survivability, the two domestic camps must arrive at some accommodation on the issue of counterforce weapons. Nuclear weapon strategists will have to give ground on the extent to which they would like to reconfigure Soviet forces away from MIRVed land-based missiles, and the extent to which they would like to emulate these forces. For their part, arms controllers will have to give ground on the acquisition of some new counterforce capabilities. Since definitions of the utility of counterforce weapons are so far apart and constraints on them are so difficult to enforce, the primary criterion on whether to deploy new counterforce weapons must be their survivability.

SLBMs are the most reasonable choice for new U.S. counterforce weapons. Fears within the arms control community concerning the Trident II missile can be allayed. The Trident II poses the greatest threat to opposing forces only if it is deployed in the most vulnerable way—close to Soviet targets. The Trident II, however, has greater range than its less accurate predecessor, the Trident I. The purpose of this additional range is to place it farther beyond the reach of projected improvements in Soviet anti-submarine warfare (ASW) capabilities. It is therefore reasonable to assume that submarines carrying the Trident II missile will not move up close to Soviet shores to carry out a surprise attack, because doing so places the submarine in greatest jeopardy, while nullifying the element of surprise: the closer U.S. ballistic missile submarines operate to Soviet shores, the more likely they are to be detected and prosecuted.

The same applies for Soviet counterforce missiles at sea, only more so. Since U.S. anti-submarine warfare capabilities are far superior, the Soviets have a greater incentive to deploy most of their missile-carrying submarines in protected waters. Attempts to move these forces close to U.S. shores will be detected by under-water listening devices, a sure tip-off for U.S. political leaders and military commanders.

Another scenario of concern to some in the arms control com-munity has both sides flattening the ballistic trajectories of missiles launched from submarines, so as to speed their time of arrival to targets ashore. But "depressed trajectories" would require time and effort to develop while still yielding uncertain results — reasons why neither side has shown much interest in them to date. Moreover, these unnatural trajectories can be detected quite readily by moni-toring the flight tests necessary to perfect this technique. A ban on depressed trajectory tests is eminently sensible and verifiable. For these reasons, new SLBM counterforce capabilities need not pose severe hardships for a stable balance of forces at lower levels.

Survivability is the primary, but not the only, criterion for new counterforce weapon programs. It is also important to avoid, wher-ever possible, new deployments that complicate subsequent methods of control and the potential for reductions. In this respect, sea-launched cruise missiles pose more troublesome problems than sea-launched ballistic missiles. While both have counterforce potential, SLCMs can be carried on a wide variety of platforms, some of which can routinely be deployed nearby each nation's shores. Moreover, unlike SLBMs, SLCMs stored internally cannot be counted precise-ly, thereby raising questions about the utility of negotiated con-straints. To make matters worse, SLCMs have already been de-ployed. Determining ranges and distinguishing between conventional and nuclear-armed versions are extremely difficult. As a result, any agreements that limit SLCMs can be subject to continuous chal-lenges over Soviet compliance — challenges that can progressively erode domestic confidence in the terms of any agreement of which SLCM constraints are a part.

Cruise missile deployments will therefore be quite difficult to con-trol, but there is no choice but to try. An absence of controls in-vites unending deployments, particularly as other avenues of com-petition are closed off in negotiations. Like their predecessors, future negotiators will find there are no simple formulas for placing limits on cruise missiles. A differentiated approach toward deploy-ments and controls is therefore unavoidable. Continued cruise mis-sile deployments on bomber aircraft make the most sense and can be regulated by methods already devised in the SALT II Treaty. Similar bookkeeping methods will be required to curtail SLCM deployments. A useful precedent utilizing counting rules was established for deployed missile warheads during the SALT II negotiations. Since neither side could tell exactly how many warheads existed on individual missiles, both agreed to assess a standard number of warheads for every type of missile deployed. For example, every MX and SS-18 was characterized as carrying ten warheads, because that was the maximum number of warheads flight tested on them. The same general formula could apply to SLCMs: agreed counting rules for deployed SLCMs could be assessed to every boat of each class on which they have been tested or deployed. The total number of SLCMs thus assessed would have to fall within aggregate ceilings to provide a disincentive to unending deployments.

Arms control and nuclear weapon strategists can continue to do battle on counterforce weapon programs, or they can attempt to define guidelines for consensus bargaining on this issue. The guidelines suggested here call for some increments in survivable counterforce capabilities in return for decrements in vulnerable counterforce weapons. In operational terms, this means decreased reliance on land-based missile forces that are both threatening to opposing forces and vulnerable to them. As difficult as this may be for nuclear weapon strategists to accept, they must weigh their preferences against the growing opposition on cost, environmental, strategic, and political grounds to new missile bases on American or NATO soil.

Even the Midgetman missile which has initially gained broad-gauged support will eventually generate debates similar to those that beset the MX missile. These missiles are planned to be mobile in order to be survivable. Mobile ICBMs are extraordinarily costly, however: each missile requires its own launcher, security detachment, and high operational expenses. Another presidential blue ribbon commission may well conclude, like the Scowcroft Commission before it, that the best of a poor series of choices is to place single warhead missiles in existing, vulnerable silos. This may not be a bad choice given circumstances at the time of deployment, but it is one that should be made in the context of steady improvements in the overall survivability of U.S. nuclear forces.

The best way to defuse contentious debates in the future over the expense, purposes, and basing schemes of new land-based missiles is to shift gradually to greater reliance on the other two legs of the triad. Land-based missiles should not be abandoned altogether, but they should be progressively reduced, their place supplanted by more survivable forces. The continued failure of political and military leaders to do so is a testament to the triumph of bureaucratic and doctrinal myopia over sound military and arms control policy.

Consensus bargaining of the kind described here can succeed only when both domestic camps accept the proposition that added survivability must outweigh improvements in counterforce capabilities. One camp must temper its passionate opposition to counterforce weapons in general, while the other relents in its demands for threatening, yet vulnerable weapons. Over the long haul, if both camps stick to an agreed framework for reductions and choose wisely in deploying new forces, actions by the United States can promote a stable strategic balance at lower levels even if Soviet leaders continue to choose foolishly. By placing increased emphasis on the bomber and sea-based legs of the triad, we can negate whatever Soviet advantages may accrue from their heavy reliance on MIRVed land-based missiles, by removing an increasing percentage of U.S. forces out from under the cross-hairs of Soviet military planners.

10 Tacit Agreements

Consensus bargaining is most possible over common objectives that can readily be reduced to numerical calculations, like parity, reductions, and greater survivability. Arms control and nuclear weapon strategists will have far more difficulty working on common approaches to broader concepts like strategic stability and the requirements of deterrence where there are no agreed definitions or means of implementation. In general, the more diffuse the objective, the greater the difficulty there can be in bridging differences between the two domestic camps.

The bargaining process can still work in areas where common approaches do not exist, as long as operationally-minded strategists tacitly agree to avoid taking positions that lead to stalemate. Three areas where tacit agreements would clearly be beneficial relate to the role of nuclear weapons in U.S. defense policy, linkage, and compliance diplomacy. Operationalists within both camps can easily assume positions on these questions that will result in periodic, bruising confrontations. Alternatively, they can manage their differences in more constructive ways by working toward informal understandings to de-emphasize nuclear forces, downplay linkage, and depoliticize compliance issues. Unlike consensus bargaining that will yield concrete program choices, tacit agreements on these issues can only suggest guideposts to follow and dead ends to be avoided. Political pressures will continue to be severe on denuclearization, linkage, and compliance questions. Tacit agreements, however, can moderate the intensity and duration of positions taken by the two camps, and suggest trade-offs that serve the interests of the nation as a whole.

Trade-offs are regularly made within the Congressional arena and between the executive and legislative branches that reflect consensus bargaining and tacit understandings. Maneuvering over the defense budget provides yearly examples of how this process works. Regardless of what level of funding is requested for defense programs, there will always be difficult choices over force levels and programs. The results of this bargaining process yield specific funding and procurement levels as well as agreements over some of the purposes of defense expenditures. Other military programs and missions generate heated debates. Still, disagreements are submerged enough to allow for annual cycles of defense funding. A similar bargaining process can be discerned on issues as diverse as public works projects, environmental legislation, and tax policy. The process of reconciliation that is applied so naturally to most domestic issues is strangely underutilized for the critical issues of nuclear weapons and arms control.

Denuclearization

Consensus bargaining over parity, reductions and survivability fits squarely within a framework that de-emphasizes the role of nuclear forces in the overall U.S. defense effort. Operationalists may differ on how to achieve this objective, but they can at least tacitly agree on its value.

Tacit agreements over denuclearization will be stillborn if, as an entry test, one must choose between appreciation of the threat of Soviet expansionism or the threat of nuclear war. Regardless of how small one feels either likelihood may be, both are worthy of concern and both can be addressed in ways that do not require added reliance on nuclear forces.

A strong case can be made that the Soviet Union is both a status quo power where that power now resides and an opportunistic power searching for geopolitical advantage where it does not. The standard metaphor for Soviet risk-taking is that of the burglar testing for unlocked doors. Concern over unlawful Soviet entry has grown with the steady increase in the Kremlin's capabilities to project its military power far afield and the sustained care and feeding of its military forces at home. The Soviet occupation of Afghanistan in December 1979 presented a new and disturbing extension of Kremlin risk-taking beyond the sphere of influence ceded to it after the Second World War.

Even accepting the premise that the Soviet occupation of Afghanistan was defensively motivated and not part of a new offensive thrust toward the Persian Gulf is to accept a disturbing corollary: the Kremlin's conception of its legitimate defense interests has become enlarged to the degree where it poses new threats to its neighbors.

This does not mean that Soviet risk-taking threatens to unhinge Western security. There is nothing particularly out of the ordinary about Soviet attempts to increase influence abroad; it would be peculiar for a superpower not to look beyond its back yard to shape events more to its liking. On the other hand, the Kremlin surely has much to be preoccupied about at home without additional foreign entanglements. Perhaps the invasion of Afghanistan may prove to be the high water mark of foreign adventurism by Soviet ground forces. But there is none among us wise enough to forecast the future in this way.

Whether one believes the Politburo is going for the West's jugular or simply chancing modest gains whenever possible, simple prudence dictates improved conventional forces to defend that which we hold dear and to de-emphasize reliance on nuclear weapons. Continuing global violence on a large scale makes clear that the international political system is built on at least as much kindling as in previous eras, if not more. Quincy Wright once calculated an average of three wars every five years between 1480 and 1941. In the summer of 1982, three major conflicts were being waged concurrently.

In this uncertain environment, it makes good sense to have conventional forces that are well-trained and well-equipped. After all, these forces can plausibly do what nuclear weapons cannot: defend U.S. interests against threats from the Soviet Union or from any other quarter. One purpose of statecraft is to distinguish between what Bernard Brodie once labeled as prestige and vital interests. The purpose of military planning is to be prepared to protect the latter.

Weapon strategists have not shown how nuclear forces can be used to secure U.S. vital interests. There is no effective rebuttal to the argument by arms controllers that attempts to use nuclear weapons to achieve military objectives would be profoundly misguided and incalculably tragic. Finely embroidered nuclear war-fighting options cannot answer fundamental questions that provide the basis for broad and sustained public support. Wars are, after all, fought for political objectives. But no strategist over the past four decades has convincingly explained how nuclear weapons could be integrated into a military campaign to secure political objectives. How would individual soldiers or entire divisions react in the fog of nuclear war? How would the delegation of authority to use nuclear weapons actually work? How can the initiative necessary for offensive operations or negotiations from strength mesh with the objective of terminating the war at the lowest level of destruction?

A weapon that travels thousands of miles in a matter of minutes to deliver an explosive force many times more powerful than the Hiroshima bomb might appear to be an instrument of advantage until one recognizes that the enemy can respond to it in kind—and that he may have no alternative but to respond in kind. Such weapons do not lend themselves to discrete objectives; there is nothing discrete about their damages, even if their initial nuclear effects are directed accurately against a specific target. The deeper one goes into the target lists on both sides, the more catastrophic the consequences.

This assertion is contested by the right wing of the domestic political spectrum, but it is no less true in the fourth nuclear decade, when some claim the United States is behind in the arms race, than in the halcyon years of strategic superiority: U.S. retaliatory capabilities are far greater now than in earlier decades. If the writings of Clausewitz have any meaning for Soviet leaders—as nuclear weapon strategists insist they do—then they, too, must come to the same conclusion. Whatever geopolitical gains the Kremlin may hope to achieve, nuclear warfare is not the means to do so. The only realistic objective to be gained by nuclear detonations is one of stalemate. If either side attempts to achieve anything more by repeated use, the resultant "gains" would be dwarfed by damages. What will matter most in the event of a nuclear exchange is not the military ability of one side to apply leverage on the other through escalation, but the ability of political leaders on both sides to effectively stop escalation from occurring.

Unfortunately, threats to U.S. vital interests, such as the defense of Western Europe or petroleum lifelines to the industrial democracies, are precisely those most difficult to guard against and finance, even in full partnership with our allies. The implausibility of these threats isn't that much of a comfort since implausible threats can be no less consequential than expected ones, if and when they materialize.

The dilemma of somehow matching military requirements to budgetary constraints has confronted Western military strategists and political leaders throughout the four nuclear decades. It has been answered in a variety of ways — sometimes by emphasizing nuclear forces and other times by building up conventional capabilities. Neither answer has been very satisfactory for very long. The defense of Europe by nuclear weapons may have been credible at one point, but few find it completely plausible today. On the other hand, most are uncomfortable with the economic, social, and political burdens associated with a high confidence, conventional defense of Europe.

There is no ideal solution to this dilemma, which helps explain why policy has continually vacillated between the two poles of nuclear defense and conventional mobilization. We are left with the same familiar yet discomforting mix of military risks and budgetary constraints. The United States has values and interests to defend; there is no choice but to maintain large standing armies for these purposes, particularly in light of Soviet military capabilities. U.S. and NATO conventional force levels will not fulfill all military requirements, but they must nevertheless demonstrate the capability for a determined defense of Western interests.

Those in the arms control community who maintain that such military preparations make the use of force more likely have little in the way of historical precedent to back up their claims. The United States has habitually been unprepared to use force before the outbreak of hostilities.[1] Military preparedness doesn't make the political decision to use force any easier; it makes realization of U.S. objectives more likely if political leaders have chosen to use force wisely. Traditional instruments of statecraft are in no way impaired and are a good deal strengthened by having strong conventional forces, whether the Soviet Union is the object of concern or not.

As for direct Soviet expansionism by force of military arms, what purposes would be served by not making it extremely costly for such efforts to succeed? To say this is to do no more than rehearse the diplomatic dispatches of Averell Harriman and George Kennan from earlier decades. This is not to deny the Soviet Union other forms of entry into distant parts of the globe. The Kremlin has the same entry rights we do — a desire for bilateral relations on the part of host countries. But we are lost if we cannot distinguish between certain forms of entry by the Soviet Union and its allies that are of little consequence and those that directly threaten our vital interests.

Operationally-inclined weapon strategists will always feel the tension between their recognition of arms control as a political prerequisite and their animosity toward the Soviet Union and its enlarged role in the world. Success in reconciling the two will depend in part on their ability to distance themselves from the kind of "permanent antipathies" and "passionate attachments" that George Washington warned against in his farewell address — attachments which their ideologically-inclined brethren hold so fiercely. Our first President's insight, lost amid wider-noticed passages, was that "the nation which indulges toward another an habitual hatred or an habitual fondness is in some degree a slave. It is a slave to its animosity or to its affection, either of which is sufficient to lead it astray from its duty or interest." This is not to ask that those of the hawkish persuasion recant their opposition to Soviet expansionism. It is merely to ask that they pursue a differentiated approach toward the Kremlin, one that accepts and supports controls over nuclear weapons as well as opposition to Soviet imperial adventures.

It is unrealistic to expect weapon strategists to be more receptive toward denuclearization if arms controllers passionately continue to resist spending for conventional forces and prudent measures to protect U.S. interests and objectives abroad. Just as it would be helpful for one camp to refrain from interpreting every Soviet move in the Third World as a certain prelude to checkmate, it would also be helpful for the other to refrain from seeing U.S. military assistance abroad as an automatic prelude to intervention. In the words of former Deputy Secretary of Defense Roswell T. Gilpatric, "We cannot afford a policy which, in effect, deliberately avoids seeking a reduction of tensions in order to keep the public alert to dangers. Nor can we afford a policy which deliberately seeks to lull the public, and ignore the dangers where they exist, in order to build support for a policy of peaceful accommodations."[2]

A differentiated approach is needed by arms controllers no less than by nuclear weapon strategists. Defense-related initiatives need not be incompatible with arms control or the development of more stable relations between the superpowers. A strong case can be made that neither objective can succeed without a judicious combination of arrows and olive branches. The key question is, of course, what sort of arrows are being sharpened.

New nuclear weapon programs should presumptively be questioned unless they contribute directly to survivability and overall parity. Programs that are primarily justified on the basis of their counterforce potential or bargaining leverage are, on their face, deeply suspect. Instead, prudence and political realities both dictate tacit agreements that de-emphasize the role of nuclear weapons within the overall U.S. defense posture, while beefing up conventional forces to defend vital interests.

Tacit understandings to de-emphasize nuclear weapons can be reflected in a variety of ways: reductions in deployed forces by means of negotiated agreements, withdrawals of short-range, tactical nuclear weapons, lesser reliance in strategic doctrine on prompt counterforce capabilities, and changes in U.S. declaratory policy regarding the weight we place on nuclear and conventional forces to defend national interests.

Some weapon strategists will balk at several of these initiatives, but their assertions that added nuclear capabilities are needed to check Soviet adventurism will sound hollow as long as funds directed at improving U.S. conventional capabilities are so obviously more appropriate to this objective. The means to check Soviet expansionism have little to do with the use of nuclear weapons. When former Secretary of Defense Melvin Laird reaffirmed the need "to keep open the sea and air links that bind together the NATO alliance, to hold ground on the borders of Europe and elsewhere, and to project and sustain power at great distance," he flatly stated that "none of these objectives requires nuclear weapons."[3]

Operationally-minded strategists from both camps have repeatedly endorsed denuclearization. Former Secretary of Defense James Schlesinger has called our "overreliance" on nuclear deterrence "the fatal flaw in the Western alliance system"; former Secretary of State Henry Kissinger has also warned that our "excessive" reliance on nuclear weapons has been a severe detriment to Western defense strategy. Improving conventional defenses was an explicit corollary to the "no first use" proposals of George Kennan, McGeorge Bundy, Gerard Smith, and Robert McNamara.[4] A working coalition appears ready to adopt this formula; it remains for their political leaders to implement it.

During past debates over arms control agreements, the price of admission for operationally-minded skeptics has been a wide variety of new nuclear weapon programs. The nature of this trade has served neither domestic camp. Subsequent arms control agreements have not been easier to achieve, and they have been less meaningful as a result. Nor have these trade-offs produced a broad commitment to improve U.S. conventional forces. A significantly more useful political compact would instead call for the pursuit of progress in strategic arms control and improvements in conventional forces. After all, this equation has the powerful advantage of clearly promoting the nation's security interests while easing a host of domestic and alliance problems. Another set of problems will rise, however, through attempts to formalize objectives and links between achievements in arms control and improvements in conventional forces. Both goals stand on their own merits and must be pursued. There is no sense in making necessary defense measures contingent on arms control successes, just as there is no sense in shackling arms control with this new form of linkage. The most important aspect of the tacit agreement described here is recognition of its importance and avoidance of actions that are destructive to it.

A de-emphasis on nuclear weapons does not suggest making the European continent safe for a prolonged conventional war, an almost equally appalling prospect for all concerned. Even an extraordinarily successful process of denuclearization will not lift the shadow of the mushroom cloud falling over any confrontation between the superpowers, especially in Europe. The fate of all members of the NATO alliance are bound together, particularly with several hundred thousand U.S. soldiers and citizens stationed across the Atlantic. If for no other reason than to symbolize this bond, it makes sense for the arms control community to support an indefinite commitment of U.S. troops in Europe, particularly in conjunction with steps toward denuclearization.

Movement toward denuclearization is unlikely to result in major shifts of funding within the defense budget, or even in cost savings. Nuclear forces absorb only a small fraction of the overall defense budget; conventional forces are far more costly to maintain. It is true that efficiencies can be found to get more bang for the conventional buck, and changes in roles, missions, and defense organization can save money. A redivision of labor within NATO over military activities within the European Theater and those "out of area" may also be useful.

The focus on military roles and missions within NATO is helpful because it highlights the conclusion that our conventional forces need not be the mirror-image of Soviet forces; we and they have far different military organizations, objectives, and can expect different contributions from our allies. We can also reduce the burden of defense expenditures for conventional forces by means of negotiated agreements. Nevertheless, the myriad of U.S. commitments abroad requires large standing armies, and large standing armies cost considerably more than nuclear-tipped missiles. The objective of denuclearization is necessary for reasons other than cost. The resulting financial burdens can be shared more easily in the expectation that they serve the common defense far more sensibly than does a heavy reliance on nuclear weapons.

Linkage

The superpowers will no doubt continue to maneuver for advantage in the international arena. The record of previous negotiations yields no evidence that arms control solutions can somehow transcend this fundamental political rivalry between two great powers. While arms control solutions must necessarily be somewhat modest, even modest constraints can be critical if they channel the competition into less dangerous pursuits.

It follows, then, that a primary task of political leaders in both countries is to divorce the nuclear arms race as much as possible from their other competitive pursuits. In a democracy, this is extraordinarily difficult to do, particularly when the twin drives of competitive gain and risk avoidance are not easily compartmentalized. Still, operationally-minded strategists from both camps must recognize by now that they cannot sustain the pristine positions on linkage held by their ideologically-inclined brethren. Tacit bargains to accept linkage as a political necessity rather than a political issue are therefore both wise and unavoidable.

Each camp in the domestic debate has carefully outlined positions on linkage that have been hastily redrawn by subsequent events. As arms controllers in the Carter Administration can attest, the state of U.S.-Soviet relations in other spheres cannot help but have an impact on progress in arms control negotiations. On the other hand, formally linking progress in arms control to other political issues leads to a dead end, and attempts by Presidents Nixon and Reagan to do so at the outset of their Administrations were not logically or politically sustainable. The actions of both Administrations constituted the most effective rebuttals to the feasibility of an effective linkage policy. President Nixon signed SALT agreements while American soldiers were being killed in Southeast Asia with Soviet military equipment; President Reagan followed the shooting down of a Korean Airlines 747 with a more negotiable START proposal. The American public wants progress in nuclear arms control. Reprehensible Soviet behavior in unrelated areas will dampen this desire, but not for very long. As a result of this political dynamic, arms controllers have to accept linkage as a powerful fact of life, while nuclear weapon strategists have to accept the pursuit of negotiated agreements.

Political maneuvering over linkage will arise as frequently as deplorable Soviet activities. During these periods, conservative administrations are most immune when they reject linkage while arms control-oriented presidents are most immune when they embrace it. Over time, the contradictions and embarrassments of making a political issue out of linkage will be felt by those expressing outrage as well as those receiving abuse: the accusers will doubtless have the opportunity to reverse themselves on the linkage issue whenever they assume the responsibilities of negotiations. Tacit agreements between the two camps to downplay the linkage issue are therefore in the long-term interests of both.

Compliance Diplomacy

At the outset of the SALT I negotiations, President Richard Nixon vowed, "I am determined to avoid, within the Government and in the country at large, divisive disputes regarding Soviet compliance or non-compliance with an understanding or agreement. Nor will I bequeath to a future President the seeds of such disputes."[5] Despite these intentions, the SALT I accords generated considerable controversy over Soviet compliance, contributing to President Jimmy Carter's failure to secure ratification of the SALT II Treaty. Subsequently, compliance problems grew progressively worse, symbolized by the release of U.S. and Soviet reports charging each other with noncompliance. As a result of this public record, arms control-oriented presidents can expect verification and compliance issues to figure prominently in upcoming treaty debates.

From the Partial Nuclear Test Ban to the SALT II Treaty, American Presidents supported a flexible approach to verification requirements: the United States had to be in a position to detect Soviet cheating of any consequence in time to take appropriate countermeasures. This operational construct became known as "adequate" verification during the Nixon, Ford, and Carter Administrations. President Kennedy used a different lexicon but a similar standard for verification during the Limited Test Ban Treaty debate.

During the SALT I and II debates, Administration officials did not contend they could detect every instance of Soviet cheating; they asserted they could monitor any cheating that mattered. President Nixon explicitly stated this formulation in his instructions to the SALT I negotiating team:

> No arms limitation agreement can ever be absolutely verifiable. The relevant test is not an abstract ideal, but the practical standard of whether we can determine compliance adequately to safeguard our security — that is, whether we can identify attempted evasion if it occurs on a large enough scale to pose a significant risk, and whether we can do so in time to mount a sufficient response. Meeting this test is what I mean by the term "adequate verification."[6]

Verification issues were of far greater concern during the SALT II hearings because of the difficulty in monitoring the qualitative limits included in the SALT II Treaty and because of the compliance issues that arose from the SALT I accords. The Carter Administration's defense of the "verifiability" of the SALT II Treaty was therefore more comprehensive and detailed than that of the Kennedy and Nixon Administrations before it, but similar in substance:

> The anticipated SALT II agreement is adequately verifiable. This judgment is based on assessment of the verifiability of the individual provisions of the agreement and the agreement as a whole. Although the possibility of some undetected cheating in certain areas exists, such cheating would not alter the strategic balance in view of U.S. programs. Any cheating on a scale large enough to alter the strategic balance would be discovered in time to make an appropriate response. There will be areas of uncertainty, but they are not such as to permit the Soviets to produce a signifi-

cant unanticipated threat to U.S. interests, and those uncertainties can, in any event, be compensated for with the flexibility inherent in our own programs.[7]

The mix of operationally- and ideologically-inclined strategists in the Reagan Administration rejected this litany. They asserted that "adequate" verification was insufficient, and concluded that political judgments as to adequacy in the past had been notably lax. Because previous arms control agreements had been poorly drafted, the Kremlin exploited ambiguities in ways that injured U.S. national security and altered the strategic balance. For all of these reasons, ideologically-minded strategists demanded a more exacting standard for verification. To distinguish their standard from the previous one, Reagan Administration officials referred to the need for "effective" verification. Henceforth, U.S. monitoring had to be more intrusive and verification requirements tougher. For medium-range and strategic forces, Reagan Administration officials expressed concerns about stockpiled missiles, silo reloads, covert production and the resulting possibilities of "breakout" against treaty constraints. Presumably, alleviating these concerns would require difficult negotiations and significant Soviet concessions.

Behind the distinctions between "adequate" and "effective" verification lay fundamental differences of view concerning Soviet objectives and the value of arms control. A more flexible standard for verification requirements made sense for those who believed the United States and the Soviet Union had common interests in maintaining the viability of agreements reached and in foreclosing destructive avenues of competition. As arms controllers readily asserted, this did not entail trusting the Kremlin to abide by its commitments; it merely required trusting them to act in their own best interests. Little trust seemed necessary for arms controllers, because Soviet leaders were unlikely to sign agreements that required cheating in order to protect their security. In addition, there were bureaucratic reasons to expect Soviet compliance, once the Kremlin made the necessary internal trade-offs to reach agreement. As Abram Chayes argued,

An agreement that is adopted by a modern bureaucratic government will be backed by a broad official consensus generated by the negotiating process, and will carry personal and political endorsement across the spectrum of bureaucratic and political leadership. These are exceedingly hard to undo or reverse, the more so since, once the treaty goes into effect, they are reinforced by the ponderous inertia of the bureaucracy.[8]

Complementing these forces for restraint were sophisticated national technical means of verification which could serve as a deterrent to Soviet cheating. Detection of cheating would be, at the very least, embarrassing, and could prompt unwanted reactions.

The resulting matrix of forces argued for flexible standards of verification, depending on the benefits of the agreement in question and the risks of undetected cheating. The Kennedy Administration did not argue with those who contended that monitoring capabilities for a limited test ban could not detect all instances of Soviet noncompliance; only that these were risks worth taking in the light of the perceived benefits. As President Kennedy said in his transmittal message to the Senate:

> The risks in clandestine violations under this treaty are far smaller than the risks in unlimited testing. . . . No nation tempted to violate the treaty can be certain that an attempted violation will go undetected, given the many means of detecting nuclear explosions. The risks of detection outweigh the potential gains from violation, and the risk to the United States from such violation is outweighed by the risk of a continued unlimited nuclear arms race.[9]

As one moves to the right along the political spectrum, this calculus of benefits and risks changes. For those most skeptical of Soviet intentions, arms control agreements backstopped by "adequate" verification couldn't be trusted to protect and advance U.S. security interests. This belief was often unstated because of the widespread popularity of arms control, at least in the abstract. But it could be inferred from the specific proposals championed by skeptics: proposals deemed worthy of support were also wholly unacceptable to the Kremlin.

For ideologically-minded weapon strategists, there were few incentives—bureaucratic or otherwise—for Soviet compliance with arms control agreements. On the contrary, the Kremlin's impulse was not to comply with agreements that constrained military forces needed to achieve their national objectives. Failure to detect Soviet noncompliance did not necessarily mean that the Kremlin was be having itself; it meant only that violations had not yet been detected. Of particular concern was the Kremlin's high priority on the arts of deception and concealment. The potential for noncompliance was therefore great for most sorts of arms control agreements. Since the United States has never found anything that the Soviets have successfully hidden, the possibilities of cheating and the resulting harm are considerable. The best checks against nefarious Soviet practices are precisely drafted agreements, highly intrusive monitoring provisions, and a forceful policy of sanctions and unilateral actions once detection has occurred.

As a result of these contrasting viewpoints, Congressional debates over verification issues have had a ritualistic quality. In every debate, critics called attention to problems of detection and the potential military significance of undetected Soviet cheating. During the Partial Test Ban Treaty debate, critics pointed to the difficulties in detecting weapon tests in remote ocean areas, in space, behind the moon, adjacent to the Chinese border, under Lake Baikal, or even in the atmosphere during periods of heavy cloud cover. Another concern expressed by Congressional skeptics was that the Soviets could test "legally" under a few feet of dirt, thereby gaining unfair advantages over the U.S.[10] For these reasons, some in Congress called for on-site inspections. Treaty opponents also pointed to blatant gaps in U.S. detection capabilities, since the first VELA satellites to monitor atmospheric testing had yet to be placed in orbit.

President Kennedy parried concerns over verification when he decided to forgo a comprehensive treaty in favor of an agreement allowing underground tests. Thereafter, the Joint Chiefs of Staff reversed their opposition to an agreement. General Maxwell Taylor, speaking for the Chiefs, effectively argued that whatever clandestine progress the Soviets might make would be minor, especially with safeguards supported by Congressional skeptics, including a strong underground test program and improved monitoring capabilities. Harold Brown, then the Pentagon's chief scientist, persuasively assuaged concerns over Soviet cheating, noting the difficulty and expense of carrying out clandestine tests in remote areas, compared to the relative ease with which tests could be carried out underground. A reservation to the treaty, making ratification contingent on a system of on-site inspections, offered by Senator John Tower was easily defeated. Tower maintained that such inspections were necessary to ensure compliance; seventy-six of his colleagues felt otherwise.

One reason for Tower's overwhelming defeat was that four out of five Americans gave their "unqualified approval" to the Partial Test Ban Treaty before the Senate vote, up from 52% at the start of the Senate's deliberations. The Treaty offered an end to radioactive fallout from U.S. and Soviet tests, and the promise of subsequent agreements. Concerns expressed by treaty opponents over verification appeared petty by comparison.

Verification concerns were similarly inconsequential during Congressional debate over the SALT I accords. Secretary of Defense Melvin Laird and Chairman of the Joint Chiefs Admiral Thomas Moorer flatly declared U.S. verification capabilities to be adequate, and few cared to argue the point. Operationally-minded strategists in the Nixon Administration could also point to treaty provisions which secured, for the first time, formal Soviet acceptance of national technical means of verification (NTM). Moreover, the Kremlin agreed not to interfere with NTM, nor to use deliberate concealment measures which impeded verification of treaty provisions. These provisions seemed more than sufficient for the kinds of controls embodied in the SALT I accords. With President Nixon's strong political position and assurances from Pentagon officials, skeptics of the agreements were in a poor position to make a strong case against the accords on verification grounds. Critics of SALT I were far more concerned about the emerging strategic balance, not our ability to verify it.

In stark contrast to preceeding debates, verification issues were prominent during the SALT II hearings. The treaty's qualitative constraints placed more demands on U.S. monitoring capabilities, and compliance questions arising from the SALT I accords heightened sensitivities to verification capabilities. Finally, events during the Congressional review process drew attention to verification, particularly the loss of Iranian monitoring stations and the "discovery" of the Soviet military brigade in Cuba.

As in the Partial Test Ban Treaty debate, SALT II critics cited treaty provisions and Soviet activities that would be difficult to monitor. Carter Administration officials provided the same assurances as their predecessors, but with considerably less success. Administration spokesmen could point to new treaty provisions that aided verification — such as counting rules, "cooperative measures," and a ban on encryption when it impeded verification of treaty provisions — but few were swayed by such arguments. Technical issues relating to verification became surrogates to broader political concerns during the SALT II debate, symbolized by Senator John Glenn's vote against the treaty in the Senate Foreign Relations Committee. Glenn withheld his support for the treaty until gaps in U.S. monitoring capabilities could be closed. Long before the Soviet invasion of Afghanistan, the treaty was in trouble because of perception of abrogation if the Kremlin did not fulfill treaty obligations. ing trend lines in superpower fortunes and military capabilities.

As with the verification issue, Congressional debates over treaty compliance have followed a discernible pattern. Critics have pointed out the potentially dire implications of noncompliance as well as previous instances of Soviet transgressions, while supporters dwelt on the benefits of the agreement at hand and the ultimate sanction of abrogation if the Kremlin did not fulfill treaty obligations.

During the Partial Test Ban Treaty debate, President Kennedy was in a strong position to defuse concerns over Soviet noncompliance. Despite his reluctance to break the moratorium in place since 1958 on atmospheric testing, he did so in 1961, following the example of France and the Soviet Union. If the Soviets reneged on their treaty commitments in the Kennedy Administration, the possibility of U.S. abrogation was more than an idle threat. Moreover, the scenarios for possible compliance problems such as testing behind the moon or in deep space seemed far-fetched, and the presumed value for clandestine cheating quite marginal. Ideologically-minded treaty opponents compiled long lists of Soviet violations and broken promises from the Bolshevik Revolution to Yalta, but with little effect. The perceived benefits of the Partial Test Ban Treaty clearly seemed worth the risk of Soviet noncompliance.

During the SALT I debate, Congressional critics offered mixed messages on prospective compliance problems. On the one hand, supporters of the Jackson Amendment expressed concern not that the Kremlin would cheat, but that it could do so much harm without resort to cheating. On the other hand, Senator Jackson and his allies were quite concerned over ambiguities in the agreements that could be exploited by the Kremlin, particularly the Interim Agreement's provisions governing new ICBMs.

Later, this issue would be a springboard for contentious debates over Soviet SALT violations, but at that time, compliance questions did not loom large on the horizon. President Nixon did not need to defend his credentials as a staunch defender of U.S. interests in negotiations with the Soviet Union. Whatever criticism was levied at the SALT I accords was deflected by the President's accept-

ance of the Jackson Amendment and his firm commitment to proceed with the B-1, Trident and various other programs to strength-
en his hand in subsequent negotiations. In addition, the SALT I
accords established a special channel, the Standing Consultative
Commission, to handle any compliance questions that might arise.

Concerns over Soviet noncompliance with the SALT I accords
figured prominently in the SALT II debate, where one-quarter to
one-third of the Senate appeared irreconcilably opposed to the treaty.
As in the past, committed treaty opponents compiled lists of Soviet
transgressions. Unlike Presidents Kennedy and Nixon, President
Carter was in a poor position to rebut these charges: the perceived
benefits of the SALT II Treaty were not greatly appreciated, and
the President's resolve in dealing with the Kremlin was widely questioned.

To make matters worse, President Carter and his predecessors
were hard-pressed to defend the record of the Standing Consultative Commission in the political arena. To be most effective, the
S.C.C.'s deliberations required privacy, yet some accounting of the
Commission's work seemed necessary since periodic leaks of Soviet
"violations" undermined the S.C.C.'s credibility as well as the SALT
accords themselves.

To clear up this record, the Carter Administration released an
unclassified report of U.S. and Soviet concerns raised in the S.C.C.
since its inception in 1973. The report did not dispute those who
argued that the Kremlin repeatedly exploited definitional ambiguities and pressed at the margins of the SALT I accords. But the
Carter Administration's compliance report did refute assertions of
violations, finding that in every instance of troublesome Soviet practices, "the activity has ceased or subsequent information has clarified the situation and allayed our concern."[11] These conclusions were
supported by several case studies sketching out patient efforts by
Presidents Nixon, Ford and Carter to maintain the viability of the
SALT I accords. From 1973 to 1979, the S.C.C. was able to establish common definitions of permissible activity in ambiguous
cases and to halt military practices that could, over time, undercut treaty provisions. Every substantive problem raised at the
S.C.C. required more than one negotiating round to be resolved.
Despite their complexity, earlier problems could be ironed out, because both sides adopted a problem-solving rather than a prosecutorial approach to the issues at hand.

President Carter's compliance report had a negligible impact
on the SALT II Treaty debate. Once a President has lost his polit-

ical standing or once perceptions of troubling Soviet activity have become widespread, official reports asserting correct, if unhelpful Soviet behavior are hardly a prescription for success in the political arena. To put it another way, once critics have captured the political high ground on compliance issues, they are exceedingly difficult to dislodge.

Occasionally, allegations of Soviet wrongdoing are completely devoid of substance, such as reports in the fall of 1975 that the Soviets were blinding U.S. satellites. The source of this problem turned out to be fires along Soviet gas pipelines. Sometimes, however, allegations of violations reflect worrisome activity requiring addressal by the S.C.C. Regardless of their veracity, reports of Soviet violations have a damaging cumulative effect, leaving the arms control community in a bind, since it is difficult to rebut charges without focusing more attention to them and without seeming to defend questionable Soviet behavior. Rebuttals must also be sanitized through the national security bureaucracy to protect intelligence sources and methods as well as the privacy of diplomatic communications. For these reasons, timely rebuttals are unlikely, while *ex post facto* summaries of how the S.C.C. ironed out compliance questions rarely dispel built-up perceptions of Soviet wrongdoing.

Critics of the SALT process, including many operationally-minded strategists formerly associated with the SALT I accords, rejected the Carter Administration's conclusions about the work of the S.C.C. and the record of Soviet compliance. These concerns were fully aired during the bitter SALT II debate, and were reflected in positions subsequently taken by the Reagan Administration.

During the Senate Foreign Relations Committee's SALT II hearings, Paul Nitze was asked if he knew of any compliance issues not resolved at the S.C.C. He responded, "No, but how were they resolved? They were resolved by accepting that which had been done in violation."[12] To buttress this view, hard-line critics of the SALT process compiled lists of Soviet "violations and circumventions" of arms control agreements, while leaks of new violations appeared periodically in newspapers and journals with a strong editorial stance against Soviet "cheating." The willingness of the Carter Administration to acknowledge these violations was also called into question. During the SALT II debate, Richard Perle wrote:

. . . from a political point of view, the last thing we will desire is to catch the Soviets in a violation—and especially in a viola-

tion of a provision that careless negotiating had rendered unen
forceable. . . . In the real world we would face a choice betweer
precipitating a political crisis of enormous proportions or ignor
ing evidence of the Soviet violation. If past history is any guide
our officials will find an endless list of excuses to justify doubt
ful Soviet behavior.[13]

Moreover, the ability of the Carter Administration to lodge future
complaints was called into question due to skillful maneuvering by
Soviet negotiators. For example, before he was appointed Assistant Secretary of Defense in the Reagan Administration, Richard
Perle asserted that the Kremlin could deploy all of their new ICBMs
under development within the lax "new types" provision of the
SALT II Treaty. Similarly, the United States could not verify treaty
provisions relating to the SS-16 missile.[14] The Republican Party's
campaign platform during the 1980 election formally pledged to enc
the "cover-up" of Soviet SALT violations.

As ideologically-minded strategists settled into key positions of
responsibility in the Reagan Administration, conditions were ripe
for compliance problems to come to the fore. Concerns over noncompliance will arise even in periods of détente, because every arms
control agreement will contain ambiguities that can be exploited
and because there will always be those in Washington and Moscow
who will wish to do so. During periods of bad political relations,
the impulse to seek advantage by defining treaty obligations in permissive ways is far greater, and the checks against doing so are
weakened. When the downturn in U.S.-Soviet relations that began
during the latter half of the Carter Administration accelerated after
the election of Ronald Reagan, compliance issues became more intractable. With bilateral relations increasingly strained, it also became far more difficult for both sides to iron out problems in private channels like the S.C.C.

Statements by Reagan Administration officials further undermined the possibility of ironing out compliance issues once they
arose. President Reagan set the tone at his first press conference,
when he characterized his negotiating partners as "liars and cheats."
His first Secretary of State, Alexander Haig, declared that "We consider SALT II to be dead. We have so informed the Soviet Union
and they have accepted and understood that." His Secretary of Defense, Caspar Weinberger, declared that U.S. defense programs
were in conformity to SALT I and II restraints as a matter of coin-

cidence rather than design, and the President's White House Counselor, Edwin Meese III, stated that the Reagan Administration had no moral or legal commitment to abide by expired or unratified SALT agreements. When challenged by the State Department and Arms Control Agency legal experts on this assertion, the White House issued a defense of Meese's position, calling it "entirely accurate."[15]

Several military initiatives of the Reagan Administration lent force to these public pronouncements, since they could not be pursued within the confines of existing arms control agreements. The "Dense-Pack" deployment scheme of clustering MX missiles closely together would have required digging holes for new missiles, an activity prohibited by the SALT I Interim Agreement and the SALT II Treaty. Administration officials explained that the excavations would be allowed because they were for new "hardened capsules" rather than silos, and would be completed after the expiration of SALT II, in any event. Later, the President agreed to press ahead with a second new ICBM — the Midgetman — to complement the MX. Again, its deployment would begin after the terms of the SALT II agreement — which permitted only one new type of ICBM — were to expire. Then the President endorsed a "Star Wars" defense against nuclear attack which could not be tested in space or deployed without violating the ABM Treaty. More conventional ABM ballistic missile defense research projects continued, which would also pose treaty compliance problems.

While U.S. military programs suggested prospective compliance problems, Soviet activities were of immediate concern. Questions of Soviet compliance with the Geneva Protocol and Biological Weapons Convention were generated by evidence that Soviet troops and Soviet-equipped Vietnamese forces used "yellow rain" in Afghanistan and in Southeast Asia. In addition, concerns over Soviet compliance with the Biological Weapons Convention (BWC) were raised by an accident at a suspected biological weapons facility in Sverdlovsk in 1979. This incident resulted in an outbreak of what appeared to be pulmonary anthrax. The BWC bars development, production and stockpiling of biological warfare agents "in quantities that have no justification for prophylactic, protective or other peaceful purposes." The Kremlin blamed infected meat as the cause of the events that transpired at Sverdlovsk, an explanation that did not seem plausible.

The evidence of Soviet chemical and toxic warfare magnified concerns over SALT compliance questions. Initially, the Reagan Administration declined to endorse the long list of "violations and circumventions" prepared by bitter critics of the SALT I accords. As new compliance issues relating to the unratified SALT II agreement arose, pressures from conservative members of Congress began to mount for a public accounting of Soviet transgressions. As was the case after the Interim Agreement was signed, the flight testing of new Soviet ICBMs became a highly contentious issue, fueled this time by earlier assurances from Carter Administration officials that only one new type of ICBM would be allowed under SALT II. The high level of encryption associated with these missile flight tests was inconsistent with the SALT II provision barring these practices when they impeded verification of treaty constraints. Of greater concern was the unexpected construction of a new, phased array radar in Siberia, discovered in mid-1983.[16]

When SALT II questions arose, protracted debates took place within the Reagan Administration over whether and how these questions should be discussed in the Standing Consultative Commission. The most ardent SALT II opponents within the Reagan Administration argued against raising them in the S.C.C., since to do so would provide unwarranted standing for an agreement whose ratification they helped to block.[17] A compromise was reached whereby the U.S. delegation was directed to express concern about SALT II compliance while refusing to become engaged in discussion of specific issues. As U.S.-Soviet relations continued to slide downhill, S.C.C. proceedings became adversarial and tendentious. The United States finally raised the Siberian radar and ICBM compliance issues in the fall 1983 session of the S.C.C. When Administration officials were not satisfied with the initial Soviet explanations, President Reagan responded to a Congressional initiative by publicly issuing a report on Soviet noncompliance. Included in the Administration's findings were the "new types" and SS-16 citations previously considered to be either unverifiable or within the permissive boundaries of the SALT II Treaty.

The Reagan Administration's report on Soviet noncompliance reflected a different approach to compliance diplomacy than that practiced by his predecessors — one no less important than the difference between "adequate" and "effective" verification. For the mix of ideologically- and operationally-minded strategists in the Reagan Administration, Soviet compliance with arms control agreements could not be presumed, even though the agreements conferred advantages to the Kremlin. Thus, in two of the citations of possible

Soviet violations—testing nuclear weapons underground above the 150 kiloton ceiling established in the Threshold Test Ban Treaty and deploying SS-16 missiles—the Reagan Administration reached conclusions different from those of its predecessors, although it was drawing from essentially the same evidence.

The Reagan Administration's list of Soviet SALT violations related to problems over treaty definitions and Soviet concealment practices. In this sense, the issues in dispute had many antecedents. In previous cases, however, Presidents Nixon, Ford, and Carter were able to hammer out new agreed definitions and to curtail Soviet concealment practices at the S.C.C. The objective for these Presidents was not necessarily to re-establish the *status quo ante,* but to maintain the viability of the SALT I accords. In their view, as well as in the view of Pentagon officials at the time, they succeeded: no compensating U.S. military actions were deemed necessary to counter the Kremlin's actions.

The process of fencing in Soviet testing at the margins was often an arduous one, as was evident with the compliance problem relating to Soviet SA-5 radar tests "in an ABM mode." Article VI of the ABM Treaty barred such testing, in order to impede the upgrading of surface-to-air missile batteries to the point where they might have some capability to intercept strategic missiles. The picture was clouded, however, because there was no common agreement on what constituted tests in an ABM mode and because the United States maintained that tests for "range safety and instrumentation" were permitted.

Characteristically, U.S. intelligence began to notice Soviet encroachment on treaty provisions. In this instance, a SA-5 radar had been turned on during flight tests of strategic ballistic missiles. At first, the Nixon Administration declined to raise this issue at the S.C.C., in deference to the intelligence community's sensitivity about disclosing sources and methods. This position changed, and when the Ford Administration raised the issue of the SA-5 radar, the practice stopped within three weeks. It then required approximately two years of private diplomacy in the Carter Administration to work out a common agreement governing these practices.

Operationally-minded arms control strategists considered this case study an example of successful compliance diplomacy: a potentially serious problem was ironed out, ambiguous provisions of the ABM Treaty had been clarified to the satisfaction of both parties, and the viability of the agreement remained intact.

Operationally-minded nuclear weapon strategists generally found this case study a troubling example of how the Kremlin's malpractices were grandfathered into the S.C.C.'s "solutions." Ideologically-minded nuclear weapon strategists were convinced that the Soviets had gained advantage from this and other instances of SALT "compliance." For them, the *status quo ante,* or something close to it, should be the outcome of S.C.C. deliberations, and if prompt and satisfactory solutions couldn't be reached at the S.C.C., a President should go public with findings on Soviet violations, even in ambiguous cases.

When President Reagan went public with his concerns, he further politicized the compliance-resolution process, making it far more difficult to iron out compliance problems in private. For the Kremlin, public disclosures raised questions about U.S. intentions and the utility of trying to revise official judgments. Thus, in operational terms, the compliance diplomacy practiced by the Reagan Administration — unlike that of the Nixon, Ford, and Carter Administrations — tended to make diplomatic solutions more remote.

Ideologically-minded weapon strategists might evaluate this turn of events as a success, but the progressive unravelling of what few constraints exist on the nuclear arms competition can hardly be judged a positive development by most Americans or their elected officials. Both camps of operationally-minded strategists have a stake in preventing compliance concerns from becoming heated political issues. Both also have a considerable stake in protecting the process where these concerns can be ironed out in private. The interests of arms controllers are clear: negotiated agreements can be blocked or undermined by politicizing compliance problems. Operationally-minded weapon strategists have difficult choices to make on these issues, since they have legitimate grievances concerning the Soviet approach to treaty compliance. Nevertheless, if they side with their ideologically-minded brethren, the nation will be considerably less secure as a result: the road chosen by ideologues leads to the absence of nuclear arms control and the breakdown of compliance diplomacy.

The far-right has no better alternative to the compliance-resolution process, whether to achieve Soviet compliance within existing treaty obligations or to improve U.S. security in the absence of treaty constraints. There is always political mileage to be gained by raising compliance issues, but no mileage to be gained by closing off avenues of communication and abrogating existing agreements. Operationalists will always feel uneasy about the compliance-resolution process; but unless they are willing to protect it against unrealistic expectations and uphold its consultative provisions, the entire fabric of negotiated agreements between the U.S. and U.S.S.R. will be placed at risk.

Arms control and nuclear weapon strategists have generally recognized that absolute assurance of detecting Soviet violations is not within the realm of the possible. Simple prudence — a marriage of U.S. security interests as well as the dictates of domestic politics — led both camps to support precise treaty texts and impressive, redundant monitoring capabilities to track Soviet compliance. But assessments differed on weighing monitoring risks against the risk of failing to reach an agreement, and on the ability of the United States to respond in an appropriate and timely fashion in the event of violations. Nuclear weapon strategists have always been troubled by formulations that left definitions of risk and assessments of injury in the hands of more trusting souls.

In the past, weapon strategists insisted on excessive verification requirements for Soviet forces in order to protect deployment of new U.S. weapon systems. On-site inspections were demanded in order to ban MIRV deployments, a senseless exercise when MIRV flight tests could have been detected by sophisticated monitoring devices. Assessments of risk and benefit for an anti-satellite treaty remain far apart, as is the case with a comprehensive ban on nuclear weapon testing. Ideologically-minded strategists will continue to insist on extreme verification provisions; arms controllers will need the help of operationally-minded strategists to scale verification requirements to more reasonable assessments of risk and benefit.

The gap between these assessments has remained wide because many in the arms control community have tended to assume that strategic arms control agreements with the Soviets were in the interest of both parties not only to sign, but to observe. In this view, once treaties were in place, the competition between the two nations would be dampened, at least within the confines of agreements reached. But Soviet practices have not conformed to this view. The Kremlin has habitually pressed on the margins of agreements reached or exploited their ambiguities when some advantage could result. These practices helped take the bloom off détente, and became progressively worse as bilateral relations began to slide.

In response, arms controllers must join forces with operationally-minded nuclear weapons strategists to endorse an effective compliance strategy. The purposes behind such a strategy are to foreclose destructive avenues of competition and to assure the public that the nation's security is being advanced—precisely the same reasons for entering into agreements in the first place.

Both camps of operationalists will lose if they do not join forces on a positive and persuasive compliance strategy when the Kremlin presses at the margins of negotiated agreements. Otherwise, affirmations of negotiated agreements by arms controllers will ring hollow if they are contested by weapon strategists, just as any corrective action needed to maintain the integrity of agreements will be undermined if questioned by the arms control community. Stated in this way, a tacit understanding begins to emerge between the two camps: operationally-minded weapon strategists must help to combat the prosecutorial approach to compliance issues championed by ideologues, while arms controllers must be more assertive on compliance questions, lending support to countermeasures when appropriate.

No compliance strategy can work effectively if signatories have lost interest in maintaining the viability of an agreement. A compliance strategy can work, however, when the Kremlin knows that the United States will respond in predictable ways to actions that undermine existing agreements, and when the political center feels that their President has a coherent approach to handling the ambiguities of treaty compliance.

The components of an effective compliance strategy can be inferred from the definitions of adequate verification used by every President from John F. Kennedy to Jimmy Carter: the U.S. should first try to achieve a satisfactory explanation or solution of the compliance problem through diplomatic channels, moving when necessary to countermeasures if diplomatic channels fail.

With the unravelling of U.S.-Soviet relations and increased concerns over treaty compliance, it would be wise to make this common sense, two-track strategy explicit. For SALT-related issues, the diplomatic track starts with the S.C.C., where there are procedures and precedents to iron out problems in mutually acceptable ways. Other diplomatic channels should be used sparingly, since the S.C.C. is specifically tailored to address these problems. Nevertheless, it may be necessary to reinforce or facilitate the work of the S.C.C. by higher-level diplomatic exchanges. While the diplomatic track is being used, it makes little sense to issue public reports or presidential findings of noncompliance since "going public" will only make satisfactory solutions in private harder to achieve.

If compliance diplomacy does not yield a satisfactory solution and if our objective is to maintain the agreement in force, offsetting actions may be required. If this second track is needed, counter-measures should be proportional to Soviet activities and within trea-ty constraints. Countermeasures must be chosen carefully, however, since their impact can be interpreted either as further hedges against treaty abrogation, depending on the Kremlin's reading of U.S. in-tentions.

A positive two-track compliance strategy will allow operationally-minded strategists to respond to the substantive and political prob-lems arising from troubling Soviet actions. This approach will not alter the opinions of those who reflexively assume violations have taken place, but it will help assure the political center that compli-ance questions are being addressed in a purposeful and sequential way. Public assurance can also be fostered by cooperative meas-ures and better ways of conveying the work of the Standing Consul-tative Commission, such as by declassifying common agreements devised under its auspices, or by issuing periodic summaries of its deliberations.

Differences over verification and compliance between the two do-mestic camps can also be bridged by the judicious use of safeguards to accompany new agreements. Like the use of proportional coun-termeasures in ongoing disputes, safeguards against prospective compliance problems can have multiple purposes, encouraging stricter Soviet compliance and assuring the American public that U.S. interests will be protected in the event of troubling Soviet be-havior.

For example, an anti-satellite weapons agreement clearly poses risks if the Kremlin fails to comply, although these risks seem less ominous than the risks of an unfettered competition in space war-fare. Nuclear weapon strategists are concerned about "breakout" scenarios or covert Soviet cheating against ASAT provisions. To deal with these concerns arms control strategists can consider several alternative safeguards to shorten the timelines of an appropriate U.S. response. These possibilities include allowing a certain number of ASAT tests prior to an agreement, restricting tests in ways that limit operational capabilities, or banning flight tests altogether but establishing a production line which can be opened in the event the Kremlin resumes ASAT tests.

In the past, safeguards were accepted by Presidents after they had concluded arms control agreements. In the future, operationally-minded strategists would be wise to initiate this process early in negotiations to lower potential hurdles to ratification, and to ensure that safeguards do not undercut treaty provisions.

As in the case of proportional countermeasures, there is no substitute for choosing safeguards wisely, and on a reasonable scale. If nuclear weapon strategists believe the risks of entering into an ASAT or any other arms control agreement are inordinately large, the preferred safeguards are likely to be so excessive as to foreclose the possibilities of an accord or to minimize its value. Arms controllers are not likely to share this calculus of benefits and risks. However, they cannot deny the need for safeguards of any kind, because safeguards can make a difference in the record of Soviet compliance and in the outcome of domestic debates.

The bargaining process suggested here will cause discomfort to operationally-minded strategists from both camps, but the tensions that will arise will be far less injurious than those that accompany knock-down, drag-out debates over arms control agreements. Both camps bring leverage into these consultations. If nuclear weapon strategists are concerned over Soviet compliance, they need the arms control community to support effective countermeasures. Corrective action, when needed, will be difficult to carry out unless the arms control community lends continuing credence to the official U.S. government position. For their part, nuclear weapon strategists can undercut arms control by lending support to the unreasonable expectations and demands of their ideologically-inclined brethren, or they can assume a more reasoned stance.

Arms controllers and nuclear weapon strategists are stuck with the same imperfect mechanisms for treaty compliance. Unless the two camps of operationally-minded strategists work to maintain the integrity of the compliance-resolution process, they will find themselves locking horns on more basic issues in ways far more damaging to the security of the Republic. The informal understandings suggested here, like those proposed on denuclearization and linkage, cannot be operationalized in any set fashion. Their workability depends on the willingness of key leaders from both camps to dampen the political fires that can burn so destructively on arms control and nuclear weapon questions.

Epilogue

The recommendations offered in the preceding pages for phased reductions, overall parity, and greater survivability in nuclear forces will seem maddeningly modest to those who wish for drastic disarmament and terribly naive to those who wish to nullify Soviet power. Nevertheless, these are objectives that lend themselves to broad public support and that can be operationalized by political leaders of widely different persuasions.

I would argue that these recommendations are more idealistic than modest, for they constitute an ambitious agenda based on two extraordinarily difficult goals. First, the two superpowers must effectively isolate the strategic arms race as much as possible from their other competitive pursuits. Second, the two domestic camps must try to manage better their different perspectives on arms control and nuclear weapon issues. Political differences on questions such as denuclearization, linkage, and compliance cannot be submerged, but they can be somewhat contained by effective political leadership.

Neither of these tasks will be easy. In the domestic arena, the natural tendency of both camps will be to press for decisive political advantage when opportunities arise. There is reason to hope, however, for a growing recognition that short-term advantages do not provide long-run gains, either for one's camp or for the nation as a whole.

In the international arena, great powers have not been able to isolate their most prestigious and fearsome weapons from the political aspects of their competition for very long or very well. But the stakes involved in not controlling nuclear weapons are far different from, say, the consequences of failure in the 1930s to control naval armaments. Nuclear weapons are, after all, weapons of mass destruction. There are no defenses against the consequences of their repeated use. They make citizens of the Soviet Union no less vulnerable than we are. With this recognition, leaders of both nations may, just possibly, be able to change the odds in their — and our — favor.

The two domestic camps can work together with the mutual understanding that the Kremlin will continue to press for advantage, but that it also wishes to avoid risks. These dual impulses apply to negotiated agreements governing nuclear weapons, as well as to other areas of the geopolitical competition. We can reach arms control agreements with the Soviet Union because they allow both nations to manage their risks, yet they do not foreclose attempts to gain advantage — even within the confines of agreement.

The United States is capable of meeting the challenges involved in negotiating agreements and, insofar as it is possible to do so through unilateral actions, maintaining their integrity, either through corrective military programs or diplomatic exchanges. Similarly, the United States is quite capable, again, insofar as it is possible through unilateral actions, of maintaining the nation's security through a purposeful defense effort.

Presumably, the Kremlin knows that the United States will respond vigorously to Soviet military programs that undermine our security. A more salient concern is whether we can summon the political will and the political base to make a success of arms control. In the past, we have shown far more fortitude for improving our nuclear weapon capabilities than for seeking alternatives through arms control. Can the Soviet Union be convinced to travel with us on a different road? As Henry L. Stimson said at the outset of the strategic arms race, "We do not yet know surely in what proportion unreasonable fears and twisted hopes are at the root of the perverted policy now followed by the Kremlin. Assuming both to be involved, we must disarm the fears and disappoint the hopes."[18] In the four nuclear decades, both the U.S. and the Soviet Union have been highly successful in disappointing hopes and woefully inadequate in disarming fears.

In what is arguably the best book written on this subject, *Strategy in the Missile Age,* Bernard Brodie wrote, "The one great area in our public affairs in which romanticism survives is that of national defense policies."[19] Undoubtedly, both camps in the domestic debate over arms control and nuclear weapons still hold romantic ideas. But if it is a romantic notion to mend fences on these issues, then we as a nation are in deep trouble. The penalties of strategic stalemate mandate pragmatic, problem-solving approaches, not additional pitched battles.

Notes

CHAPTER 1. TWO CAMPS

1. Henry L. Stimson, "The Decision to Use the Atomic Bomb," *Harper's*, Vol. 194, (February 1947), p. 107. Also see Henry L. Stimson and McGeorge Bundy, *On Active Service in Peace and War* (New York: Harper & Brothers, 1947), p. 633.
2. *Eindhovensch Dagblad*, August 8, 1946, reprinted and translated in Sydnor H. Walker, ed., *The First One Hundred Days of the Atomic Age* (New York: Woodrow Wilson Foundation, 1946), p. 16.
3. J. Robert Oppenheimer, "Physics in the Contemporary World," *Bulletin of the Atomic Scientists*, Vol. 4, No. 3 (March 1948), p. 66.
4. The GAC reports are reprinted in Herbert F. York, *The Advisors, Oppenheimer, Teller and the Superbomb* (San Francisco: W. H. Freeman & Co., 1976).
5. See David Alan Rosenberg, "American Atomic Strategy and the Hydrogen Bomb Decision," *Journal of American History*, Vol. 66, No. 1 (June 1979), pp. 62–88.
6. Thomas C. Schelling and Morton H. Halperin, *Strategy and Arms Control* (New York: The Twentieth Century Fund, 1961), p. 1.
7. Jonathan Schell, *The Fate of the Earth* (New York: Alfred A. Knopf, 1982), p. 216.
8. *Control and Reduction of Armaments*, Hearings before a Subcommittee of the Committee on Foreign Relations, United States Senate, 85th Congress, 2nd Session (Washington, D.C., 1958), Pt. 11, p. 1003; and George F. Kennan, *Russia, The Atom and the West* (New York: Harper and Brothers, 1958), p. 52.
9. George Kennan, "Two Views of the Soviet Problem," *The New Yorker* (November 2, 1981), p. 62.

CHAPTER 2. THE SOVIET THREAT

1. "NSC-68, A Report to the National Security Council," *Foreign Relations of the United States,* 1950, I (Washington, D.C.: Government Printing Office, 1977), p. 237.
2. Arleigh Burke, "Power and Peace," in Frank R. Barnett, William C. Mott, and John C. Neff, eds., *Peace and War in the Modern Age* (New York: Doubleday & Co., 1965), p. 28.
3. American Security Council, *U.S.S.R. vs. U.S.A., The ABM and the Changed Strategic Military Balance* (Washington, D.C.: Acropolis Books, 1969), p. 11.
4. Robert Strausz-Hupé, William R. Kintner, James E. Dougherty, Alvin J. Cottrell, *Protracted Conflict* (New York: Harper & Brothers, 1959), p. 7.
5. Robert Strausz-Hupé, Willaim R. Kintner, and Stefan T. Possony, *A Forward Strategy for America* (New York: Harper & Brothers, 1961), pp. 31, 406.
6. Strausz-Hupé, "Soviet Strategy 1962–1970," in David M. Abshire and Richard V. Allen, eds., *National Security: Political, Military, and Economic Strategies in the Decade Ahead* (New York: Frederick A. Praeger, 1963), pp. 5–6.
7. Richard V. Allen, "The Strategy of Peaceful Coexistence," in *Peace and War in the Modern Age,* p. 145.
8. George F. Kennan, "The Sources of Soviet Conduct," *Foreign Affairs,* Vol. 25, No. 4 (July 1947), p. 575.
9. "Common Sense and the Common Danger," (Washington, D.C.: Committee on the Present Danger, November 11, 1976), p. 2.
10. Kennan, "The Sources of Soviet Conduct," p. 576.
11. "Is SALT II a Fair Deal for the United States?" (Washington, D.C.: Committee on the Present Danger, May 16, 1979), p. 5.
12. Charles W. Yost, *History and Memory* (New York: W. W. Norton and Co., 1980), p. 168.
13. Retrieved from the Harry S. Truman Library Archives by Gregg Herken, *The Winning Weapon, the Atomic Bomb in the Cold War, 1945–50* (New York: Vintage Books, 1981), p. 325.
14. George F. Kennan, *Realities of American Foreign Policy* (Princeton: Princeton University Press, 1954), p. 82.
15. Marshall Shulman, "SALT and the Soviet Union," in Mason Willrich and John B. Rhinelander, eds., *SALT, The Moscow Agreements and Beyond* (New York: The Free Press, 1974), p. 116.
16. Richard J. Barnet, *Real Security: Restoring American Power in a Dangerous Decade* (New York: Simon and Schuster, 1981), p. 110, and George F. Kennan, "Two Views of the Soviet Problem," *The New Yorker* (November 2, 1981), pp. 55–56.
17. Excerpts from a speech delivered to the United Press International Editors and Publishers, San Francisco, California, September 18, 1967, reprinted in Robert S. McNamara, *The Essence of Security, Reflections in Office* (New York: Harper and Row, 1968), pp. 51–68.
18. David E. Lilienthal, *Change, Hope, and the Bomb* (Princeton: Princeton University Press, 1963), p. 40; Paul C. Warnke, "Apes on a Treadmill," *Foreign Policy,* No. 18 (Spring 1975), p. 29.
19. Maxwell D. Taylor, "The Legitimate Claims of National Security," *Foreign Affairs,* Vol. 52, No. 3 (April 1974), p. 581.

20. Charles W. Yost, *History and Memory,* p. 161.
21. Kennan, "The Sources of Soviet Conduct," p. 582.
22. See George F. Kennan, *Memoirs 1925–1950* (Boston: Little, Brown and Company, 1967), pp. 354–365.
23. George F. Kennan, "America and the Russian Future," *Foreign Affairs,* Vol. 29, No. 3 (April 1951), p. 351–2.
24. Hans A. Bethe, "The Hydrogen Bomb," *Bulletin of the Atomic Scientists,* Vol. 6, No. 4 (April 1950), p. 103.

CHAPTER 3. HOW MUCH IS ENOUGH?

1. "NSC-68, A Report to the National Security Council," *Foreign Relations of the United States,* 1950, I (Washington, D.C.: GPO, 1977), p. 253.
2. For an investigation why this was so, see McGeorge Bundy, "The Missed Chance to Stop the H-Bomb," *New York Review of Books,* Vol., 29, No. 8 (May 13, 1982), pp. 13–22.
3. Stefan T. Possony, *Strategic Air Power, The Pattern of Dynamic Security* (Washington, D.C.: Infantry Journal Press, 1949).
4. Possony, "Toward a Strategy of Supremacy," in David M. Abshire and Richard V. Allen, eds., *National Security: Political, Military, and Economic Strategies in the Decade Ahead* (New York: Frederick A. Praeger, 1963), p. 563.
5. *Nuclear Test Ban Treaty,* Hearings before the Committee on Foreign Relations, United States Senate, 88th Congress, 1st Session (Washington, D.C., 1963), p. 388. (Hereafter cited as *SFRC, Test Ban Hearings.*)
6. *Investigation of the Preparedness Program,* Interim Report by Preparedness Investigating Subcommittee of the Committee on Armed Services, United States Senate, 88th Congress, 1st Session (Washington, D.C., 1963), pp. 1–2. (Hereafter cited as *SASC, Test Ban Report.*)
7. See William W. Kaufmann, *The McNamara Strategy* (New York: Harper & Row, 1964), p. 95.
8. *Military Aspects and Implications of Nuclear Test Ban Proposals and Related Matters,* Hearings before the Preparedness Investigating Subcommittee of the Committee on Armed Services, United States Senate, 88th Congress, 1st Session (Washington, D.C., 1963), Part 1, p. 365. (Hereafter cited as *SASC, Test Ban Hearings.*)
9. "The Need for a National Strategy of Peace Through Strength," Coalition for Peace Through Strength membership drive pamphlet, undated.
10. *Military Implications of the Treaty on the Limitation of Strategic Offensive Arms and Protocol Thereto,* Hearings before the Committee on Armed Services, United States Senate, 96th Congress, 1st Session, (Washington, D.C., 1979), Part 1, p. 414. (Hereafter cited as *SASC, SALT II Hearings.*)
11. *The SALT II Treaty,* Hearings before the Committee on Foreign Relations, United States Senate, 96th Congress, 1st Session (Washington, D.C., 1979) Part 1, p. 488. (Hereafter cited as *SFRC, SALT II Hearings*).
12. *SFRC, SALT II Hearings,* Part 3, p. 157.
13. Richard Burt, "A Glass Half Empty," *Foreign Policy,* No. 36 (Fall 1979), p. 41, and "Reassessing the Strategic Balance," *International Security,* Vol. 5, No. 1 (Summer 1980), p. 51.

14. Edward Rowny, "Integrating Defense Planning," *Defense Planning and Arms Control* (Washington, D.C.: The National Security Affairs Institute, 1980), pp. 51–52.
15. *New York Times*, May 30, 1982, and June 21, 1982.
16. Richard J. Barnet, *Real Security: Restoring American Power in a Dangerous Decade* (New York: Simon and Schuster, 1981), pp. 13, 112.
17. United States Atomic Energy Commission, *In the Matter of J. Robert Oppenheimer: Transcript of Hearing before Personnel Security Board and Texts of Principal Documents and Letters* (Cambridge: The MIT Press, 1977), p. 243; George F. Kennan, "Draft Memorandum of the Counsellor to the Secretary of State," *Foreign Relations of the United States*, 1950, I (Washington, D.C., GPO, 1970), p. 165.
18. *Bulletin of the Atomic Scientists*, Vol. 6, No. 3 (March 1950), reprinted in *The H-Bomb* (New York: Didier, 1950), pp. 160–61.
19. Bernard Feld, "The Summer Study on Arms Control," in David H. Frisch, ed., *Arms Reduction, Program and Issues* (New York: The Twentieth Century Fund, 1961), p. 5.
20. Arnold Wolfers, in Bernard Brodie, ed., *The Absolute Weapon: Atomic Power and World Order* (New York: Harcourt, Brace and Company, 1946), pp. 135–136.
21. Bernard Brodie, ed., *The Absolute Weapon*, p. 49.
22. Marshall D. Shulman, "Toward a Western Philosophy of Coexistence," *Foreign Affairs*, Vol. 52, No. 1 (October, 1973), p. 52.
23. Gerard C. Smith, *Doubletalk: The Story of the First Strategic Arms Limitation Talks* (Garden City, N.Y.: Doubleday & Co., 1980), p. 35.
24. *ABM, MIRV, SALT, and the Nuclear Arms Race*, Hearings before the Subcommittee on Arms Control, International Law and Organization of the Committee on Foreign Relations, United States Senate, 91st Congress, 2nd Session (Washington, D.C., 1970), pp. 395–6.
25. *Consideration of Mr. Paul C. Warnke to be Director of the U.S. Arms Control and Disarmament Agency and Ambassador*, Hearings Together with Individual Views, Committee on Armed Services, United States Senate, 95th Congress, 1st Session, (Washington, D.C., 1977), p. 51. (Hereafter cited as *Warnke Nomination*.)

CHAPTER 4. THE POLITICAL UTILITY OF NUCLEAR FORCES

1. Richard Pipes, "Why the Soviet Union Thinks it Could Fight and Win a Nuclear War," *U.S.-Soviet Relations in the Era of Détente* (Boulder: Westview Press, 1981), p. 167.
2. Eugene V. Rostow, "The Case Against SALT II," *Commentary*, Vol. 67, No. 2 (February 1979), p. 30.
3. Edward Luttwak, *The Strategic Balance 1972* (New York: The Library Press, 1972), p. 80.
4. Henry Kissinger, *Nuclear Weapons and Foreign Policy* (New York: Harper & Brothers, 1957), p. 10.
5. Arthur H. Compton, *Atomic Quest* (New York: Oxford University Press, 1956), pp. 280–81.
6. See McGeorge Bundy, "The Missed Chance to Stop the H-Bomb," *New York Review of Books*, Vol. 29, No. 8 (May 13, 1982), p. 14, and Gregg Herken,

The Winning Weapon, The Atomic Bomb in the Cold War (New York: Vintage Books, 1981), p. 317.

7. *Washington Post,* May 10, 1970.

8. *Congressional Record*, Senate, June 4, 1975, p. S9623.

9. *United States Military Posture for FY 1973*, Hearings before the Committee on Armed Services, United States Senate, 92nd Congress, 2nd Session (February 15, 1972), pp. 505–6.

10. *SASC, SALT II Hearings,* Part 1, p. 413.

11. See, in particular, "Congressional Briefing," reprinted in *Strategic Arms Limitation Agreements*, Hearings before the Committee on Foreign Relations, United States Senate, 92nd Congress, 2nd Session (Washington, D.C., 1972), p. 395.

12. *SFRC, SALT II Hearings,* Part 3, p. 155.

13. *National Security Policy and the Changing World Power Alignment*, Hearing-Symposium before the Subcommittee on National Security Policy and Scientific Developments of the Committee on Foreign Affairs, House of Representatives, 92nd Congress, 2nd Session (Washington, D.C., 1972), p. 75.

14. *Status of U.S. Strategic Power*, Hearings before the Preparedness Investigating Subcommittee of the Committee on Armed Services, United States Senate (Washington, D.C., 1968), Pt. 1, p. 126.

15. "News Conference at Moscow, July 3, 1972," *Department of State Bulletin* (July 29, 1974), p. 215. See Kissinger's *Years of Upheaval* (Boston: Little, Brown and Company, 1982), pp. 1175–76, for qualifications.

16. Bundy, "To Cap the Volcano," *Foreign Affairs,* Vol. 48, No. 1 (October 1969), p. 11.

17. Cited in William W. Kaufmann, *The McNamara Strategy* (New York: Harper and Row, 1964), p. 96.

18. Maxwell D. Taylor, "The Legitimate Claims of National Security," *Foreign Affairs*, Vol. 52, No. 3 (April 1974), p. 582.

19. "The Lessons of the Cuban Missile Crisis," *Time*, September 27, 1982.

20. *Nuclear Weapons and Foreign Policy*, Hearings before the Subcommittee on U.S. Security Agreements and Commitments Abroad, and the Subcommittee on Arms Control, International Law and Organization of the Committee on Foreign Relations, United States Senate, 93rd Congress, 2nd Session, (Washington, D.C., 1974), p. 58.

21. Hans Morgenthau, "The H-Bomb and the Peace Outlook," *The H-Bomb* (New York: Didier, 1950), p. 174.

22. James Franck, et al., "A Report to the Secretary of War," *Bulletin of Atomic Scientists*, Vol. 1, No. 10 (May 1, 1946), pp. 2–3.

23. *New York Times Magazine*, June 23, 1946, reprinted in Julia E. Johnsen, *The Atomic Bomb* (New York: The H. W. Wilson Co., 1946), p. 102.

24. Albert Einstein, *The H-Bomb* (New York: Didier, 1950), p. 14.

25. David E. Lilienthal, *The Journals of David E. Lilienthal: The Atomic Energy Years, 1945–1950* (New York: Harper and Row, 1964), pp. 581, 591.

26. *Airpower,* Report of the Subcommittee on the Air Force of the Committee on Armed Services, United States Senate, 84th Congress, together with Minority Views, Washington, D.C. (January 25, 1957), p. 105.

27. Donald A. Quarles, "How Much is 'Enough'?" *Air Force Magazine*, (September 1956), pp. 51–53; Alsop column in *New York Herald Tribune*, April 24, 1959.

28. *National Security Policy and the Changing World Power Alignment*, Hearing-Sympo-

sium before the Subcommittee on National Security Policy and Scientific Developments of the Committee on Foreign Affairs, House of Representatives, 92nd Congress, 2nd Session (Washington, D.C., 1972), p. 93.

29. Bundy, "To Cap the Volcano," p. 9.

CHAPTER 5. THE MILITARY UTILITY OF NUCLEAR FORCES

1. *Study On Airpower,* Hearings before the Subcommittee on the Air Force, Committee on Armed Services, United States Senate, 84th Congress, 2nd Session (Washington, D.C., 1956), p. 96. (Hereafter cited as *SASC, Airpower Hearings.*)

2. William R. Kintner, "Arms Control and National Security: A Caveat," in James E. Doughtery and J. F. Lehman, eds., *Arms Control for the Late Sixties* (Princeton: D. Van Nostrand Co., 1967), p. 35.

3. James R. Killian, Jr., *Sputnik, Scientists, and Eisenhower* (Cambridge: MIT Press, 1977), p. 73.

4. *SASC, Airpower Hearings,* p. 213.

5. See Morton H. Halperin, "The Gaither Committee and the Policy Process," *World Politics,* Vol. 13, No. 3 (April 1961), pp. 360–85, and James R. Killian, Jr., *Sputnik, Scientists, and Eisenhower,* pp. 96–102.

6. *New York Times,* November 13, 1957.

7. Henry Kissinger, *The Necessity for Choice,* (New York: Harper and Brothers, 1961), p. 20.

8. *Military Implications of the Proposed SALT II Treaty Relating to the National Defense,* Report of the Hearings on the Military Aspects and Implications of the Proposed SALT II Treaty, together with additional views, Committee on Armed Services, United States Senate, 96th Congress, 2nd Session (Washington, D.C., 1980), p. 2. (Hereafter cited as *SASC, SALT II Report.*)

9. Pipes, "Why the Soviet Union Thinks It Could Fight and Win a Nuclear War," *Commentary,* Vol. 64, No. 1 (July 1977), reprinted in *U.S.-Soviet Relations in the Era of Détente* (Boulder: Westview Press, 1981), p. 136.

10. Colin Gray, "Presidential Directive 59: Flawed But Useful," *Parameters, Journal of the United States Army War College,* Vol. 11, No. 1 (March 1981), p. 33.

11. *SASC, SALT II Hearings,* Part 1, p. 310.

12. Paul Nitze, "Is SALT II a Fair Deal for the United States?" (Washington, D.C.: Committee on the Present Danger, May 16, 1979), p. 6.

13. *U.S.-U.S.S.R. Strategic Policies,* Hearings before the Subcommittee on Arms Control, International Law and Organization of the Committee on Foreign Relations, United States Senate, 93rd Congress, 2nd Session (Washington, D.C., 1974), p. 41.

14. Bernard Brodie, ed., *The Absolute Weapon: Atomic Power and World Order* (New York: Harcourt, Brace and Co., 1946), p. 181.

15. Bernard Brodie, "The Atomic Bomb and American Security," Memorandum Number Eighteen (New Haven: Yale Institute of International Studies, November 1, 1945), p. 2. Brodie later toyed with the idea of using nuclear weapons under some circumstances, only to return later to his original precepts.

16. J. Robert Oppenheimer, "Atomic Weapons," *Proceedings of the American Philosophical Society,* Vol. 90, No. 1 (January 1946), pp. 8–9.

17. Albert Einstein, "Real Problems in the Hearts of Men," *New York Times*

Magazine (June 23, 1946), reprinted in Julia E. Johnsen, *The Atomic Bomb* (New York: The H. W. Wilson Co., 1946), pp. 101–2.

18. Hans Bethe and Edward Teller, *The Future of Nuclear Tests*, Headline Series No. 145 (New York: Foreign Policy Association, January-February 1961), p. 35.

19. *Arms Control Implications of Current Defense Budget*, Hearings before the Subcommittee on Arms Control, International Law and Organization of the Committee on Foreign Relations, United States Senate, 92nd Congress, 1st Session (Washington, D.C., 1971), p. 58. (Hereafter cited as *Arms Control Implications*.)

20. Herbert Scoville, Jr., *MX, Prescription for Disaster* (Cambridge, Mass.: MIT Press, 1981), pp. ix, 1.

21. "Let Us Pledge Not to Use H-Bomb First!", *Bulletin of the Atomic Scientists*, Vol. 6, No. 3 (March 1950), p. 75.

22. James L. Buckley and Paul C. Warnke, *Strategic Sufficiency: Fact or Fiction?* (Washington, D.C.: American Enterprise Institute for Public Policy Research, 1972), p. 74.

23. McGeorge Bundy, George F. Kennan, Robert S. McNamara, and Gerard Smith, "Nuclear Weapons and the Atlantic Alliance," *Foreign Affairs*, Vol. 60, No. 4 (Spring 1982), p. 768.

24. See *Military Aspects and Implications of Nuclear Test Ban Proposals and Related Matters*, Hearings before the Committee on Armed Services, United States Senate, 88th Congress, 1st Session (Washington, D.C., 1963), Pt. 1, pp. 366–7.

25. See Alton Frye, *A Responsible Congress: The Politics of National Security* (New York: McGraw Hill, 1975), and *Congressional Record*, Senate, July 29, 1970, p. 26386.

26. For the Senate debates over the Schlesinger initiatives, see the *Congressional Record*, June 10, 1974, pp. 18483–505, and June 4, 1975, pp. S.9616-39.

27. *Nuclear Weapons and Foreign Policy*, Hearings before the Subcommittee on U.S. Security Agreements and Commitments Abroad and the Subcommittee on Arms Control, International Law and Organization of the Committee on Foreign Relations, United States Senate, 93rd Congress, 2nd Session, (Washington, D.C., 1974), p. 55.

28. Gerard C. Smith, *Doubletalk, The Story of the First Strategic Arms Limitation Talks* (Garden City, N.Y., Doubleday & Co., 1980), p. 24.

CHAPTER 6. ARMS CONTROL

1. Strausz-Hupé, "The Disarmament Delusion," *U.S. Naval Institute Proceedings* (February 1960), reprinted in Ernest Lefever, ed., *Arms and Arms Control* (New York: Frederick A. Praeger, 1962), p. 167.

2. *SFRC, Test Ban Hearings,* p. 507.

3. Remarks at a news conference, October 16, 1957, reprinted in Paul E. Zinner, ed., *Documents on American Foreign Relations, 1957,* (New York: Harper and Brothers, 1958), p. 163.

4. *Arms Control and Disarmament*, Hearings before the Preparedness Investigating Subcommittee of the Committee on Armed Services, United States Senate, 87th Congress, 2nd Session (Washington, D.C., 1962), p. 65. (Hereafter cited as *SASC, Hearings on Arms Control and Disarmament*.)

5. *Control and Reduction of Armaments*, Hearings before a Subcommittee of the Com-

182 STRATEGIC STALEMATE

mittee on Foreign Relations, United States Senate, 85th Congress, 2nd Session (Washington 1958), Part 11, p. 1041. (Hereafter cited as *SFRC, Control and Reduction Hearings.*)

6. *ABM, MIRV, SALT and The Nuclear Arms Race*, Hearings before the Subcommittee on Arms Control, International Law and Organization of the Committee on Foreign Relations, United States Senate, 91st Congress, 2nd Session (Washington, D.C., 1970), p. 343.

7. See Zbigniew Brzezinski, *Power and Principle* (New York: Farrar, Straus, Giroux, 1983), p. 189, for Brzezinski's explanation of why "SALT lies buried in the sands of Ogaden").

8. *The SALT II Treaty,* Report of the Committee on Foreign Reations, United States Senate, 96th Congress, 1st Session (Washington, D.C., 1979), p. 491.

9. *SASC, SALT II Hearings*, Part 3, p. 1308.

10. Paul Nitze, "Is SALT II a Fair Deal for the United States?" (Washington, D.C.: Committee on the Present Danger, May 16, 1979), p. 12.

11. *SASC, Test Ban Report*, p. 2.

12. James Hubert McBride, *The Test Ban Treaty: Military, Technological, and Political Implications* (Chicago: Henry Regnery Company, 1967), pp. 110, 151.

13. *Military Implications of the Treaty on the Non-Proliferation of Nuclear Weapons*, Hearings before the Committee on Armed Services, United States Senate, 91st Congress, 1st Session (Washington, D.C., 1969), p. 76.

14. *Congressional Record*, March 12, 1969, p. 6192.

15. *Congressional Record*, August 3, 1972, p. S.12615.

16. *SASC, SALT II Report*, p. 15.

17. *SFRC, SALT II Hearings*, Part 1, p. 302.

18. *SFRC, SALT II Hearings*, Part 1, p. 436.

19. *SFRC, SALT II Hearings*, Part 4, p. 2.

20. "The Signs of the Times," Address by Senator Henry M. Jackson before the Coalition for a Democratic Majority, June 12, 1979.

21. Richard Pipes, "Why the Soviet Union Wants SALT II," (Washington, D.C.: Committee on the Present Danger, September 17, 1979), p. 7.

22. *SFRC, Test Ban Hearings*, p. 84.

23. *SFRC, Test Ban Hearings*, p. 75.

24. *SFRC, Test Ban Hearings*, p. 678.

25. *SFRC, Test Ban Hearings*, p. 516.

26. *Military Implications of the Treaty on the Limitation of Anti-Ballistic Missile Systems and the Interim Agreement on Limitation of Strategic Offensive Arms*, Hearings before the Committee on Armed Services, United States Senate, 92nd Congress, 2nd Session (Washington, D.C., 1972), p. 3. (Hereafter cited as *SASC, SALT I Hearings.*)

27. *SFRC, SALT II Hearings,* Part 1, p. 511.

28. *SFRC, SALT II Hearings*, Part 4, p. 245.

29. *SFRC, SALT II Hearings*, Part 1, p. 373.

30. *SFRC, Test Ban Hearings*, pp. 275–76.

31. *SFRC, Test Ban Hearings*, p. 510.

32. *Non-Proliferation Treaty*, Hearings before the Committee on Foreign Relations, United States Senate, 90th Congress, 2nd Session (Washington, D.C., 1968), p. 130. (Hereafter cited as *SFRC, Non-Proliferation Treaty Hearings.*)

33. *Congressional Record*, March 12, 1969, p. 6201.

34. *SFRC, SALT II Hearings*, Part 2, pp. 148-9.

35. Robert Strause-Hupé, William R. Kintner, and Stefan T. Possony, *A Forward Strategy for America* (New York: Harper and Brothers, 1961), p. 403.

36. See Robert Gilpin, *American Scientists and Nuclear Weapons Policy* (Princeton: Princeton University Press, 1962), p. 43.

37. James Franck, et al., "A Report to the Secretary of War," *Bulletin of the Atomic Scientists*, Vol. 1, No. 10 (May 1, 1946), p. 3.

38. J. Robert Oppenheimer, "The Scientific Foundations of World Order," in Ernest Llewellyn Woodward, et. al., eds., *Foundations for World Order* (Denver: University of Denver Press, 1949), p. 43.

39. James Franck, et. al., "A Report to the Secretary of War," pp. 2-3.

40. *Congressional Record,* April 11, 1946, p. 3509.

41. United States Atomic Energy Commission, *In the Matter of J. Robert Oppenheimer: Transcript of Hearing Before Personnel Security Board and Texts of Principal Documents and Letters* (Cambridge, Mass.: The MIT Press, 1971), p. 1019. Also, see Philip M. Stern, *The Oppenheimer Case: Security on Trial* (New York: Harper and Row, 1969), p. 406.

42. Jerome Wiesner, in Donald G. Brennan, ed., *Arms Control, Disarmament and National Security,* (New York: George Braziller, 1961), p. 14.

43. F.A.S. Newsletter, Vol. 22, No. 5 (May 1969), p. 1.

44. *Congressional Record*, June 4, 1959, p. S.8864.

45. Arthur H. Dean, *Test Ban and Disarmament, The Path of Negotiation* (New York: Harper and Row, 1966), p. 65.

46. *Warnke Nomination*, 1977, p. 18.

47. *Control and Reduction of Armaments*, Hearings before a Subcommittee of the Committee on Foreign Relations, United States Senate, 85th Congress, 2nd Session (Washington, D.C., 1958), Pt. 11, p. 1008.

48. Marshall Shulman, "What Does Security Mean Today?" *Foreign Affairs*, Vol. 49, No. 4 (July 1971), pp. 616-17.

49. Richard J. Barnet, *Real Security: Restoring American Power in a Dangerous Decade* (New York: Simon and Schuster, 1981), p. 118.

50. Strobe Talbott, "Behind Closed Doors," *Time*, December 5, 1983, p. 19.

51. Grenville Clark and Louis B. Sohn, *World Peace Through World Law, Two Alternative Plans*, Third edition, enlarged (Cambridge: Harvard University Press, 1966), p. xlvi.

52. Richard J. Barnet, *Who Wants Disarmament* (Boston: Beacon Press, 1960), pp. 52, 134.

53. Jerome Wiesner, in Donald G. Brennan, ed., *Arms Control, Disarmament, and National Security* (New York: George Braziller, 1961), p. 14.

54. "Arms Reduction in the 1960's," in David H. Frisch, ed., *Arms Reduction, Program and Issues* (New York: The Twentieth Century Fund, 1961), p. 37.

55. Grenville Clark and Louis B. Sohn, *World Peace Through World Law, Two Alternative Plans*, p. xlviii.

56. Dexter Mathews and Katherine Way, eds., *One World or None, A Report to the Public on the Full Meaning of the Atomic Bomb* (New York: McGraw-Hill Book Co., 1946), inside jacket and p. 76.

57. Norman Cousins, *Modern Man is Obsolete* (New York: The Viking Press, 1945), p. 20; *Saturday Review of Literature*, August 18, 1945.

58. Arthur H. Compton, "Atomic Energy as a Human Asset," *Proceedings of the*

American Philosophical Society, Symposium on Atomic Energy and its Implications, Vol. 90, No. 1 (1946), p. 70.

59. Grenville Clark and Louis B. Sohn, *World Peace through World Law, Two Alternative Plans*, p. xlvi.

60. J. Robert Oppenheimer, "International Control of Atomic Energy," *Bulletin of the Atomic Scientists*, Vol. 4, No. 2 (February 1948), pp. 41–42.

61. Henry L. Stimson and McGeorge Bundy, *On Active Service in Peace and War* (New York: Harper and Brothers, 1948), p. 644.

62. J. Robert Oppenheimer, "International Control of Atomic Energy," *Foreign Affairs*, Vol. 26, No. 2 (January 1948), p. 245.

63. See Alice Kimball Smith, *A Peril and a Hope, The Scientists' Movement in America: 1945-47* (Chicago: University of Chicago Press, 1965).

64. Richard J. Barnet, *Real Security: Restoring American Power in a Dangerous Decade*, p. 101.

65. George F. Kennan, *Russia, The Atom and the West* (New York: Harper and Brothers, 1958), p. 28.

66. *Control and Reduction of Armaments*, Final Report of the Committee on Foreign Relations Subcommittee on Disarmament, United States Senate, 85th Congress, 2nd Session (Washington, D.C., October 13, 1958), p. 3.

CHAPTER 7. THE ART OF NEGOTIATION

1. *SASC, Hearings on Arms Control and Disarmament*, p. 113.
2. Colin Gray, "Strategic Stability Reconsidered," *Daedalus*, Vol. 109, No. 4 (Fall 1980), p. 138.
3. "NSC-68, A Report to the National Security Council," *Foreign Relations of the United States*, 1950, I (Washington, D.C., GPO, 1977), p. 273.
4. *SASC, Hearings on Arms Control and Disarmament*, p. 90.
5. See Coral Bell, *Negotiation From Strength, A Study in the Politics of Power* (New York: Alfred A. Knopf, 1963), p. 5.
6. *SASC, Airpower Hearings*, p. 1.
7. *SFRC, Control and Reduction of Armaments Hearings*, Part 2, p. 51.
8. *Disarmament Agency*, Hearings before the Committee on Foreign Relations, United States Senate, 87th Congress, 1st Session (Washington, D.C., 1961), p. 87. (Hereafter cited as *SFRC, Disarmament Agency Hearings*.)
9. *SFRC, Disarmament Agency Hearings*, p. 71.
10. *SFRC, Control and Reduction of Armaments Hearings*, Part 2, p. 51.
11. "NSC-68, A Report to the National Security Council," *Foreign Relations of the United States*, 1950, I (Washington, D.C., GPO, 1977), p. 273.
12. *Nomination of Eugene V. Rostow*, Hearings before the Committee on Foreign Relations, United States Senate, 97th Congress, 1st Session (Washington, D.C., 1981), p. 23.
13. *The Limitation of Strategic Arms*, Hearings before the Subcommittee on Strategic Arms Limitation Talks of the Committee on Arms Services, United States Senate, 91st Congress, 2nd Session (Washington, D.C., 1970), Part 1, pp. 35–36.
14. Strobe Talbott, *Endgame, The Inside Story of SALT II* (New York: Harper and Row, 1979), p. 61.

5. *SFRC, SALT II Hearings*, Part 1, p. 544, 587.

6. *SASC, SALT II Hearings*, Part 3, p. 949.

7. Nitze, "Is SALT II a Fair Deal for the United States?" (Washington, D.C.: Committee on the Present Danger, May 16, 1979), p. 12.

8. *SASC, Hearings on Arms Control and Disarmament*, pp. 90–91.

9. *SFRC, SALT II Hearings*, Part 1, pp. 573–74.

0. *New York Times*, May 1, 1981.

1. Strause-Hupé, et. al., *Forward Strategy for America*, p. 324.

2. Strause-Hupé, "The Disarmament Delusion," *U.S. Naval Institute Proceedings* (February 1960), reprinted in Ernest Lefever, ed., *Arms and Arms Control* (New York: Frederick A. Praeger, 1962), p. 159.

3. *SFRC, Non-proliferation Treaty Hearings*, p. 129.

4. Cited in Curtis E. LeMay, *America is in Danger* (New York: Funk and Wagnalls, 1968), p. 275.

5. "Integrating Defense Planning," *Defense Planning and Arms Control*, Proceedings of a Special National Security Affairs Institute Conference (Washington, D.C.: National Defense University, 1980), pp. 52 and 55.

6. *SASC, Test Ban Report*, pp. 5–8.

7. *Congressional Record*, September 16, 1963, pp. 17041–2.

8. Strause-Hupé, et al., *Forward Strategy for America*, p. 303.

9. See Glenn T. Seaborg, *Kennedy, Khrushchev and the Test Ban* (Berkeley: University of California Press, 1981), p. 188.

0. *Diplomatic and Strategic Impact of Multiple Warhead Missiles*, Hearings before the Subcommittee on National Security Policy and Scientific Developments, House of Representatives, 91st Congress, 1st Session (Washington, D.C., 1969), p. 246. Also see Alton Frye, *A Responsible Congress: The Politics of National Security* (New York: McGraw Hill, 1975), p. 62.

1. *SASC, SALT I Hearings*, p. 414.

2. Miscellaneous Committee Prints, *Full Committee Hearings on the Military Limitations of the Strategic Arms Limitation Talks Agreements*, Committee on Armed Services, House of Representatives, 92nd Congress, 2nd Session (Washington, D.C., 1972), pp. 15092, 15119, 15135–36.

3. *SASC, SALT I Hearings*, pp. 60–61.

4. *Consideration of Mr. Paul C. Warnke to be Director of the U.S. Arms Control and Disarmament Agency and Ambassador*, Hearings together with individual views, Committee on Armed Services, United States Senate, 95th Congress, 1st Session (Washington, D.C., 1977), p. 192.

5. *SASC, SALT I Hearings*, p. 125.

6. Henry Kissinger, *White House Years* (Boston: Little Brown and Company, 1979), pp. 540, 549.

7. Gerard C. Smith, *Doubletalk, The Story of the First Strategic Arms Limitation Talks* (Garden City, N.Y.: Doubleday & Co., 1980), p. 119.

8. Henry Kissinger, *White House Years*, p. 543.

9. *Arms Control Implications of Current Defense Budget*, Hearings before the Subcommittee on Arms Control, International Law and Organization of the Committee on Foreign Relations, United States Senate, 92nd Congress, 1st Session (Washington, D.C., 1971), pp. 176–7. (Hereafter cited as *SFRC, Hearings on Arms Control Implications*.)

0. *SFRC, Hearings on Arms Control Implications*, p. 182.

41. *SFRC, Hearings on Arms Control Implications*, p. 184.
42. *Congressional Record*, June 10, 1974, p. 18486.
43. *Congressional Record*, June 4, 1975, p. S.9635.
44. *Investigation of the Preparedness Program*, Report by Preparedness Investigating Subcommittee of the Committee on Armed Services, United States Senate on Status of U.S. Strategic Power, 90th Congress, 2nd Session (Washington, D.C., 1968), p. 17.
45. *Warnke Nomination*, p. 50.
46. *SFRC, Hearings on Arms Control Implications*, p. 251.
47. Ralph Earle II, "The Bargaining Chip Theory," *The Christian Science Monitor* December 17, 1982.
48. James Franck, et. al., "A Report to the Secretary of War," *Bulletin of the Atomic Scientists*, Vol. 1, No. 10 (May 1, 1946), pp. 3–4.
49. See Herbert F. York, *The Advisors, Oppenheimer, Teller and the Suberbomb* (San Francisco: W. H. Freeman and Co., 1976), pp. 155–59.
50. *Strategic and Foreign Policy Implications of ABM Systems*, Hearings before the Subcommittee on International Organization and Disarmament Affairs of the Committee on Foreign Relations, United States Senate, 91st Congress, 1st Session (Washington, D.C., 1969), Pt. 1, p. 127.
51. *SFRC, Hearings on Arms Control Implications*, p. 210.
52. *Strategic Arms Limitation Agreements*, Hearings before the Committee on Foreign Relations, United States Senate, 92nd Congress, 2nd Session (Washington, D.C., 1972), p. 1.
53. *Review of Arms Control and Disarmament Activities*, Hearings before the Special Subcommittee on Arms Control and Disarmament of the Committee on Armed Services, House of Representatives, 93rd Congress, 2nd Session (Washington, D.C., 1974), p. 19.
54. *SFRC, Hearings on Arms Control Implications*, p. 99.
55. McGeorge Bundy, "To Cap the Volcano," *Foreign Affairs*, Vol. 48, No. 1 (October, 1969), p. 17.
56. U.S. Department of State, "A Report on the International Control of Atomic Energy," reprinted in the *Bulletin of Atomic Scientists*, Vol. 1, No. 8 (April 1, 1946), p. 9.
57. David E. Lilienthal, *The Journals of David E. Lilienthal, The Atomic Energy Years 1945–1950* (New York: Harper and Row, 1964), p. 628.
58. George F. Kennan, *Russia, The Atom and the West* (New York: Harper and Brothers, 1958), p. 94.
59. Hans A. Bethe and Edward Teller, *The Future of Nuclear Tests*, Headline Series No. 145 (New York: Foreign Policy Association, January–February, 1961) p. 34.
60. Paul C. Warnke, "Apes on a Treadmill," *Foreign Policy*, No. 18 (Spring, 1975) pp. 28–29.

CHAPTER 9. CONSENSUS BARGAINING

1. Lawrence Freedman, *The Evolution of Nuclear Strategy* (New York, St. Martin's Press, 1981), p. xv.
2. *Nuclear Test Ban Treaty*, Hearings before the Committee on Foreign Relations

United States Senate, 88th Congress, 1st Session (Washington, 1963), p. 910.

3. Bernard Brodie, "Technology, Politics and Strategy," in *Problems of Modern Strategy* (London, Chatto and Windus, 1970), p. 167.

4. *Foreign Relations of the United States*, 1929, I, p. 241.

5. Senator Henry M. Jackson's term. See *Congressional Record*, August 8, 1972, p. S.12948.

6. Robert Strausz-Hupé, William R. Kintner, and Stefan T. Possony, *A Forward Strategy for America* (New York: Harper and Brothers, 1961), pp. 322, 292.

7. See Michael Krepon, "Assessing Strategic Arms Reduction Proposals," *World Politics*, Vol. 35 (January, 1983), pp. 216–244.

8. See McGeorge Bundy, "MX Paper: Appealing, But Mostly Appalling," *New York Times*, April 17, 1983.

9. *Report of the President's Commission on Strategic Forces* (Washington, D.C.: Government Printing Office, April 1983), p. 16.

CHAPTER 10. TACIT AGREEMENTS

1. See Barbara Tuchman, "The American People and Military Power in an Historical Perspective," *Adelphi Papers*, No. 173 (Spring, 1982), pp. 5–13.

2. Gilpatric, "Our Defense Needs," *Foreign Affairs*, Vol. 42, No. 3 (April, 1964), pp. 368–69.

3. *Washington Post*, April 12, 1982.

4. "The Handwriting on the Wall May be a Forgery," *Armed Forces Journal*, March 1982, p. 28; Henry A. Kissinger, "Strategy, Trade, and the Atlantic Alliance," Address Inaugurating the Geri Joseph Lectureship on Public Affairs, The Hague, (May 12, 1982); McGeorge Bundy, George F. Kennan, Robert S. McNamara and Gerard Smith, "Nuclear Weapons and the Atlantic Alliance," *Foreign Affairs*, Vol. 60, no. 4 (Spring, 1982), p. 759.

5. Gerard C. Smith, *Doubletalk: The Story of the First Strategic Arms Limitation Talks* (Garden City, N.Y.: Doubleday & Co., 1980), p. 99.

6. President Nixon's instructions appeared in *SFRC, SALT II Hearings*, Pt. 2, p. 241.

7. "SALT I Compliance and SALT II Verification," U.S. Department of State, Bureau of Public Affairs, Selected Documents, No. 7, 1978, p. 12.

8. Abram Chayes, "An Inquiry into the Workings of Arms Control Agreements," *Harvard Law Review*, Vol. 85:905, 1972, p. 968.

9. *SFRC, Test Ban Hearings*, p. 4.

10. *SFRC, Test Ban Hearings*, pp. 241–2, 461; *Congressional Record*, September 13, 1963, pp. 17099–100; September 19, 1963, pp. 17511–15; September 20, 1963, pp. 17605–6, 17638.

11. "Verification of SALT II Agreements," U.S. Department of State, Bureau of Public Affairs, Special Report No. 56, August 1979, p. 3.

12. *SFRC, SALT II Hearings*, Pt. 1, p. 493.

13. Richard N. Perle, "What Is Adequate Verification?" *SALT II and American Security*, (Cambridge: Institute for Foreign Policy Analysis, Inc., 1980), p. 58.

14. Richard Perle, "SALT II: Who Is Deceiving Whom?", *Intelligence Policy and National Security*, Robert L. Pfaltzgraff et al., eds., (Hamden, Conn: Archon Books, 1981), pp. 151–154.

15. Presidential Press Conference, January 29, 1981; *Nuclear Arms Reduction Proposals*, Hearings before the Committee on Foreign Relations, United States Senate, 97th Congress, 2nd Session, 1982, p. 118; *Strategic Weapons Proposals*, Hearings before the Committee on Foreign Relations, United States Senate, 97th Congress, 1st Session, 1981, Part 1, p. 15; *Los Angeles Times*, May 21, 1981.
16. Testimony of the Honorable Richard Perle, Assistant Secretary of Defense (International Security Policy) before the Special Panel on Arms Control and Disarmament, Subcommittee on Procurement and Military Nuclear Systems, House Armed Services Committee, February 22, 1984, p. 2.
17. Michael R. Gordon, "Can Reagan Blow The Whistle On the Russians While Saying No On Salt II?" *National Journal*, May 7, 1983, pp. 953–57.
18. Henry L. Stimson, "The Challenge to Americans," *Foreign Affairs*, Vol. 26, No. 1 (October, 1947), p. 9.
19. Bernard Brodie, *Strategy in the Missile Age* (Princeton University Press, 1959), p. 266.

Index